*The
Emotionally
Disturbed
Family*

Ernest E. Andrews

The Emotionally Disturbed Family

And Some Gratifying Alternatives

Jason Aronson   New York

Copyright © 1974 by Jason Aronson, Inc.

LIBRARY OF CONGRESS CATALOGING IN PUBLICATION DATA

Andrews, Ernest E. 1932–
  The emotionally disturbed family (and some gratifying alternatives)

  Bibliography: p.
  1. Problem family—United States. 2. Family psychotherapy. I. Title. [DNLM: 1. Family therapy. WM430 A566e 1974]
HQ536.A558   301.42'7   73–17734
ISBN   0–87668–112–7

Manufactured in the United States of America
DESIGNED BY SIDNEY SOLOMON

To Janet, Kathy, and Dave

Contents

Preface

This book is intended as an intelligent person's guide to understanding the psychology of family relationships. It will bring together, in understandable language, recent professional experience, scientific thinking and research findings on the function of the family as a system of behavior. The thought, experience, and research are specifically concerned with: (a) the nature of human relationships, (b) the perpetuation of emotional disturbance, and (c) the relationship of rational and irrational behavior to what happens in marriage and family life.

As a stimulator of intense feelings, both positive and negative, and as a mutual emotional experience for better or worse, there is no place like home. The family has the power to influence, to sustain, or to destroy a person's potential for psychological survival.

It is hoped that this book will help the reader to develop a transactional awareness of his own family; an awareness of the reciprocal nature of the relationship between a you and a me—a parent and a child or a husband and a wife; and an emotional understanding of the systematic and mutual nature of emotional interaction and its consequences. It presents a philosophical point of view that is swiftly emerging not only from research in the fields of family behavior but also from the mental health field. The viewpoint is basically "existential" in nature; that is, it emphasizes the personal meaning of existence as it is derived from a relationship with another.

Numerous professionals have contributed to this emerging philosophy. While this book reflects many influences, there are a number of authors whose work has particularly influenced my understanding. Hugh Mullen has written much about the reality aspects of the relationship between a psychotherapist and a patient; much of this information is germane to relationships between any two or more people. Eric Berne's writings on transactional analysis and his well-known book *Games People Play* are other rich sources of thinking about relationships in the here and now, especially about their repetitive and systematic nature. The whole area of communications research has also been a valuable source of theories and constructs in developing a psychology of family relationships. The work done by Watzlawick, Shefflen, and Birdwhistell points specifically to the unbelievable subtleties of communicative behavior between people. Nathan Ackerman, an early pioneer in the study of emotional family life, has contributed much to the understanding of observed family behavior and underlying irrational motivation and frustration. Probably the largest contribution to the understanding of the psychology of family relationships has come from the original members of the Mental Research Institute at Palo Alto, California. They have spent nearly two decades in the study of the family as a social system, as a living, patterned organism. I have principally been influenced by the work of the late Don Jackson, Jay Haley, and Gregory Bateson. Most important has been the influence of Virginia Satir, who has also been affiliated with the Esalen Institute at Big Sur, California, and the Department of Psychiatry of Johns Hopkins University, among her varied and extensive experiences.

The
Emotionally
Disturbed
Family

Introduction

What Is a Family?

It may seem easy to define a family, since almost everyone has grown up in one. Each person will inevitably say a family is what he or she experienced or is experiencing in his or her own family. But observation of numerous families reveals that some rather sizable differences exist between families. In fact, they appear to have "personalities," in the sense that each, in general, behaves in a predictable, characteristic, and unique way: The Joneses are quiet and reserved; the Smiths all dislike blacks; the Browns all have been or are in college. The behavior, beliefs, and goals shared by members of one family at the same time distinguish them from members of another. These are differences, however, fundamentally of the *content* of shared family experience. Is there also an underlying *process* that is largely common to human families and not tied to the idiosyncratic content that distinguishes between them? If the family is viewed as a system of interlocking and interdependent relationships that structure life experience, we can concentrate on the structure of family systems. We would focus on how family members mutually influence and affect one another. In what way do they contribute to what happens within the family?

Consider the following situation in a troubled family that seems to center on ten-year-old Tommy. The school principal has recently called Alice, Tommy's mother, to report with concern that Tom's classroom work and attention have gradually but progressively declined over the semester. Alice's reaction is to sigh deeply and then to feel angry at Tom. After supper Alice tells her husband Bob about the news, expecting Bob to handle it from there: "The principal called and said Tom just isn't doing his work or paying attention." What in fact ensues is a series of episodes that quickly escalate into a deadly but rather low-key family row.

Bob calls Tommy in, and in succession both Bob and Alice upbraid Tom for his lack of adequate performance in school. More or less concurrently:

1. Tom becomes angry at both himself and his parents' *manner* of discussion. Soon he has tuned them out and is daydreaming about his favorite tree hideaway. (The same thing occurs in school when demands are made on him.)

2. Bob, while he both criticizes Tom's efforts and exhorts him to do better, seems to think that words in themselves are all Tom needs. Turning to Alice, he criticizes her for "never handling the boy firmly." He looks a bit harassed, however, and soon after "the discussion" (to which Alice responds with hurt resignation), he leaves for his office to do some piled-up work.

3. Alice, in her criticism of Tom, offers no support of either his past or future effort. Her manner with Tom, as well as with Bob, is one of resignation. She does not want Bob to go back to his office but after a weak and somewhat desperate plea accepts his decision with resigned disappointment.

4. Tom's sisters, Jane, twelve, and Connie, thirteen, have overheard what has occurred and, as Tom leaves the house for outside (just like their father), they tease him about his school problem. He retorts angrily at them, and a secondary row between the children ensues, which father breaks up with a few loud, abrupt words. Tom sulks outside, and the girls run off to their rooms in fear of Bob. Alice sinks into a chair and looks blankly at the opposite wall.

The careful observer of this family situation would be struck first of all by the interrelatedness of the behavior of the family members. Not too far under the surface the marital relationship appears unsatisfying, leaving the family with a depressed mother and a sanctioning and withdrawal-prone father. Tom picks up much of his behavior from his father, especially the pattern of copping out when the going gets unpleasant. The girls join the "criticize Tom" party to keep on the side of the good and powerful parents. Tom appears to have nobody on his side, and withdraws to happier fantasies.

These are not solely individuals in reaction to emotional stress but members of a family who systematically and characteristically respond this way when together. A contagious emotionalism is unleashed in such situations that, in part, reveals the patterned nature of their relationships. Another family might deal differently with a similar situation; such a situation might not even come up in many families.

The Family Is an Emotional System

Persons in a family have feelings about themselves as well as about the others with whom they live. Both sets of feelings are part of family existence: They result from family experience and play a part in the determination of subsequent behavior. Because of the daily "sandpaper" of eating, sleeping, working, and communicating in such repetitious and close proximity, the intensity of feelings in a family is often considerable and spreads into every facet of life. In the family described, Tom is angry both at himself for not doing well and at his parents for their inability to deal with him as a person rather than a problem. Alice's feelings about her husband's withdrawal from her range from disappointment in herself for not being more interesting to him to anger over his abandonment, but all feeling is encapsulated in her chronic depression. Bob is not only disappointed in his inadequacy at dealing with others in the family but feels frustrated and bewildered by their fear and lack of communication with him. The two girls, who can be emotionally closer to each other than to anyone else in the family, often feel apart and left out—the result, in part, of a critical, escapist father and a depressed mother.

The Family Is a Living System

With the family, as with all living organisms, there is growth and an unfolding life cycle. Nothing ever remains the same in the joint life of family members. Continuous change and growth, even in disturbed families, create new problems, new dilemmas, and new courses of action. Family members themselves are always changing: The "terrible two's" give way to more placid threes and fours; the considerate and communicative bug collector of ten becomes a teen-ager and all that changes forever. Parents are changing too. The bright eager parents of the new baby look more haggard, less patient, and more experienced fifteen years later. If the promise of marital fulfillment gradually erodes into indifference and depression, the entire family shares the consequences.

The Family Is a Social System

To understand the family, we must view individuals within a family as part of a relationship system. A person's behavior is a result of forces both within *and* outside him. Besides instinctive needs, he has needs learned in a social context, needs stimulated by the transactional interchange with other people. Each of us has a learned history that we bring into every new transaction. It is the combination of this learned history plus the stimulation of new experience that results in our behavior. We are shaped as a person by both past experience and current relations with others.

The quality of the relationships is the most manifest aspect of a family's emotional life and can be considered a mutual process. In essence, the family is a social system with interdependent and interrelated forces of influence; each member of this system is mutually involved with each other member, and the systematic pattern of behavior that is the result of living together is due to the wholly interlocking nature of the human emotional relationships. This is illustrated diagrammatically in Figure 1.

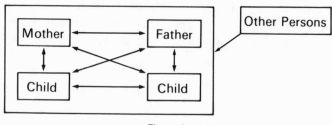

Figure 1

In a family of four, for example, there exist six dyadic, reciprocal relationship possibilities. These tie each member of the family to every other member both directly and indirectly through another person to whom he is directly related. One might construct a physical model of this diagram by using paper clips to represent each family member and connecting rubber bands to represent the relationship vectors in the diagram. If the paper clips are each fastened down and the rubber bands drawn taut, the model will assume a stability that can be altered at any time. Plucking any of the rubber bands will reverberate the entire model. Similarly, any action or reaction pattern between any two family members will resonate throughout the entire family. Marital difficulties between parents will often manifest themselves in symptomatic behavior in one of their children.

This "family resonance" phenomenon is the perpetuating mechanism of characteristic behavior within a family. Reinforcement of certain kinds of behavior is not unilateral or even bilateral but multilateral; thus, change can either be encouraged or resisted.

In addition to the relationship reciprocity and resonance just described, the family social system also has certain other characteristic qualities:

1. The family system possesses a boundary delimiting expected or prescribed behavior within the system. The boundary can be relatively open to interchange—agreement or mutual exchange with other systems outside of it (e.g., church, school, friends)— or relatively closed to external influence—that is, the family somewhat resembles an alienated secret society.

2. Behavior within the family is regulated by overt and covert "rules" that maintain the system in balance. These rules are a system of beliefs about what is right and wrong, good and bad, acceptable and unacceptable in human relationships. They evolve over time from a "mythology" shared first between the marital pair and later with the children, who have been taught the rules or learned them by imitation and observation. This mythology results from perceptions on the part of the parents about the nature of the human world as they have experienced it, especially certain learned convictions about the relationship between self and others that came from their families of origin. The place of rules in the family system may be seen in Figure 2. Their primary function

is the maintenance of stability within the system by encouraging redundant behavior and, thus, the self-perpetuation of the system.

MYTHOLOGY ⟶   RULES   ⟶   BEHAVIOR IN
                                                                    FAMILY

(Learned convictions   (How relationships   (How, in fact, family
from past family   are conducted)   members do relate to
experience)   one another)

Figure 2

3. In order to survive together, a family must maintain a kind of dynamic unity that allows the members of the family to grow, while at the same time the intactness of the family is preserved— this is the task of the functional family.

To do this, the balance of emotional relationships within the family takes on certain protective and often deceptive or displaced properties. Difficulties in one person or within a particular complex of relationships in the family tend to be compensated for in other areas of family living. For example, for the marital pair who can survive only with a troubled child, the child keeps the focus of family life off the parental relationship and on himself. He (not they) becomes the problem, and the parents together will help him (and not have to look at their own relationship).

While the way in which the family lives inevitably alters and changes with time and new demands, it also tends inevitably to be highly resistant to any change that runs counter to or threatens to destroy the established emotional balance. For example, when any one member of the family does not seem to fit into the existing pattern of relationships (he may be frustrating family success by failing in school), attempts are made by the other members of the family to deal with this maverick. Families who are comprised of mainly passive people may be substantially disrupted by the birth of a rather aggressive individual. He often will tend to become the scapegoat for difficulties in the family and not infrequently will develop symptomatic behavior. Symptomatic behavior in a family member really represents an area of dysfunction within the total family unit that the one member is acting out in his own behavior. Disturbed symptoms (e.g., school failure, withdrawal, depression, etc.) are an indicator of family dysfunction rather than exclusively internal, individual disturbance.

4. It is also necessary to look for changes of behavior within the family system. What causes it to alter? What is the source of behavioral deviations from generally accepted, shared family norms? Behavior within a family system is related to the degree to which certain emotional needs are met by family living. Dysfunctional changes or unexpected alterations of behavior occur when these needs are not met by relationships with other family members. There are two sets of need patterns that must be met in the living together in a family. The first can be termed the idiosyncratic needs of the individual, needs that are peculiar and particular to a specific individual. A more passive person, because of his constitutional nature, requires generally more reassurance. A more aggressively constituted person requires adequate outlets for his aggression. The second class of needs is what Virginia Satir calls "basic survival needs." In order to survive psychologically in a matrix of relationships, all persons must have their needs for sense and order, productivity, and intimacy met by the family.

The need for *sense and order* implies that the behavior of people around oneself must make some kind of sense: the environment in its totality—the people, how they live and how they relate— must follow a predictable and meaningful sequence. One must be able to rely and depend upon this sense and order within the family to stabilize himself and eventually to orient himself to a larger world outside the family. For the parents, this familial sense and order acts as an anchorage from the trials and tribulations of their lives outside the family.

The need for *productivity* means that persons in the family must have a productive place in its work output. They must feel worthwhile, useful, and able to perform adequately in assisting with the multitude of practical and necessary tasks the family has to carry out. This includes not only who cleans the basement but who gives support, encouragement, enjoyment, and regulation.

The need for *intimacy* calls for a degree of emotional closeness to others in the family that permits people to know one another deeply and to be aware of their full range of human uniqueness. Intimacy permits trust and confidence in relationships; it allows one to grow without fear and to be confident in experiencing others. These basic needs for survival are essential if one's self-esteem is to be raised in relationships; only then can psychological growth occur in a person within a family.

5. What goes on inside the social system we call the family is a whole variety of communication, subtle and flagrant, hidden and apparent, spoken as well as acted out in behavior. In fact, it has become increasingly clear that *all* behavior between people in a relationship is communication—communication about the relationship between self and other. The communication may be in the form of language that is plain and direct or that uses metaphors, similes, and symbolic analogies. The communication may also include a whole variety of nonverbal gestures: as voice tone, facial expression, posture, skin-color phenomena (blushing), and a whole host of nonverbal or analogic forms of communication. In fact, the nonverbal forms of communication are often the most meaningful communication between people, even though their significance is frequently denied or expressed in a covert fashion.

To understand the transactional nature of family relationships it is necessary to develop a way of thinking about human behavior that accounts for both individual personality and the human relationships of the family. One way of doing this is to think of the personality as a kind of "self-system" and the relationships in the family as a variety of "self–other negotiations." Both the self-system and self–other negotiations operate at the same time and the result is relationship outcome. This can be visualized readily by looking at Figure 3. The circles in the middle of the diagram represent the individual person. The lines inside the circles represent what goes on "inside" him; the lines outside the circle represent relationship exchanges between people, what goes on "outside" him.

The "self-system" gives us living potential. It is what the unique individual brings into relationships. It is what is inside of us that we manifest to the outside and use in meeting the reality of our social environment, especially in meeting those people with whom we have close relationships. "Self–other negotiations" are merely a way of conceptualizing the obvious reciprocity and mutuality involved in any two-person relationship. When B manifests any kind of behavior toward A, A can respond functionally only if he takes into account his own needs *and* the initial action of B. When B then replies to A, he must do exactly the same. The relationship between two people then becomes circular in its causality. Each stimulates and perpetuates responses in the other and consequently between the two of them. An oversimplified example would be

Self-System
(What goes on inside of us—thoughts and feelings)

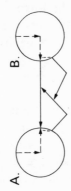

A.

Consists basically of:
(a) perception of reality
(b) picture of self relative to others

Self-Other Operations
(How self and other relate)

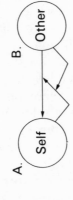

A. Self   B. Other

Consists principally of:
(a) games—a one person payoff to gain self-esteem
(b) intimacy—a secure encounter to enhance self-esteem

Relationship Outcome
(How it turns out when two self systems form a relationship system)

A.   B.

Results in:
(a) functional outcome when psychological survival needs are met
(b) dysfunctional outcome when psychological survival needs are not met

Figure 3

the relationship between an alcoholic husband and a nagging wife. He says, "I only drink because you nag." She says, "I only nag because you drink." Therefore, the more he drinks the more she nags and the more he drinks, and so on. The cycle is unending and mutually supported. The joint consequence of their relationship is mutual despair and frustration.

Any relationship eventually results in a choice between "games" and intimacy. (It is possible to have some of both, but there is usually more of one or the other.) Games, as Eric Berne uses the term, are an avoidance of intimacy. They are an attempt through the use of interpersonal maneuvering to work for a one-person payoff in the hope of gaining self-esteem. Intimacy, on the other hand, can be seen as a kind of secure and meaningful encounter with another that enhances self-esteem. Transactional behavior, the result of the blending of self-systems and self–other negotiations, is reciprocal and mutual behavior between persons. Within a family system, transactional behavior means that the consequences of this behavior are meaningful and influential on all the people of the family. All are linked together in a system of relationships that binds them in mutual responsibility and obligation, as well as in enjoyment and growth. In fact, looking at human behavior within the context of the family, we are looking at the reciprocal nature of change and survival, for better or for worse. Living together may lead to growth or to danger, fear, and defensive anxiety.

This book deals with basic areas of information and concern about the family. It is broken down into seven parts, each of which is further divided into brief chapters that illustrate common patterns of familial behavior. The behavior patterns will be given in the form of a "syndrome" or a pattern of behavior that forms a typical "transactional sequence"—how A's behavior is related to B's behavior, which, in turn, affects A's behavior (A ⇆ B). The colloquial descriptive titles are not intended to convey any humor or enjoyment in the relationships themselves; they are merely easily-recognizable designations for particular sequences of behavior within a family.

The first five parts of the book deal primarily with dysfunctional processes in the family, while the final two are concerned with functional relationships. Each part has its own brief introduction so that the syndromes are seen in relation to the family as a system. The syndrome descriptions are not intended to be a complete lexicon of family patterns. They are meant only to illustrate more prominent behavior and to indicate the rather complex interlocking of elements in a dysfunctional pattern. Certain phenomena will be repeated in several chapters; these are the vital and redundant elements in human interaction. Their repetition emphasizes this and places these phenomena in their several common patternings.

Since the self–other dyad is the basic unit of transactional relationship, many of the patterns will be discussed in terms of self and other. Both are seen as givers and recipients in the relationship on an alternating basis.

PART I

How We Affect One Another

Because the network of relationships in a family is mutual and reciprocal, all members of the family are affected by dysfunctional behavior anywhere in the system. If, for example, the head of the family is alcoholic, his problem affects all the others in the family. Conversely, it has often been discovered that the other members of the family have indeed contributed to and been a part of the "problem" one member of the family appears to possess. When families develop seriously dysfunctional relationship patterns, there is usually one particular "identified patient," even though realistically the whole family's pattern of behavior is involved. This dysfunctional pattern both stimulates and perpetuates the symptoms of the identified patient; often all family members experience some distress. With disturbed families it is, in fact, difficult to tell who has the symptom, or, in other words, "who's got the button."

The family will become unconsciously convinced that the only way to maintain themselves as a family—that is, to survive together psychologically—is to continue to allow one member of the family to have a symptom. The tension and stress dysfunctional relationship patterns promote are drained off in that one person. All the hurt, anger, frustration, etc., are focused on and embodied in his symptoms. The relationship process, which evolved in their living together and led to the accumulated hurt, is thereby over-looked and avoided. Overall family tension is, moreover, lessened. Any attempt to change symptomatic behavior, either within the family or from outside, is met by a "stop rocking the boat, please" response.

Chapter 1

"Who's Got the Button?"

Clinicians in the mental health field have for some time been aware of a curious and alarming phenomenon. When one member of a family comes to seek help for a symptom he is experiencing, it often turns out that other members of the family are likewise experiencing symptoms. It often seems as if the most functional and healthiest member of this family comes in for help first. If his symptom is alleviated, other members of the family may subsequently come in with even more severe difficulties. Who exactly has the symptom may be the wrong question. Examining the family as a total unit, the more reasonable question is: What patterns of interrelationship within the family led to progressive dysfunction and symptomatology on the part of the members of the family? In other words, it is not so much "who's got the button?" but "why is the button necessary in the first place?"

Suppose, for example, that a family of three is involved in the "Who's Got the Button" pattern. One might initially see an adolescent son with a recalcitrant attitude, a poor school record, and a propensity for marginal delinquent involvement with the law. This young man has parents who are also experiencing difficulties but in a different manner: The mother seems quite depressed and is prone to wide mood fluctuations; the father suffers from a periodic ulcer flare-up. The parents complain that the boy is difficult to control, never seems to pay attention, and is uncooperative. The young man feels that his parents do not understand him.

When the three members of this family are together, the father at times appears to become somewhat angry with his wife. However, he does not direct his anger at her but rather turns toward his son with a tirade of personal criticisms. At the same time the father, who insists the son cannot be controlled, never really attempts to enforce his or his wife's expectations of the boy. The mother, while she can be subtly critical of her husband, is much less so of her son. It is apparent that the triangle of mother, father, and son at times involves the mother and son in a coalition against the father, while at other times the father and son form a coalition against the mother. The father, by not enforcing his and his wife's expectations of the boy, is tacitly allowing the youth to act up in a manner that will justify his criticism of his son (really meant for the mother). Secondarily, the son's behavior is upsetting to the mother and reinforces a sense of failure on her part. Unable to deal with her husband, she transfers her concern and affection to her son, thereby "showing" her husband that she can survive without him.

The other point to be noted in this pattern is that the son is involved alternately in coalitions with each parent against the other. Such a position is confusing and insecure for a family member. The family in general appears to lack direction and authoritative responsibility. Each tries to align with the others in order to avoid being left out.

The germ of this interaction lay in a parental contract, unconscious, of course, made when they first married in which they agreed not to disagree openly. This was one of the rules crucial to their relationship and evolved from the belief—or mythology— that open disagreement between people only dissolves relationships. (Very heightened amounts of disagreement *are* disintegrative in their influence on relationships, but this occurs only in the extreme.) At the same time, open communication of differences between people is absolutely essential in order to negotiate a joint outcome. Because, in fact, these parents were different from one another and were at times resentful, disappointed, and perplexed with one another, their feelings needed to be handled in some manner. Because they could not disagree, the angry and resentful feelings were shifted to their son. Under these circumstances, his recalcitrance, poor schoolwork, and delinquency pattern were not at all surprising. The mother at the same time had much to be depressed about; images and expectations about her marriage and her family had been rather rudely and progressively destroyed. The father's evasive and vague way of relating kept his feelings deeply bottled up and eating away at him. Not only was his self-esteem gradually eroding, so was his stomach lining.

This pattern represents a kind of psychological family collusion; an attempt, albeit desperate and dysfunctional, to maintain family "togetherness" in order to keep the family intact. The collusion is based on an unconscious conviction that a minimum of conflict at all costs will result in a maximum of security in being together. It was better, they felt, to live this way than not live together at all. This was the only alternative they felt existed.

Often the relationships in a family are a living example, in the form of a neurotic reenactment, of unsolved conflicts, false assumptions, and defensive fears of abandonment. In other words, each member of this family says to himself, "I may be abandoned, deserted, or not cared for if I don't——." The mother and father fill in the blank space by their denial of anger in order to preserve the relationship. For the son, the blank space represents his role as a volunteer scapegoat for the submerged, but ever-present, resentment in the family. This pattern represents a kind of cooperative "survival," even though it is growth-inhibiting.

The potential for helping this family to become more functional resides in their ability to grasp the false assumption involved in their dangerous-disagreement mythology and in their ability to become aware of their pain and to express their feelings to one another. They must learn not to be taken for granted but to be listened to and understood, even disagreed with. In short, they need to learn to live with, learn about, and tolerate differentness without feeling that they do not belong or are not cared for. The symptoms they have are the result of a progressive, but thoroughly patterned, interaction.

Chapter 2

"Stop Rocking the Boat!"

This pattern is often seen in families where the parents appear to have a satisfactory marital adjustment. The symptom behavior arises, however, when one or more of the children does not accept the rules of relationship the parents have thoroughly accepted and agreed to. The child therefore represents a threat to the mythology about behavior that the parents have been able to tolerate.

Underlying this interaction is the false assumption that relationships can exist only if the individual uniqueness of a person is denied. The parents come from very similar families of origin in which their own uniqueness as children was ignored, denied, and in general not reacted to. It is relatively easy for them together to accept the same assumption in their marriage. They must still, however, convince their children to accept it. The "rule" itself represents a basic violation of the survival need for intimacy, which can occur only where uniqueness and individuality have been recognized. Otherwise each self is denied real significance in his relationship to others.

Two factors conspire in the initiation of this syndrome. First, since the child is a unique individual, he has a survival need for intimacy—for closeness and for recognition of his uniqueness. He cannot accept the false assumption. (Only if he is eventually beaten down will the child "tolerate" the situation in order to survive with the parents.) Second, the parents, involved in finding their own individuality, are somewhat prone to give their child what they did not have—to allow him more individuality. These two influences result in the child's breaking the rules. If the parents expect all the children to sit quietly and take orders, the one who questions or rebels to unburden his resentment and express his unique identity will rock the boat. The child may manifest this in a recalcitrant attitude, open argumentative rebellion, or hostile and destructive behavior, but the child's behavior is tantamount to the destruction of mutual capacity to survive in the family. When the child resists the trampling of his uniqueness, the parents feel they are failures. The child, on the other hand, can never please his parents, so he feels a failure. Nobody succeeds. Everybody feels hurt, but nobody admits to it. Identity denied is often replaced by helplessness and rage, resulting in this kind of family pattern and, once again, the progressive destruction of self-esteem.

Family members in this pattern are generally unemotional but experience periodic outbursts of "temper." These outbursts, in fact, are quite frightening to the members of the family and result in considerable ensuing guilt and often depression. For the most part, however, the family seems rather passive and superficially harmonious. Usually their complaint is, "Our only trouble is ——." The blank here is filled in with the name of a family member who has not gone along with the rules of relationship the parents have established for themselves. Often the child's behavior is de-linquency-oriented, which represents an expression of the inner feeling of "badness" on the part of the identified patient—the child with the symptom. It also tends to be extremely destructive to the parents' perception of the family as a "good family," leaving the parents feeling guilty and helpless.

Expressing any kind of feeling is difficult for members of this family. It is feared even positive feelings may be rejected but negative feelings pose a larger problem. Conflict means difference, which is tantamount to, "You don't love me" and, hence, abandonment and rejection. Family members often subsequently feel hurt and disillusioned with one another. This hurt is often seen in terms of who's to blame, rather than who will take action next. Few, if any, overtures are made to face up to the inherent and expectable conflicts present. In such a system the fate of the nonconformist or the identified patient (who is open with his feelings) is not to be loved. Consequently, he cannot risk expression of positive feelings toward the parents for fear that only further rejection will ensue. This, of course, only adds to the futility and helplessness on the part of the parents, who then deal with their frustration by further rejecting their own child. The dysfunctional circle becomes self-reinforcing, and after a while they all conclude that only by having "their way," can they feel worthwhile as an individual. This then brings them in conflict with the needs and wants of others in the family. They cannot all have their own way at all times. The cycle is unending.

Differences between people living in any family can be negotiated only if they are freely communicated. But fear of such free communication is the hallmark of this pattern. The only potential for growth, therefore, lies in exposing the family members to the experience of free communication without threat and injury—with the experience of uniqueness and differentness and occasional hurt that is the lot of us all.

Frequently in such families the child's behavior reaches the point of legal intervention, at which time he is removed from the family. The tension in the system is relaxed and, therefore, the family once again resumes its dysfunctional but relatively stable balance, only to produce another symptomatic child within a short time (unless the children have all learned to "play ball" with the parents rather than get out or be thrown out).

The basic difficulty in dealing with this family is the largely nonverbal quality of their patterns of communication. Meaning is more often expressed by gesture, looks, and voice intonation than by words, which tend either to be sparse or superficially reassuring. Seldom are their words truly indicative of how they feel and perceive their own relationships within the family. Second, action or change is difficult to initiate since it is *blame* rather than *responsibility* that is the hallmark of this type of interaction. The family will feel hurt, they will experience much frustration, and they will feel very guilty. But their self-esteem is so low that it is extremely difficult for them to be aware of and admit to their role or their participation in the dysfunction of the family. They cannot assume responsibility for the difficult task of change toward functional living.

PART II

Communication and Relationship

Both marriage and family life are kinds of relationships. Content differs, but they are essentially the same relationship process. The most vital elements in a close emotional relationship are (a) the realization of uniqueness, and (b) the negotiation of human differentness. Each of us, whether a spouse in a marriage or a member of a family, is unique. The emphasis in marriages and in families, however, is often on sameness and likeness rather than on differentness. This may take the form of a compromise: "You don't find fault with me, and I won't find fault with you." It may involve an attitude of ignoring obvious differences. It also takes the form of outright denial and suppression of the family members' unique qualities. But it is all too apparent when people live together in a family or marital relationship that differences are inherent in such an association and that these serve as a pool or reservoir of conflicts. These conflicts are necessary for close relationships because the basic, real qualities of a person emerge most genuinely under an assertive encounter with another. The full quality of one's thoughts, feelings, and actions comes forth under the stress of making room for unique selves in a joint-outcome system. The aggressive encounter, whether a verbal argument or the sudden, silent awareness of differentness, provokes a commitment to openness or to deception,

23

to solving the riddle and the anguish or to retreat from defeat (the discovery that you are not the center of the universe, after all). Uniqueness that is not manifest cannot be dealt with in terms of any process of negotiation of differences. Unexpressed individuality results in simmering resentment that periodically erupts in argumentative or emotional outbursts or, on the other hand, in a depressed and detached relationship.

Virginia Satir has repeatedly emphasized how the communication of uniqueness and the negotiation of difference are vital to insure psychological survival. If uniqueness is to be realized, it is essential that a person in a close relationship manifest himself openly and clearly to the other person. All the processes of communication (speech, gestures, posture, voice intonation, etc.) play an important role in this. It is essential that we let the other know how we think, feel, see, and hear about ourself and about them. Only in this way can true uniqueness be revealed, and only then do we have a basis to negotiate differences.

In this country we have a whole series of romantic notions and myths in regard to certain aspects of relationship in marriage and family. Although the rationale for marriage is largely based upon a romantic attachment, there is also a considerable romanticizing and idealizing of "motherhood," "the dear child," and "my wonderful parents." These notions, while they contain some obvious reality, are generally quite overstated. They refer to an idealized conception of a relationship that only rarely occurs. Many parents, spouses, and family members realize that working together in such a close relationship is often a difficult and arduous task. It requires a great deal of effort, thought, and consideration to adjust to a spouse, a parent, or a child. It has its rewards, certainly, but it also has demands, responsibilities, and frustrations.

These idealizations often screen or cover up the uniqueness of the people involved and therefore make it difficult to negotiate differences and eventually to negotiate joint outcome. This, however, is extremely important. The systematic nature of a marital or family relationship implies that what affects one affects all; outcome is always joint, not a singular, individual matter without effect on family members.

Those who have the greatest difficulty in dealing with "differentness" generally prefer to live in a state of "relationship fusion," denying human uniqueness and avoiding the negotiation of differ-ences. Sameness (fusion) is taken to imply security from criticism and fault, from attack and loss of self-significance (if perfection is the only allowable significance). The real differences between self and other are wiped away in fantasy only; human uniqueness still remains. The denials and evasions only destroy the opportunity for satisfactory joint outcome.

A family begins when two persons coming from separate families reach a committed decision to live together. It is also, of necessity, a commitment to work together and to love together, to fulfill both idiosyncratic and survival needs in the relationship. Both marital partners, in their families of origin followed a pattern of alternately coming together for nurturance and leaving one another for growth and maturity, a pattern that will continue to characterize their life. Originally mother and child are almost one. The birth process then separates them. Yet in terms of physical and emotional nurturance they remain close together. Gradually the child leaves the mother to join playmates, and later a larger separation occurs when the child leaves home to enter school. This same kind of critical separa-tion again occurs with the completion of high school when the child, then a young adult, leaves home to pursue either an occupation or a college education. What goes on during this eighteen-year period between parent and child is a constant alternation between being together and being apart. Both are necessary, one for nurtur-ance, which makes growth possible, and the other for independent maturity, which is necessary for self-sustaining direction. When the child–young adult finally leaves his parents to marry, he again comes together with another. In fact, it is quite apparent that the ability of the marital partners to be together and to nurture one another is what makes it easy, comfortable, and secure for them to assume mature and independent responsibilities within the family and outside the home as well. In relationships where the nurturance aspect is poorly developed, there is a heightened degree of jealousy, mistrust, and insecurity. Still later on, the two who have come to-gether in marriage have children and serve as the source of nurturance for yet another generation. The whole process begins anew.

Because the exact content of prior family experience varies widely for each individual, spouses bring more differentness than similarity to marriage and family life. Culturally accepted romantic notions often delude partners into assuming similarity where there is really difference. What is involved when two people come together in marriage and initiate a family is graphically illustrated in Figure 4.

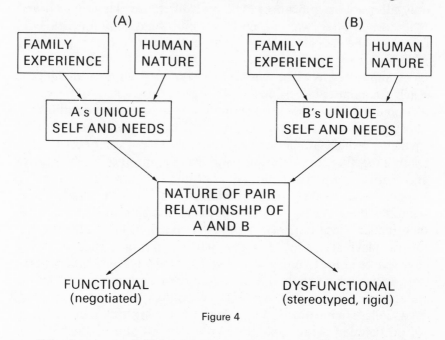

Figure 4

Whether a particular initial pair relationship (marriage) results in a functional (negotiated) relationship or a dysfunctional (stereotyped, rigid) relationship depends considerably on the degree to which each spouse has been able to separate himself from his own parents. The separation from parents is a critical indicator of the person's ability to realize his or her own uniqueness, to grasp the rather sizable generational difference between parents and children, and to negotiate that difference into a new kind of relationship between parent and child—namely, into the relationship of a younger adult and an older adult—who, while they differ in experience, are alike in their ability to assume responsibility and to exercise judgment. Only then can a successful marital relationship be originated. Marriage too, is a relationship of adults in mutual responsibility and judgment, but there is room for only two. The presence of another (in-laws), whether it presents a well-meaning involvement or an outright interference, is detrimental to the fulfillment of a mature relationship for the young married couple. It only helps to perpetuate an infantile parent–child relationship among adults and thwarts the development of a mutually responsible adult-to-adult relationship.

Methods and the devices of communication that have been learned in the family of origin are carried by each spouse into his or her marital relationship and, later on, into their gradually emerging family system of relationships. Where there has been avoidance, denial, and cover-up in the family of origin, these same maneuvers will be tried in the newly formed marital relationship. Where there has been a more open manifestation of self, a value placed on uniqueness, and where negotiation of differences has taken place, this likewise will be carried into the new marital relationship. Some families teach children a potential for functional relationship, others do not. This is not an inborn characteristic; it is learned, and it is difficult to change. Romantic love does not change people at all—it only glosses over obvious differences and hides productive uniqueness.

The awareness of the need to negotiate joint outcome in marriage evolves from the kind of policy that families develop to deal with essential aspects of relationship. George Bach has described five essentials of relationship formation that all couples and families must learn how to handle:

1. *Trust Formation*   "How far can I go?" This is the degree to which a person is able to reveal himself to another. Trust formation is enhanced when revelation of self leads to repeated support and when the conflict of differences that emerges from mutual self-revelation is repeatedly survived. This process may also be interpreted as self-exposure—a more negative perception that tends to lead to defensiveness and anxiety. Thinking in terms of self-revelation is a more positive, growth-directed conception.

2. *Affirmation*   "What do I want you to think of me, and, in fact, what do you actually think of me?" This represents the confirmation of one's identity in a relationship with another. It often leads to certain recognized discrepancies between one person's self-perception and another's, and leads to alterations and growth in one's identity. If the discrepancies are perceived as a threat to a needed sufficiency or perfection, then further inflexible and rigid self-deception occurs.

3. *Distance–Closeness* "How much can you be different from

me and similar to me as well?" It is necessary to communicate how much difference one can stand in a relationship with another. Open and direct manifestation of expectations and needs is required, involving distance and closeness in ideas and in actions. It also involves the negotiation of the closeness in the physical-sexual relationship.

4. *Power Role Relation* "Who leads and who follows, and under what circumstances?" This necessitates a clear and mutual understanding of how decisions are made. It deals with the very crucial matter not only of what the rules of relationship are, but who decides what rules of relationship are in play. The policy may be *symmetrical* (a policy of power equals, with debate and logical resolution to a decision), *complementary* (each has "spheres" or areas of decision making in the relationship), or alternately symmetrical and complementary.

5. *Outside Relationships* "Whom can you see and whom can I see apart from each other and under what circumstances?" This deals with the whole area of the management of envy, rejection, hostility, and hurt that may arise from relationships outside of the marriage and the family. It is related to the separation of self from others and has its precedent in the self's separation from his family of origin.

Each newly married couple will have to establish their own policies regarding these areas of relationship formation. They will bring with them, however, a considerable amount of prior experience from their own family of origin. These differences of experience will need to be renegotiated, hopefully into an *emergent policy pattern* that fits this particular couple uniquely rather than as stereotypes from their own families of origin. An emergent policy allows the mutual exploration of wants, needs, and real possibilities and of willingness to work toward "what fits" rather than "who's boss." For example, a husband may want to live in New York City and a a wife to live in San Francisco. An emergent solution would begin with an exploration of what each *wants* in his city of choice. They would then look for cities that encompass most of these qualities. Eventually a most suitable (not ideally suitable) choice would emerge. Each, therefore, might well get most of what he wants, rather than their sacrificing or compromising equally. Human needs are more important than interpersonal power alignments.

Relationships do not just happen; they are built on assumptions on the part of each individual involved in the relationship. They proceed along the lines of experience and expectation of the spouses— experience in their families of origin and expectations of how hurts, failures, and unmet needs in the family of origin can be corrected in the current marital relationship. One can readily say, therefore, that a relationship is conducted (usually unconsciously); it does not just happen. It is necessary, however, that mutual open communication be a vital part of how a relationship is conducted if the relationship is to be directed toward a mutually satisfactory joint outcome. This includes how one feels about marital experience as well as what one thinks about it.

The process of communication in a close, intimate relationship is an extremely complicated phenomenon. While we all speak the same language, we nevertheless have great difficulty in communicating with one another. Communication is not only the use of words— which can be complicated, vague, and ambivalent—but also involves a wide variety of nonverbal forms of communication. In fact, *how* something is said is often more important than what is said. The manner is what communicates the intent of the message. Words are not a clear enough indicator of meaning. The verbal message must be bracketed by other cues to give the receiver a more accurate indication of meaning. We talk with our eyes as well as our lips; we also talk with our posture.

Perhaps the most subtle nonverbal cue in communication between intimates is the historical context of the relationship. As they have lived together, certain repetitive patterns of message giving and receiving have emerged. This is most clear, for example, in messages between parents and children. Often a request is really not a request but a command. It is the obvious difference in power-role relations and the difference in degree of responsibility that gives a context to the parent–child relationship. Aside from this general context, there is an idiosyncratic context in any specific parent–child relationship. If, for example, in the past the parent has always asked or made a request in the form of a question, then it may well be perceived as a question when asked in the future. If, however, the child has always been asked to do something when he has really had no choice, then a command context has been part of the communication between this parent and this child. Asking a question indicates that a true choice of answers exists for the respondent. If this is in reality not so, the parent is using what might be termed "the democratic manipulation ploy." If mother asks Mary if she *would like to* do the dishes tonight, it would seem to follow that Mary has the choice of answering, "Yes," she would like to; or "No," she would not like to. The question appears to be about what Mary "would like to do." However, if mother asks in a sweet tone of voice, with a tired smile, and never requests help when she obviously needs it, a command rather than a question is being put forth.

In communication between intimates, a real dilemma arises when the different vehicles of communication (verbal and nonverbal) are not congruent with one another; that is, the words say one thing but the nonverbal gestures indicate something entirely different. Confusion, misunderstanding, and mistrust are the usual results of such communicational double binds. In the previous example, Mary can answer the question logically and run the risk of hurting mother because of lack of loving concern. Or Mary can take the past relationship experience with mother as a disqualification of the question, and respond to the pseudodemocratic ploy as a request to do it "lovingly and voluntarily." The evasiveness and basic dishonesty of such communication becomes difficult to field at times, however. Both mother and Mary require their unique needs met but not at the expense of each other. Several similarly chronic patterns of communication dysfunction will be illustrated in the subsequent chapters.

The realization of a successful relationship derives from working for congruent and clear communication between intimates. Achieving a functional relationship depends upon (a) our ability to reveal uniqueness openly, (b) our ability to understand clearly the differences between us that this uniqueness makes imperative, and (c) negotiating these differences to fit the persons involved rather than to establish who is boss.

In a dysfunctional relationship there exists a process that is termed "pathogenic relating." This implies that such relationship patterns continue to perpetuate false relationship assumptions and painful joint outcome. Basically, a dysfunctional relationship does not meet either idiosyncratic needs or survival needs and reveals itself characteristically in the following ways:

1. *Psychological "Games"* These are ways of getting "one up" on the other in the relationship in order to enhance one's own self-esteem at the expense of the other.

2. *Neurotic Relationship Compulsions* The spouse and other current family members are seen as representative of siblings and parents in the family of origin and are so treated. This obviously deprives the spouse and children of their uniqueness and leads to stereotyped, repetitive, but inappropriate ways of relating to them.

3. *A Collusive Relationship* We agree to ignore the problems, romanticize our few successes, and decide we like one another when it is quite apparent that we don't.

4. *Communications Snafu* What we say and do to one another is vague and indirect, and we never bother to check it out with one another.

A dysfunctional relationship pattern is based upon wishes of how things "should be" and images of how things are "thought to be." What results are actions based on false images and unreal wishes, fostering anxiety, pain, and diminished self-esteem. Inevitably no growth can occur in the people involved. They are constantly on the defensive, protecting themselves from pain and hurt. They try desperately to gain self-esteem, often at the expense of the other. The mutuality of the relationship breaks down, mutual support fails, and desperation leading to withdrawal takes place. Because dysfunctional relationships are conducted on assumptions and not on reality, there is often confusion between what is intended an what, in fact, actually happened. For example, after a bitter exchange, Mary says to Bob, "I didn't mean to hurt your feelings." This is somewhat akin to expecting an injured pedestrian to "feel better" (less hurt) if the automobile that just ran him down was driven by an absent-minded but kindly old friend, rather than a homicidal enemy. Because what actually happened is more important than intent, it is necessary that we report back to one another and help one another check out what actually *did* happen if we really want to avoid hurting. It is the hurt we must deal with, not the intentions. In fact, it is not an uncommon ploy in dysfunctional relationships to express hostility under the guise of good intentions. This, of course, is unconscious in the sender but the receiver of these messages seems to be continually confused and hurt to the dismay of both. Since the family functions as a system, in order to correct its own errors the members of the system must report back to one another what is going on in the system. In other words, if the system is to be error-activated, it must utilize its own feedback routes and check out meaning by open comment.

What is reacted to in a dysfunctional relationship is an image or an expectation and not a real person. If the reaction to the original communication is in actuality a misperception, any resultant behavior is inappropriate. This, then, leads to further inappropriate behavior and a pathogenic circle of causality. A husband's response to his wife is based in part upon the wife's original response to him. Their pattern of relationship is circular and mutual—this is true in either functional or dysfunctional relationships.

The dysfunctional pattern may still be perpetuated even if one person guesses the intent of the other correctly. The correct guessing results in a "mind-reading assumption" in the relationship, and leads only to a further pattern where nobody ever checks messages out, they simply mind read. Few married people or family members are, in fact, actual mind readers. It is commonly assumed in our romantic myths about marriage and the family that mind reading to some degree comes from living together, but the reality of human uniqueness makes this impossible. Uniqueness in fact is not stable; it changes with time. Any person who grows evolves from his new experiences. He is continuously changing. Growth cannot come from stereotyped assumptions about a person, it can only come from experiencing his emerging and growing uniqueness. Only a corpse is entirely understandable and predictable.

Failures in communication that perpetuate a dysfunctional relationship are derived from four sources:

1. Sender's message is unclear (vague inappropriate use of language).

2. A distorted message is received (present seen in terms of past).

3. An inability to check out the meaning between the persons occurs (defensive reluctance to avoid "hurt").

4. Combinations of the above.

Chapter 3

"Shall We Sit and Talk in Silence?"

This pattern is most refined in families where the sullen stare is the favorite defensive maneuver. Hurt is expressed in silence, and the anger that ensues is revealed in the stare. The obvious dysfunctional value of silence is that one can project anything on to it he so desires—rejection, or every fantasy, hope, wish, and vindication imaginable. The absence of open, clear, and direct communication allows for this projection of private meaning. Persons cannot experience a relationship encounter without an awareness of what the encounter means to self, to other, and to the relationship as a whole; it is necessary to give sense and order to the ongoing relationship. When private meaning is substituted for openly communicated negotiation of conflict, only private, individual outcome is possible. Self and other become alienated.

The silent pattern often occurs between people who have deep needs for recognition and support but, at the same time, possess a consistent conviction of their own unworthiness and a fear that rejection is just around the corner. Any attempt to really express their needs goes unsaid because of this fear.

The self-martyred wife (A) and the strong, silent husband (B) are one possible set of partners in this mutual standoff. Eventually tears may flow or someone may "give in," but little is ever really said as to who wants and needs what or how they really feel. Frequently, nothing is said, and with the passage of time the incident is pushed aside. If an apology should eventually be offered in hopes of "breaking the ice," two possibilities may result; neither resolves the conflict. The adroit martyr has a distinct advantage here: 1. If B confesses lack of understanding, A can respond ʼby a condescending "Of course you didn't, dear." This, of course, implies that A is the innocent victim of B's stupidity. 2. A can give in out of sheer "goodness of heart," which B will accept. This leads to the rather elegant double payoff in that A's goodness is vindicated and B's churlish inconsideration is highlighted as well. From A's point of view this only confirms what she knew in the first place—that she was right. At no point is the hurt recognized or the need for recognition and support in any way fulfilled. Whenever conflict arises again there will be a clash, hurt will ensue, and they will sit and talk in silence again.

In all likelihood the communication that occurred during the silence was nonverbal but nevertheless meaningful. Watzlawick, among others, clearly demonstrates that we "cannot not communicate." Posture and facial expression take care of that. Amazingly what is obvious to most of us is difficult to recognize in a situation where our feelings are highly aroused. We are often "nonverbally blinded," yet the message is present.

If it is possible for the person involved to develop an awareness of these cues, however, they can then begin to do something about the pain they are mutually experiencing. This is largely a matter of introducing a new "rule" into the relationship system: When silence accompanies a disagreement (or any other form of conflict), each of the persons involved is required to note facial and postural "signs" and openly report them to the other. Mutual exploration of the significance of these signs must then occur. This allows the focus to be shifted to how one feels and away from defensive evasion via sullen silence. The focus is on "I feel hurt" rather than on self-vindicated martyrdom.

Nathan Ackerman concluded that there is often an inverse relation between verbal and nonverbal communication. In highly charged emotional situations where silence reigns, nonverbal communication is considerable. It would appear that the more we are able to clearly verbalize with one another, the less necessary it is to overstate meaning with gestural, postural, and voice-tone clues. Feelings of hurt, resentment, and anger are powerful; they always seem to find expression, if not verbally, then nonverbally. Over time, if their expression receives no recognition, they will eventually spill into symptomatic behavior—depression, an extramarital affair, or alcoholism. It is the behavioral manifestation of an underlying, circularly reinforced pattern of hurt—resentment—fear—withdrawal—low esteem—hurt, etc. If the silence interchange between the couple is to be altered into more clear and direct information exchange, the sequence pattern beneath it must be altered.

Among intimates, a breakdown of communication is also a breakdown of survival potential. Any relationship in which we risk our total being as a valued person is significant to our psychological survival (the will to live with purpose and commitment). In marital and family relationships, if meaning between the persons is unclear and vague, it is also threatening because of its unknown nature. In the place of sense and order, anxious guesswork and/or fatalistic withdrawal emerge. "Intimacy" is fraught with fear of loss of self-esteem. Mutual emotional support is not possible under apprehensive self-protectiveness. Only the specter of personal defeat and loneliness presents itself.

Even if we observe the nonverbal cues, without verbal reinforcement or validation we again run into the problem of possible misinterpretation and distortion. Guessing at intended meaning or surmising another's reaction, even when occasionally correct, is unpredictable and unreliable. Eventual direct and clear verbal clarification is necessary. Otherwise we fall prey to the "crystal ball" syndrome, that is described in the next chapter.

Families can also engage in "silencing strategies." Gerald Zuk has elaborated on a number of patterns which occur in families where there are areas of "dangerous information." This avoided information is a reservoir of feelings of resentment, hurt, anger, and fears of rejection that cannot openly be talked about in the family. The members fear that what they neurotically anticipate will indeed come to be, that these feelings will disintegrate the family. Secondarily, such silencing strategies involve a power tactic, frequently found between parents and children, that implies that "if you talk, you will be punished." Thus, silence is a strategy in interpersonal relations. As a power in and of itself, however, its value lies in keeping the other person guessing; the best defense against any perceived attack is to refuse to engage in any transactions at all with the other person (deny them any importance to you).

The underlaying assumption in the use of silence is that it is better than an outright dissolution of the relationship. This, of course, is predicated on the fallacy that conflict automatically dissolves a relationship. A person may be convinced that if you do not agree with him, you do not like him, and he, therefore, is less of a person. The fear of psychological annihilation of the self by another is presumed to be present. Many people cannot feel worthwhile unless they are the center of the relationship and therefore free from insignificance. Any conflict, however small, exerts a threat to this position and leads to expected loss of self-esteem. In other words, if you can't beat 'em, don't join 'em, just collapse.

To sum up, the biggest problem that verbal silence presents to a relationship is the reinforcement it gives to a fear of the unknown. Almost everyone is somewhat fearful and anxious about new situations and meeting new people. Knowing little about the quality of the new situation or person, one must risk one's own skin, initially, in order to find out. This, of course, is a chance we must all take in order to grow. For people who have been taught that growth itself is dangerous, the fear of the unknown becomes overwhelming. To obtain a feeling of security, of sense and order and to convey meaning in a relationship, it is necessary to be clear in our communication of thoughts, feelings, and perceptions. Any defensive posture that utilizes silence as a tactic results in diminution of our security about psychological survival in a relationship.

Chapter 4

"Those Are My Toes, Friend!"

Since no one person at any one time or even over a period of time is wholly functional in his communication, we must all use "corrective feedback" with others in our family to accomplish clarity, delineation, specificity, and congruency. Realistically, any one person's communication to any other person is usually a mixture of functional and dysfunctional features. This may take such forms as:

1. The message is clear, but the intended receiver is not clear. (E.g., "I wish someone would take the garbage out.")
2. The sender assumes that the receiver "knows" what he really means. (E.g., "Take the thing out there, you know"—the waste paper to the garage.)
3. The message is vague to cover up a suspected retaliation. (E.g.—after a request—"Well, I suppose I *could* do the typing for you.")

It is not as important to see communication as functional or dysfunctional *in toto* as to see in which ways it is functional or dysfunctional.

In human communication perfection and consistency are behavioral myths. Any value of good or bad, or right or wrong attached to these ideas is both false and unproductive in human relations. We are imperfect by nature and, therefore, our communication is imperfect. We must rely on communicational feedback to check out meaning. All systems (and also the family) are characteristically functional only as long as the errors that block progress are openly acknowledged. In communication between people in a family, problems of communication may be resolved only if each of the partners is receptive to the plea of reclarification from the other person and can report back what he doesn't understand and why the message is unclear.

Consider the following situation: A male graduate student at a large university is engaged in time-consuming research to complete his doctoral thesis. His wife, among other things, works part-time to provide financial support for the marriage, types his thesis, repairs the automobile, cleans the apartment, and makes many small but supportive gestures to help her husband feel like an acceptable man. This kind of relationship is taken for granted by both. At times the reaction of both seems to be: "That's all she does." Her "toes" are apparently his. She seldom reacts when they are frequently stepped on by his considerable demands and her own aptitude for getting them in the way. Who decides when and where reciprocity begins in this relationship? They could begin with smoldering resentment and proceed to alienation or begin with honesty and work toward shared intimacy. When psychological toes are stepped on it hurts and, if not expressed openly and directly, this soon becomes smoldering resentment. Persons do not enhance the emotional closeness in their relationship by concealing feelings. A gradual alienation will evolve that is supposed to protect one from further "hurt," and "show" the other how undesirable he is because he is imperfect. Marital and family intimacy derives from shared experiences of feelings, reactions, and conflicts—experiences that are mutually acknowledged. As long as there is no open commentary, especially on the wife's part, on the obvious imbalance in the above relationship, it is doomed to begin with smoldering resentment and end in alienation. On the other hand, if the wife can be honest with her husband about the load placed upon her, they can negotiate other alternative arrangements. They may then share the burdens and responsibilities and thereby develop more meaningful intimacy. This type of marital system began with a somewhat dysfunctional alignment and needs to be readjusted to a different kind of mutuality between the partners.

A second type of marital system begins with a suitable balance of responsibilities, but as time goes on vagueness and unclear communication results in progressive resentment. The following conversation is characteristic of this pattern:

Husband: I'm just overwhelmed with work.
Wife: Poor dear, you work so hard.
Husband: I can't seem to get it all done.
Wife: There never seem to be enough hours in the day.
Husband: Well, you could help more!
Wife: What would a man be without a woman?
Husband: Women are always nags!
Wife: What would you rather have me do, dear?
Husband: Never mind!

The conversation usually ends with nothing having been settled. A certain degree of resentment and confusion has arisen. How vague he was about what he really needed help with, how she could, in fact, actually help! In her attempt to be helpful the wife is superficially but vaguely supportive. The husband is not making his request clear in any way, and she assumes no responsibility by not asking for clarification when she is confused.

Consider a similar conversation now with functional communication:

Husband: I'm worried because I have fallen behind in my accounts. Would you have time to type some of them up for me?
Wife: I know how much that means to you. How much typing is there to do?
Husband: Well, I am about twenty billings behind, which amounts to about twenty typed pages.
Wife: Since I both work and take care of the home, too, I am also a little hard put for time. But if I didn't vacuum or wax the floors this week, I think I could work it in; if that would be all right with you.
Husband: I think I could live with that, and I would appreciate your help.
Wife: Well, why don't we try it out this week and see how it works then?
Husband: Okay, I'll bring them home tomorrow night and

if it doesn't seem to work out for you, let me know right away.

Notice the greater clarity about what is being asked, how each reports his feelings about what is being asked, and how the negotiation of the problem at hand is arrived at mutually. In the end, room is allowed for further negotiation and a reorganization of the initial scheme if, in practice, it should not work out. Because of the clarity, delineation, and specificity of their communication, the focus remains on the task at hand, rather than on whose self-esteem is to be diminished. Clarity of communication involves expression of what we want in terms of a task and our feelings about that task. Delineation is the appropriateness of the words that accurately and adequately describe both feelings and task requirements. Specificity involves the identification of a particular request that is a need of mine and that I am asking your help with in this particular way. It specifies the message, the sender, the receiver, and the expectation of an outcome.

When any of these aspects is missing from verbal communication, the receiver of such messages must report that it is unclear, undelineated, and nonspecific and ask for further clarification. It is then the functional responsibility of the sender to accept this feedback and to use it to clarify his messages so that the task may be completed. This is especially true in regard to how we feel about one another in a relationship.

The one very important aspect of communication that has not been touched upon so far is congruency: whether what we say in words is matched by what we convey in voice tone, facial expression, posture, etc. If the message is not congruent, it is also necessary for the sender to report the incongruency and the confusion that results. Incongruencies are a mismatch of human communication channels. They often occur in relationships when there is an "ought" or "should" assumption in the thinking of the partners, for example, where it is thought husbands should always be appreciative, wives should always be supportive, and children ought to know that what I am doing is for *their* own good. Since actual relationship behavior is reciprocal, response is stimulated by other prior actions, not by high hopes and good wishes.

When feelings are hurt and aspirations are not fulfilled, when anger and resentment flood our consciousness, we must learn how to say "ouch!" In other words, we must communicate this transactional pain to the other member of the relationship. We must be able to say, "Those are my toes, friend!"

It is necessary to divorce intention from behavior. The other person, after all, is affected by how, in fact, we behave, not by how we intended to come across. Unresolved hurt feelings, good intentions not backed up by appropriate behavior, and refusal to use communicational feedback when messages are unclear only lead to circularly perpetuated confusion, which deprives us of the opportunity to make sense and order out of our family relationships. It leads relationships to appear threatening, unreliable and unpredictable and, therefore, to our defensive behavior.

Consider the increasing dilemma and frustration that results from the inability to comment openly and clearly on the following pattern: The mother who will do anything for her child is usually accommodated by the child, who is only too willing to have everything done for him. In terms of self-responsibility where does the mother leave off and the child begin? Martyrdom is not helpfulness. They could have a relationship that begins in indulgence but would end up in angry alienation. Or they could begin with realistic limits and end up with mutual helpfulness. Who is manipulating whom? If the mother can only feel worthwhile by being omniscient and irreplaceable, then the autonomy and individuality of her child will suffer. This will, in turn, eventually lead to emerging resentfulness in the child, whose only escape may be a complete, and abrupt breakaway from the mother. The mother is, therefore, lonely and the child, hostile. She feels she has failed, and he is unable to negotiate the realities of life on his own. The pain that comes from failure and disillusionment in relationships is more difficult to tolerate in the long run than the risk involved in the open manifestation of needs, wants, feelings, and aspirations between self and other.

PART III

The Art of Manipulation

Manipulation has come to mean several things in our society. Originally it emphasized the *control of action by management*. More recently it has come to imply an intentional and dishonest action to gain an advantage. In this sense, it has become a somewhat "dirty word." In discussing the art of manipulation manifest in human relationships within the family, the earlier meaning of the word manipulation is intended. There are none of its usual negative implications, and human relationships are viewed as manipulative by nature.

Manipulation, usually to raise self-esteem, contributes to the joint outcome of the relationship—for better or worse. If the manipulative behavior is unilateral and unconscious (e.g., martyr tactics), joint outcome is more dysfunctional—not meeting the survival needs of sense and order, productivity, and intimacy; the four following chapters elaborate on this outcome. If the manipulative behavior is mutual and conscious (e.g., it is verbally agreed that she will dry dishes and he will wash them, because she hates to wash dishes, and he hates a cluttered sink), then joint outcome is more functional—more nearly meeting survival needs.

Obviously, if a person does not manipulate his environment to insure his survival, he will soon not survive at all. This is true of the physical environment and certainly there are corollaries in psychological survival as well. Many of the manipulations that occur between persons within a marriage or a family are often unconscious to the participants. Such manipulation exists nevertheless and serves the purpose of hopefully insuring some modicum of psychological survival. If the basic survival needs, whose satisfaction gives worth to "living," are poorly, partially, or seldom satisfied, a fundamental survival desperation sets in. A person is deprived of his will to exist as meaningful.

To survive psychologically persons will instinctively manipulate others to obtain satisfaction. Unfortunately for the manipulator, unilateral action produces only resentment and anger. This process further diminishes need satisfaction, and therefore enhances and perpetuates dysfunctional outcome. When mutual need meeting declines or is minimal, the mutual value of the relationship begins to dissolve.

In family relationships, the manipulative aspect of living together may either be covert or overt; that is, it may be clearly observed, recognized, and acknowledged by the members of the family (overt), or, while it can be observed in behavior, the acknowledgement and awareness of the manipulation is not recognized by family members. Both overt and covert manipulation occur even in basically functional families. Far more characteristic of the dysfunctional family, however, is greater covert manipulation in their relationships.

In any family there is the necessity for active collaboration among its members in the mutual meeting of both idiosyncratic and psychological needs for survival. This represents more than just a give-and-take process and usually includes such devices as: (a) accommodation (this time we'll have it your way, next time we'll have it my way); (b) compromise (let's each go half-way); (c) mutual negotiation (let's see what fits all of us the best). In dysfunctional families tactics that insure the survival of one person at the expense of another prevail. The goal is to determine not "what fits" but rather "who is boss?"

The history of manipulation in a relationship, particularly among intimates, is a long process of learning from direct experience. When openness and mutuality are viewed as threatening, witholding and manipulation emerge as unconscious "policies" of survival need attainment. One's family of origin unquestionably contributes heavily to the premises and convictions of self-conduct we bring into any later relationship. Earlier experience (with whatever false assumptions, anxieties, and control "ploys" were present), serve as the prototype for one's contemporary marital and family relationships. Only if negotiated rules emerge from open exploration of a need can dysfunctional manipulation be minimized. In all instances, however, the manipulation of persons in the family represents a person's often desperate attempt to obtain the satisfaction of a genuine need, in an inappropriate and self-defeating manner. It is not meeting human needs that is dysfunctional, but the means by which one attempts to achieve that goal.

Each of the chapters in Part III, as well as all of the chapters in Parts IV and V will utilize the following format for presenting transactional patterns.

Theme: A basic explanation of what is involved as far as relationship in the pattern goes and what is required to initiate and perpetuate this pattern.

Example: Typical illustrations of what the pattern looks like in actual behavior.

Dynamics: The nature, extent, and sequence of the transactional and psychological needs that underlie the pattern.

Resolution: What is required to transform the pattern into a functional sequence.

Chapter 5

"I Don't Wanna Go to School!"

Theme: The Family That Preys Together Frays Together

The persistent refusal to go to school is the result of a joint manipulative effort that involves both parents and child. It requires a withdrawn father, a dependent, unhappy mother, and a dependent, clinging child who will play the role of an intermediary. "Trying hard," tearful scenes, and weak but ineffectual pleas are common phenomena in this family pattern. Usually only mother "understands," father openly condones, and the "helpless" child can't resist keeping momma company. The point is that all successful manipulations are the result of unconscious collaboration and are predicated on the shrewd utilization of existing family traditions. If it is traditional to never comment openly on the presence of emotional pain, then diversions and displacements of this pain will manifest itself in family behavior. The collaboration is made possible by adherence to this rule. A child who remains home from school with an understanding mother and a seemingly protesting father, is signaling a much larger problem that involves the whole family. If the child has his mother's exclusive attention, the father is free to pursue his own interests and exclude the mother without guilt. After all, mother has a friend in the family. They are all to some degree satisfied with the result of the manipulation that seems to be the child's personal problem. At the same time, however, basic survival needs (sense and order, productivity, and intimacy) are poorly fulfilled. The father lives in relative isolation without support. The mother has to look to the younger generation for intimacy. The child's autonomy and confidence is diminished by overt attachment to the mother.

Example: It's What Eats You, Not What You Eat

The scene usually begins with little or nothing said at the breakfast table. The mother is busy cooking, but she looks unhappy and scowls. The father is busy avoiding the mother. If a newspaper is not convenient to sit behind, he may utilize a cereal box, a three-month-old magazine, or a profound and thoughtful, but rather detached, look. If there is conversation, it is evident that the mother is good at criticizing the father who responds with grunts. If there are words, the child has difficulty getting a comment in at all. The father is unlikely to respond to him and the mother wants to know, very solicitously, "What's the matter now, dear?" Since something must be the matter for him to speak up, conversation is limited to the general theme of personal complaints. When it comes to dressing and getting ready for school, the child is very slow if not downright resistant. His ability to take even the simplest two-minute job and parlay it into a ten-minute creative experience is both frustrating and admirable. The father by now has already left for work, mumbling under his breath or simply saying nothing and managing to slink out unnoticed.

In the more extreme form of this pattern the father may not even eat breakfast at home. In order to avoid his wife's accusations of his imperfections and his son's dawdling or health report, he eats alone in a restaurant. Here he can usually avoid critics and hypochondriacs. A guilt-free breakfast is more digestible, anyhow. If he feels guilty over his "monstrous family," he may skip breakfast altogether as a "penance."

At home, within fifteen minutes of the time to leave for school, the physical complaints begin to pour forth from the child. These have been previously suggested by the mother's earlier question, "What's the matter now, dear?" Albeit somewhat delayed, the child answers her before leaving for school. If the participants are adroit and experienced, the concern and complaint repartee will begin almost immediately. "Good morning" is replaced by "What's the matter?" followed by a physical systems inventory that would do an internist proud. While stomachaches are greatly preferred, headaches, armaches, legaches, and the "blahs" may be utilized with equal effectiveness. At this point the mother, being both understanding and sensitive to the needs of her child, wonders if it may not be better if Johnny stays home today. Johnny "reluctantly" agrees and miraculously enough, once the school "cop-out" has been successfully negotiated is symptom-free. He and mother are then left together for the morning or the entire day to engage in such enchanting activities as cutting paper dolls or pie baking. It is to be subsequently noticed that the mother's unhappiness lifts to some degree, and she will comment openly on what a nice young man she has.

While it is possible that the mother in this type of family pattern may not be verbally expressive in her unhappiness, her actions relative to her child's school attendance always give her away. Such a dialogue, characterized by sledgehammer subtlety, might sound and look something like the following:

Mother: (standing at the range/sink/refrigerator with a hand pressed to her bowed head. She speaks slowly in a low voice.) Good . . . morning . . . Johnny.

Johnny: (sleepily) Morning, Mom. What's for (pauses) . . . Is anything the matter?

Mother: (brightening up but smiling painfully) It's nothing. Don't worry yourself over it. Just eat a good breakfast so you will feel like going to school. (coming over to examine Johnny more closely) You look a bit peaked, dear. Is everything all right?

At this point father, who has been strategically arranged behind the morning paper, suggests that mother "quit babying Johnny." The ensuing low-key argument always seems to upset Johnny, who cannot eat. Since by mother's prior instructions, he cannot possibly feel well enough to go to school unless he eats a good breakfast, the die is cast. The displacement of pain from the mother–father dyad to son is swiftly completed.

In a relatively small amount of time the school officials seem to develop a rather negative reaction to Johnny's lack of attendance in school. But an adroit school refuser and his mother, with the absentee support of the father, will manage not to do this daily but just often enough to keep mother from being grossly unhappy and school officials from saying "it happens all the time." If the school does intervene because of poor school attendance, a secondary elaboration then begins on the earlier pattern. With much anguish on mother's and on Johnny's part, he is taken to school in spite of his "symptoms." Several alternate patterns are then open to the participants.

1. The child will go painfully, weeping most of the way. Usually once he joins his classmates, however, he will enter into normal school activities in an appropriate manner.

2. He will go angrily, shouting a host of invectives at mother. Most of these amount to how she could not possibly really love him or how she is mean and cruel and is trying to kill him outright. Again, once he joins his classmates he resumes his normal school activities.

3. He can also add to the invectives thrashing, kicking, and biting. This involves parents, teachers, principals, and crossing guards. It seldom, if ever, involves classmates. When all else fails the child will initiate his battle to avoid "incarceration at school" before he leaves home, hiding, attaching himself to the furniture, and otherwise physically resisting.

The mother in all situations is "trying hard" but is always seemingly ineffective. All children are capable of utilizing the above tactical devices; the real difference depends on a parent who *wants* them to go to school and is *firm* and *direct* about her expectations of the child. When a preexisting marital disturbance is present, however, all relationships within the family become dysfunctional. Panic, ineffectualness, and despair will prevail.

If Johnny's mother, in a splurge of middle-class maternal conscience, does quietly take him to school; and if he seemed to enjoy going, the following is likely to occur:

She brings him in by the hand, tenderly, and somewhat unhappily. If he is unable to produce any tears, she will usually be misty eyed. She will then reassure him that "it is all right to go." This sounds strikingly like false reassurance intended more for her than for him. As he walks away she appears to have some difficulty disengaging her hand from his. Just as she manages to do so, however, she lurches forward, hands extended, as if to reach out for him. Her face is the picture of pain and abandonment. Any child who can survive this last drama may be considered a paragon of functional, autonomous development.

Most children, of course, cannot withstand this final emotional assault by mother and rush back tearfully into her arms for reassurance. The question is, of course, "Who is reassuring whom?" The child is caught in a double-bind communication. The mother's words say, "Go ahead, it is all right"; her gestures and facial expressions convey that should he leave, she may very well die. The child is then left with no choice at all: He can either destroy his independence, or her life.

While the typical pattern involves the mother and a male child, it may occur with a father and a female child. If there is only one child in the family, whether male or female, the mother who is at home is most likely to utilize this child; for her, some company is better than none at all.

A school-refusal pattern will often occur in families in which there is a marital sexual adjustment problem that resolves itself into a conviction of lack of affection between husband and wife. This is usually mutual and accounts for the father's detachment and the mother's clutching unhappiness. The child with the symptom is generally of the opposite sex of the "affection loser" in the relationship. (This has tended to be the mother, since the father has had potential and opportunity for relationships outside the family.) While the mother may be the more overt affection loser she is in reality no more so than her husband; her opportunities for "affection procurement," however, are most likely within the family. In a psychological sense "while vice is nice, incest is best."

If all else fails and the child will not cooperate in the manipulation, the mother may pull all the stops and make a full-fledged attempt at "dropping dead." In effect, if the child will not have the physical symptoms, she will. As the child attempts to leave for school, her response will be "It's nothing—just my heart, again." (Chapter 9 deals with this particular facet of manipulation in detail.) Thought of his mother's imminent demise is both guilt-provoking and arouses fears of precipitous abandonment in the child. Either he will turn around before he arrives at school and return home, or he will not be able to last long in the classroom before "illness" forces him home. Once he is home, mother's heart condition clears up quickly. Her son's attention is worth more than all the medicine in the world.

Dynamics: Marriage Is for Adults

This pattern emerges most fully from an originally dysfunctional marital relationship, whose dynamics go unnoticed while the more overt pattern of school refusal is obvious to the outside observer. The marital disturbance itself is most likely the result of dysfunctional communication and an inability to negotiate joint outcome. Mutual affection in general, and sexuality in particular, become the battleground for the expression of differentness. To be different and to express needs differently is taken by each as a diminution of self-esteem. Differentness is seen as a threat to identity. Each must be perfect and complete. To make room for the other in one's own self is seen as the annihilation of self.

Consequently, the spouses tend to either avoid one another or to appear progressively hostile toward one another. Either way, neither can obtain much satisfaction in the marital relationship. The needs for support, affection, and closeness (psychological intimacy) still remain, however, and must be fulfilled in some manner. As the parents turn away from one another they will displace the desire to meet these needs upon one or more children. A wife who has little satisfaction from her husband may derive her emotional gratification from a relationship with the male child. The child then becomes embroiled in the survival battle between the parents. Each parent hopes to gain an ally in a child, to form an affection coalition against the spouse.

Since children are psychologically dependent to a very large extent upon their parents for survival, the mother's plea for help from the child is coincident with an implication that, if help is not forthcoming, the mother in fact may be lost to the child. If mother cannot survive, the child cannot survive. The latter, therefore, in a kind of psychological enlightened self-interest, must attempt to meet the mother's needs in order to insure his own survival. In essence, if mother and father cannot provide productivity and intimacy in their relationship, then mother and child will attempt to compensate for this lack.

This cannot be commented on openly, as father will then know that mother is the affection loser. She would then be one-down in the "I don't need you, anyhow," contest. Loss of face is an important phenomenon in families. The child also cannot consciously admit the disruption in family life caused by the disordered marital relationship. His whole survival depends on the continued maintenance of an intact family. The focus, therefore, turns on physical complaints rather than "if mom and pop can't love one another, how can they love me?"

The father, who may seem somewhat peripheral in the pattern, is not peripheral at all. His arrogant detachment is altogether necessary to provoke the mother into other avenues of affection procurement. Frequently, he will also criticize her handling of the child and in time will berate the child as the inappropriate neuroticism of the school-refusal pattern becomes more clear. This in turn only serves to fan the flames of attachment between mother and son. It is also likely that the father is jealous of his son. The child, after all, has been able to attain the affection the father has sought and failed to receive.

Each member of the family attempts in his own way to meet his own needs. While the neurotic manipulation in this kind of family encompasses the hope that all will be winners, they, in fact, all end up being losers. The school officials will disrupt the pattern, and the parents will argue over it; the child lives in fearful anxiety of his intermediary role in the conflict between mother and father. In addition, the child's autonomous development is thwarted by his overattachment to the mother. The parents continue to diminish their own self-esteem by a gradually accumulating conviction that they are undesirable to one another and only desirable to the children; if an extramarital affair should be a part of the picture, family life will seem a mistake and a disaster. The mother continues to feel the man she married no longer cares for her. The mother and father are alienated from one another. The child becomes alienated from his peers. All feel dissatisfied, frustrated, and lonely. The child is left with the unenviable task of acting as the glue to hold the crumbling marital relationship together. The parents can express at least some feeling, though negative, toward one another over the seriousness of the child's symptoms. The previous, almost totally disrupted communication is to some degree reinitiated again—but at what cost?

Resolution: Who Wants to Be Alone?

The functional resolution of so dysfunctional a relationship pattern requires enormous effort to get all members to focus on the underlying processes in the family rather than on what appears to be a fear of school attendance. In principle, the three basic functional processes must be restored to the relationships in the family. The only way to alter behavior within a family system is to change the rules that govern that system.

First, the needs involved in attaining intrafamily intimacy must be communicated, if they are in any way to be met. If these cannot be identified in a family member because of obscure, vague, and silent communication, survival confidence is diminished. The communication blockage must be removed. This means the open identification and communication of reactions of hurt and reactions of avoidance or withdrawal as an attempt to conceal hurt. Emotional hurt signals that one's perceived uniqueness has been violated. It matters little whether the actions that precipitated the hurt were intentional or not; it is only necessary to become aware that each is unique in a family and that difference is, therefore, inherent in relationships. This differentness, with its resultant inherent conflict, must be openly negotiated to ensure satisfactory joint outcome. Without a valued and significant place in day-to-day living for each member of the family, everybody will eventually suffer. Needs that are unmet are inappropriately displaced to another person in the family. Father needs the affection, support, and encouragement of mother; she, likewise, needs the same from him. The children require support, nurturance, and protection, not exploitation and overprotection for the needs of the adults.

As long as nobody can comment on the obvious detachment in the marital pattern, the parents will refuse to see it. They will continue to displace their needs by forming coalitions in the family to include some people and exclude others; for example, the coalition of mother and son excludes father. Such a father then cannot feel secure in his own family and can, in turn, give no security to it. The result can only be a circular and dismal pattern of gradual detachment and abandonment from his relationships in the family, leading to disillusionment, despair, fearfulness, and a lessening of the security of other family members.

No one has a crystal ball; needs must be openly communicated and thereby identified in order to be met. How they are to be met is often so idiosyncratic that negotiation for joint outcome is absolutely essential. It is not important that we be perfect in meeting one another's needs, we must simply be able to comment upon one another's imperfectness so that we may together and in mutual negotiation attain what is obviously beneficial to both parties. Need meeting is reciprocal and mutual. Private coalitions only serve to damage the emerging and interlocking mutuality of family life.

Since the family can hardly be any worse off than they already are, why not replace unconscious ploys with honest reappraisal. It will be necessary to draw attention to the manipulation that is taking place, whether intended or not. Change that requires the ability to look at old repetitious family behavior from a new point of view may be associated with the unknown. Since we fear the unknown, such change may be strenuously avoided. But this only increases the psychological pain within the family. The family system must utilize an awareness of its own operation in order to correct its errors. In systems terminology, it can only be error-activated if it utilizes feedback. Each member of the family must be free to comment on what he hears, sees, thinks, and feels about himself and others in the family. Fearful coalitions, anxious detachment, and hypochondriacal depression only add to the family pattern that resembles a subtle reign of terror more than the meeting of human needs in a living context.

The functional mutuality of needs must be restored. If family members cannot depend on one another to meet their needs, it is relatively pointless for them to remain together. In fact, they do need, and often want, one another's help but are unable to communicate this to one another. A commitment to family living represents, unconsciously, a commitment to depend on others. Such mutual dependency can only be negotiated into satisfactory joint outcome if the family can function as an open system:

1. Members must openly comment on how they see themselves and others operating in the family.

2. This information must not be used as a threat but as an opportunity for growth or change and a basis for working toward an emergent solution.

3. The family system must allow itself to be influenced by external forces to help it accomplish (1.) and (2.) above.

So often the "I Don't Wanna Go to School" pattern becomes so dreadfully dysfunctional that professional intervention is necessitated. But only by working with the whole family can such intervention, however professional, hope to succeed.

The family that "preys" together *may* stay together, but it does so at an enormous expense to its individual members.

Chapter 6

"Why Don't You Do It for Me?"

The unconscious wishes and desires of parents are realized in the behavior of their children. The two basic patterns here may be designated as (a) the male pattern and (b) the female pattern. The first requires an ambivalent father, an angry mother, and a loyal, but frustrated son. The second needs an ambivalent mother, an angry father, and a loyal, but frustrated daughter. There is a specific choice (dependent on subtle communication and manipulation and not mystical process) involved in which the child, within the family, acts out the parental impulses. Evidently: The child must be of the same sex as the parent with the repressed wish or desire and must resemble in personality the latent aspects of the parent's personality that have been repressed. (E.g., if the father's aggressiveness has previously been squelched, but he eagerly wishes to be a more aggressive man, the symptom bearer will be the aggressive child.) Frequently, this is the first-born child of the same sex of the parent with the repressed wish.

Family life resembles a poor version of "cops and robbers"; that is, the cops (parents) never seem to be able to keep the robber's (child's) impulsive behavior regulated and channeled. The child is forever getting away with the most amazing behavior, both in and out of the family. He always seems to get caught, mainly because of his own "stupidity," however. If it were not for the child's ineptitude the parents would never get him, and the child's behavior, which not infrequently borders on or includes delinquency, is often encouraged by that parental ineptitude. The child promises, for example, "never to do it again," only to repeat the action *ad infinitum*. While the veracity of the child's statements cannot be trusted, the parents, in "sincere hope" punish him and then trust him again. Each time the child acts up, he manages to get caught (either by the parents or by real policemen). The child's audacious ineptitude is matched only by his parents' ludicrous trust.

Examples: So's Your Old Man and Who Were You Out with Last Night?

Some fathers will not allow their sons to assume appropriate mature decision making mainly because their fathers never allowed them to. What was good enough for them (and they resented) is good enough for their sons (who also resent it). At the same time, the father does not protest very loudly when his own strict regulations are violated by the son; this allows the son to fool the old man as the father wanted to do with *his* old man. It gets confusing after a while as to whose old man is really being fooled.

The conscious resentment that inevitably builds up between father and son is never talked about openly, though it may be alluded to indirectly ("Now, son, we've talked about these late hours before") and met by stony silence. It may be disguised in incidents that are argued about ("How many times have I told you!"). At no time, however, does son speak to father about his resentment or does father in any way allow him to.

The child's unacceptable behavior symbolizes his feelings of badness over the poor relationship with the father. The angry mother is necessary to keep the process in perpetual repetition. Husband and wife also cannot talk about feelings of resentment and anger between them; rather this always seems to emerge in their attempts to "foil" one another by expressing contradictory expectations about the symptomatic child. If father wants the boy home by 11 p.m., mother overlooks it when the son gets home at 12:30 a.m. when father is away on a business trip. If mother feels father is too hard on the boy's regrettable behavior, then father is even tougher, at least verbally. The boy's delinquent behavior still continues, however. While the parents talk about his unacceptable behavior, nobody ever does anything about it. Mothers who help this kind of pattern the most often suffer from a "social indignation" syndrome as well. The following family situation is typical of this pattern. The father, James, and the mother, Ellen, are both in their early forties. The oldest child in the family and the only son, Doug, is sixteen. There is also a younger daughter, Barbara, age thirteen. Barbara, even though she is apart from the basic pathogenic triad of mother, father, and son, is a recipient of this dysfunctional pattern.

In observing this family, one is aware of the following pattern of their relationships: It is essentially a power struggle between the father and all the other family members, most intensely involving the father and the symptomatic family member, Doug. This, in turn, is related to three other developments within the family structure:

1. A marital problem between the mother and father has resulted in the mother's repressing her resentment and anger toward the father directly but displacing it indirectly onto the only other male in the family, Doug. Doug always hears how "you men are alike" whenever he does something not to her liking. When father did something similar previously, he got a righteous scowl.

2. In order to deal with her husband, the mother has developed a guerrilla tactic of setting her husband up in a position of authority and then, when he is on precarious ground, undermining and undercutting his authority. Her attempts at siding with the childrens' open criticism of him may be both subtle and direct. While she will always state that father, as head of the family, should deal with family problems and especially a recalcitrant son, she nevertheless denigrates his ability to do so.

3. Doug has a warm regard for his father and a strong need to be like (identify with) him. At the same time he resents a father who blocks his autonomous development through a constant "I'm right, you're wrong" philosophy. This power struggle has resulted in Doug's displacing his resentment and anger from the father and onto society by what now has emerged as antisocial behavior. Most recently, this has been a series of local curfew violations. In fact this pattern began when Doug was twelve or younger in the form of passive–aggressive rebellion, that is by various forms of footdragging, malingering, poking along, and general ineptitude.

The father sees in Doug his own younger self. His relationship to his own father was similar and James still feels badly about this and has a strong need to expiate his own mistakes through over-control of Doug. James feels guilty about his rebelliousness toward *his* father and hopes to show that he really always liked him by being the same kind of father himself. ("If you like me, you will be like me. To love me is to be similar to me; to be different is to indicate that I was not good enough as a father.") With Doug, however, James does not seem to enforce his very stringent expectations. He actually allows Doug considerable freedom, perhaps, because he resented his own father's control over him. Doug is therefore able to "get away" with things, as his father wanted to but didn't dare. James's apparent stupidity with Doug is really an unconscious second chance for his own repressed self.

Further resentment and animosity within the family have accumulated around the father's lengthy and frequent absences from the home. These are due, in part, to his occupation as executive in a small manufacturing concern; however, the father's own unhappiness about his family also increases his motivation to staying away so much. In turn, the mother feels deserted and left with overwhelming responsibilities. The father has become more of an enforcer than an identification figure for Doug; he also represents a lack of support and understanding from his wife's viewpoint. The daughter, Barbara, sees the father pretty much as a checkbook to indulge her own personal wants. Barbara appears quite apathetic and withdrawn at times. She is left with only a bitter, resentful, and repressed mother to identify with as a woman.

This family pattern is typified by considerable nonverbal communication through voice tone and gestures, such as sighs. Little apparent verbal communication is used; areas of conflict are glossed over. Family members are able to do things *for* one another but seldom *with* one another. When hostility builds up between the parents they then break off their own communication and immediately displace their anger and resentment onto both of the children in the form of criticism and moral lectures.

The symptomatic child in this family would have to be the first male child, who becomes enmeshed in the power struggle with the father and is the primary object of displaced hostility of the marital situation on the part of the mother. Barbara tends to bear the brunt of the father's suppressed anger but is relatively free of entanglement with mother. While she also has symptoms of depression, these are less obvious and go largely unnoticed by family members. She is involved in the family system dysfunction, but this will very likely not show up as overtly as Doug's delinquency until he leaves the family either voluntarily or by legal removal. Then she will be left to mediate the marital tension between her parents. At that time, the "family problem" focus will predictably shift to her.

A second family pattern example involves the mother and father and the mother and daughter as the primary conflict dyads; mother, father, daughter form the primary dysfunctional triad. The "payoff" behavior in this situation usually involves sexual acting out; that is, the symptomatic behavior takes the form of poorly controlled sexual impulses, whose translation into action violates social or family limitations. This may include premarital teen-age intercourse, various forms of exhibitionism, and possibly pregnancy as an ultimatum. The mother was perhaps overprotected and overrepressed sexually in her own childhood by her parents and especially by her mother. Such women often marry sexually unresponsive men, thereby perpetuating the frustration of their own sexual needs. With her own daughter, however, the mother tends to be rather incongruent regarding sexual matters. There are stern lectures, but there is also oversight. These mothers tend to be concerned about whether their daughters will ever get married and continuously push them into heterosexual situations.

The daughter gets the message, generally, that while sex is bad, it is nonetheless forbidden fun to be sought after. In punishing her daughter's escapades the mother often, a day or so later, forgets the conditions of her own sanctions and the daughter is free once more. The mother, who could be firm and consistent, tends rather to be dictatorial and moralistic. As daughter's resentment builds up she soon realizes that the way to defeat mother is not to do what mother wants. The child's counterresentment is embodied in the form of her own sexual behavior. ("I'll show mom.") The mother, interestingly enough, while seeming overly concerned, is also absorbed in the details of her daughter's sexual experiences. Failure of the mother's sexual relationship with her husband has its indirect compensation—the behavior of her daughter.

There are several variations on these basic patterns of the "Why Don't You Do It for Me" theme that are less dysfunctional. They would appear to be related to changes that have occurred over the past three decades in our society. We seem to be going through an alternating strictness–leniency process, whose consequences are manifest in the behavior of the third generation. For example, parents whose own parents were strict tend to be strict themselves on the surface, but underneath they really allow considerable leniency. This has been illustrated in the examples above. Their children, however, show the result of this in their behavior,

Some children who come from variations of the "Why Don't You Do It for Me" pattern have become devoted and aggressive student protestors when they reach college age. Their parents are often in their forties and are frequently disillusioned and in some despair about their own unfulfilled dreams. The college student represents a chance to accomplish the parents' own unfulfilled ideals. What the parent did not, or could not, do he unconsciously encourages the child–student to do by parental "permissiveness." In essence, this is the lament of the aging radical.

Dynamics: It's Always Easier, If It's the Other Guy's Fault

This pattern of transactional behavior is evidence of a family system that operates on a displacement principle: Whatever is undesirable in thought and fantasy in oneself is subtly provoked and sanctioned in the behavior of another. An actualization of the thought takes place in the undesirable behavior of another. The self is relieved of guilt over his bad thought, as another is obviously bad in behavior. At the same time, the self derives vicarious enjoyment from the other's behavior, while acting as if he disapproves of it.

This pattern is often seen in families where resentment and anger are viewed as bad. Subsequently, these feelings are denied but subtly displaced. Resentment and anger are associated with punishment, usually in the form of conflict with the most meaningful person in one's life and eventually in rejection or abandonment by that person. In other words, to express even genuine resentment is to risk alienating this person from us, since anger in any form is hurtful. ("Don't bite the hand that feeds you.") It is presumed inevitable that hurting another with anger will provoke retaliation by rejection. ("If you are *ever* angry, I can *never* love you.") The rejection is not real, however; it is fantasy. It is presumed to exist by virtue of the psychological illusions created by a "crystal ball" sort of communication and comes from the experience of protective detachment and wariness of another when we are not open about our underlying feelings. While we know of our own anger, the other does not. He is only aware of phony behavior (overdone niceness, sarcastic agreement, etc.). This awareness puts others on guard toward the self. But we interpret another's behavior as a rejection. Each person estimates the intention of the other by conclusions drawn from observed behavior without checking out these observations. Private meaning is substituted for mutual meaning, which can only result from openness and negotiation.

Once this illusion is accepted as truth, then all interaction within the family is regulated by an avoidance of anger and resentment. Realistically, this results in no one's knowing where anyone else really stands in terms of attitudes and feelings about them. The cycle is self-perpetuating—everybody in the family lives in a sea of anxiety. Guesswork is not certainty; sense and order, therefore, are not predictable. Relationships are unstable, and security vacillates. (See Figure 5.)

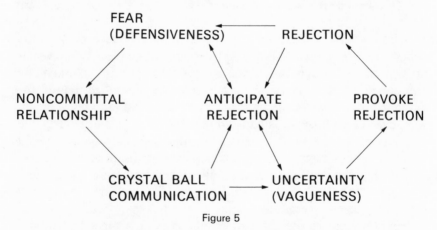

Figure 5

Since all aspects of the system are related to one another, the focus should be on the "relationships among the behaviors," rather than on how these may have originally begun.

Historically, a three-generational causal pattern is involved— grandparents, parents, and children. The parents, the intermediaries between the grandparental generation and the children generation, are in a dilemma. They must both "love and obey" their parents while at the same time allow for growth (confident expansion of self) in themselves and in their own children. The parents, in their childhood, were taught, "I must always honor my mother and father." On the other hand, the destruction of their autonomy by the strict and dictatorial regulation of the grandparents has led to their presently perceived inadequacies and disillusionments. These, in turn, are often projected or displaced onto society or the establishment, or any "scapegoat" within the family. It is, therefore, not their parents who crushed them but others (e.g., harping bosses, demanding children, a nagging spouse) in their social environment. The parents are only able to live with this dilemma if they can appear to be "good" by acting as their parents did toward them; they subtly encourage their child to express the resentment they had for their own parents in the child's overt behavior. In other words, if parents cannot be resentful and angry toward their own parents, their children will do it for them. It must be understood that parents are "good" and the child is "bad." The parent can therefore live without guilt and be justified in being punitive toward the child. After all, they are only doing what is best for the child, as they learned it from their parents.

These parents have an excessive fear that their own anger and resentment will either destroy the relationship with the grandparents or their own spouse or, even more fearful, will destroy the grandparent or the spouse. Consequently, the frequently heard phrase in this three-generational system is: "You'll be the death of me yet."

It is not at all surprising that the wife has no luck in dealing with her resentment toward her husband. He won't tolerate it, because he can't handle his own resentment. She won't push her disillusionment too far because she fears that it will disrupt their relationship completely. The frustrated wife supports her child's rebellion by being vague, indirect, and indecisive about her own regulation of the child's behavior. The father does not like it when either mother or son rebel, and he is angry at both. The dilemma is circular and without end.

The child who is the least well defended psychologically finds the damming up of such impulses to be, in reality, impossible. The feelings explode in the form of antisocial behavior outside the family. The unacceptable impulses of the parent(s) end up as the child's unacceptable behavior, which behavior allows partial fulfillment of the parents' own wish to have rebelled against constrictive regulation (parental, institutional, and societal) and drains off negative feeling within the family onto a scapegoat. Though disabled and dysfunctional, the family system is nonetheless intact. Some relationship, however dysfunctional, is usually preferred to the fantasied expectation of no relationship at all.

Resolution: Happiness Is Winning Together

The basic difficulty involved in resolving this dysfunctional pattern into a more functional outcome is to get the family members to see that anger will not destroy relationships if it is dealt with openly; it will allow greater intimacy. In the first example, the father will act as if he is now aware that he will not "kill" his own father if he is warm, open, and receptive to his own son, contrary to his own father's relationship to him. He will distinguish between fantasied disloyalty to his own father (angry rebellion) and appropriate, mature handling of his son as a unique individual. Likewise, his relationship to wife and daughter will be marked by the negotiation of a joint outcome, rather than manipulation and displacement.

Before this can occur, however, the parents and children must learn to express disagreement and anger appropriately and openly without resort to unconscious displacement or fearful anxiety. There must be a shift from "Why don't you do it for me?" to "Those are my toes, friend."

Once the basic dysfunctional rule, "anger is bad and destructive," is altered to "anger is a reaction to hurt that can be understood as an unmet need for survival," the family can begin to negotiate more satisfying joint outcome. While awareness of unmet needs for intimacy, resentment, and shattered illusions are not comfortable at first, it is certainly more functional in the longer run. The perpetuating cycle will be disrupted and will open up the system for the negotiation of need meeting without provocation and despair. The following things, among others, will finally be settled:

1. Whose father is really being provoked. This will allow the present father and son to be spontaneous rather than play at a reenactment.

2. Which spouse is *really* the loser. Since both are losers, this will allow mutual exploration of positive avenues of need satisfaction. They might just as well survive together as despair together.

Chapter 7

"Joan of Arc Rides Again"

Theme: Suffer Everybody to Come Unto Me

The use of guilt seduction on another, while in the role of the "helping martyr," is manipulation to protect oneself from a preconceived and fantasied rejection. While one does not always love a martyr, not to feel guilty in their presence is tantamount to being a cad. The martyr's role is designed to induce guilt by noble self-sacrifice in the presence of clods.

This pattern requires a guilt-ridden person of very low self-esteem with a poor self-image, often the wife-mother whose husband is also guilt-ridden but who himself enjoys seductive martyring. Because of his poor self-image, the husband is seduced by her noble efforts for him into believing the fantasy of a more positive picture of himself. To react with open opposition to her gestures and acts would be dangerous for such an unsure man. Responsibility might mean failure and resentment or abandonment; so he follows her lead. Both mother and father, it will be discovered, have a very low opinion of themselves and an inadequate picture of how they operate in relationship with others. This is true outside of the family as well as within. Their only hope for success (that is, acceptance without criticism) is potentially within the family. The mother accomplishes this through her total indispensability, continuous good works for all; the father has the goodness of heart to allow the mother to aspire to divine significance. Besides, whatever she does for him is effortless gain, albeit at times poorly fitting his own needs.

The children soon become the pawns of both parents. They realize the potential of coalition with one parent against the other. They can try to gain what they want by power alignment or play one parent against the other alternately, as needed. They may try to avoid their just deserts by hiding behind another family member at other times. The parents are quick to accept the children in coalition (that is, to support their own private brand of familial helpfulness). To have allies is to feel better, to raise one's self-esteem, and to hope to win the family popularity poll. The children eventually learn to induce guilt, arousing a state of compensable regret in another to gain one's end, as do the parents in order to obtain what they want. If the other is guilty, which is painful to endure, such guilt can be reduced by doing a favor to obtain absolution. Good works become a payoff and act as the currency of the relationship.

This pattern evolves around the validation of unworthiness perceptions by guilt induction. The other is doing things for the self, out of guilt, we will surmise, rather than because he really cares. Inevitably this acting out of guilt arouses appreciable hostility in others as well as in oneself. Several corollary reactions will soon follow:

1. Generally, the only way to get along with self is for other person to deny his own selfhood (his identity and his concept of what is of worth to him). If the other has his own values, this appears to deny the self his or her noble position. In most instances, to give up the responsibility for one's self-determination is to promptly be filled with resentment and rage. Often, responsibility for another's behavior is projected to the self. One is "forced" to act out of guilt and thereby feels resentful over acquiescence to the other's ploy. Actually, whatever rage and resentment the victim of the martyr feels, he is responsible for that choice: Only he can deny himself.

2. Specifically, the mother, however, soon becomes aware that because the others always give in to her guilt induction you can't really trust them. Do they really care? Are they weak, just giving in? Do they care so little that giving in is easier than resisting noble force? The question, therefore, of who can trust whom and under what circumstances, becomes solely a matter of presumed guilt induction, rather than sincere concern for and awareness of the other person. Mother is convinced the other family members only care for her valet

service. The children and father are constantly besieged with things "for their own good." Both sides are aware only of resentment; no one can risk any concern based on the awareness of one another's uniqueness.

3. Even if children and father should not give in to guilt induction but rather to show their concern for mother as a person rather than mother as a martyr, this leads only to a series of heart-rending pleas that almost always take the form of "You'll be sorry when I'm gone." The transactional interpretation of this unconscious message is "Go ahead and kill me if I can't have my way with you." The choice then appears to be between knuckling under and matricide. Since self-esteem has already hit rock bottom in the family, only the world's worst person could conceivably elect what appears to be the matricide alternative. Both of the supposed alternatives amount to the destruction of one for the survival of another. This is obviously no choice at all and only further diminishes self-esteem within the family.

Examples: Guilt-Inspired "Love" and Divine Servitude

Alice, after leaving her rather cold, unaffectionate, and hypercritical family of origin, began her adult life with deliberate carelessness and desperate hope. She met a man who, not unlike her family, was both exploitative and uncaring. He managed to give Alice a child but no marital contract. Alice, therefore, ends up with an illegitimate son and no husband. As time goes on she never dates or remarries. She gives all her labor and efforts, but none of her self, to the child, who grows up spoiled, craving real warmth and filled with guilt. Her servitude, while overwhelming, is given in an automatic, determined way. There is no joy when they are together, only grim determination. Her son can never do anything for her. He, in fact, learns to expect his every whim to be reacted to, with no responsibility on his part. His acquired selfishness is occasionally tainted with surges of guilt and confusion over his mother's sterile dedication to his exclusive happiness. The bitterness of her own disappointment with her "one and only man" is displaced on the child. It is not that she is suspicious of men or afraid of relationships with them but rather that she is a "good mother" who is responsible to her child. If she gives all her labor and efforts to him, nothing is ostensibly left for anyone else. And since she does everything for him, the child never learns to do anything for himself.

Their relationship is punctuated by much incongruent communication. When the child wants hugging and reassurance from his mother, for example, he receives it reluctantly and clumsily. Later on, when the child himself becomes rather overburdened with mother's continuous care, he suggests she make some time for herself or with others. This results only in further unctuous reassurance, sweet and loud, that mother only cares for him and his happiness. Consequently, he should not bother about her. Her eyes are filled with a noble glint while her stomach churns in rage. ("After all I've done for you, you want to turn me out.") The child can only be filled with guilt; he feels resentful because his emerging autonomy is blocked by maternal "concern." He can either have what *mother wants,* which is for his own good anyhow, or what he wants, without including her. The former blocks his own growth; the latter threatens to "stab mother in the back."

When her son eventually reaches late adolescence, he marries a girl because she is pregnant. The cycle repeats itself, but this time mother makes sure the man "does the right thing." She is, after all, not against pregnancy, only abandonment. When the son and his girl friend do marry they subsequently feel very guilty over a union forced by biology rather than reciprocal affection and concern. They find they cannot leave one another, even though each feels trapped in an involuntary relationship. The son feels he couldn't possibly stab another woman in the back, since mother is already his "victim." His wife, on the other hand, like his mother, would rather have some relationship rather than none. Once more the merry-go-round of behavioral reciprocity goes around: disillusionment—resentment—denial—wooden responsiveness—fear of rejection—disillusionment —etc.

Mary's family is a more typical example of the "Joan of Arc" pattern. Mary is the kind of mother who sacrifices everything for her children and even more for her dear husband. She sees to it that they have everything and she has nothing. She really feels undeserving herself, and brings a double-edged sword into play. Unconsciously, Mary has a very deep, almost delusional conviction that she does not, in fact, deserve anything. That she is truly unworthy, however, does not negate the possibility of giving her children what she did not have. Thus, by her own control and manipulation, she achieves vicariously and in spite of her own deprivation. At the same time, no one would deny Mary, after all her sacrifices, the reassurance that she does indeed deserve something for herself. A typical conversation from this pattern follows:

Son: (coming in from outside) Boy, did we have a great game!

Mary: You must be hungry. Let mother fix you some cheese and crackers.

Son: That's not necessary, mom. Some peanut butter and bread will do. I can get it.

Mary: Mother fixes cheese and crackers so well . . . Besides, it's better for you.

Son: Well, OK, mom.

Mary: Certainly—it will just take a minute. You rest up.

Father: (just coming home) Mary, are you fixing something again? Why don't you relax for a change and let someone wait on you?

Son: (somewhat guiltily) Sure mom, I can fix it OK.

Mary: Oh, it's all right. After all, what is a mother for. (The question is rhetorical and goes unanswered.)

Father: I don't know what we would do without you, Mary (even though he has already considered the possibility).

In the above two examples quite a number of significantly manipulative possibilities abound. The adroit martyr will prefer a particular constellation of ploys but will, under pressure, show a versatility of adaptation that is awe-inspiring. Some of the more common variations both Alice and Mary might be observed to use are the following:

1. *The advice giver*: "If you don't do what I suggest, you don't like me." The recipient of such advice is immediately placed in a very magnificent double bind. He can either accept the advice and, therefore, surrender his autonomy to mother, diminishing his own self-esteem, or he can refuse the advice, which places him in a position of not liking mother. It should be noted that the same would apply between husband and wife in this pattern. In fact, it may be found in its more dramatic form between Mary and her husband. Children usually are still in the process of evolving their own autonomy and

are more likely to accept the suggestion. Father, on the other hand, is still battling to keep what little he may have left.

2. *How can you be so stupid:* "It only proves that you are worthless and that I am good, if you do not accept your dependency on my indispensability." This, in actuality, amounts to the projection of Mary's own worthless image onto husband or children. Since she expiates her worthlessness by good works, the refusal by other family members to allow her indispensability would block her salvation.

There is some pragmatic reality to mother's indispensability. If they allowed her, over the years, to do almost everything, she has obviously become most adept and they have become most inadept at doing things. Should mother suddenly cease these good works, the family would, in most cases (but only temporarily), find themselves in some distress about who should do what. That mother is indispensable is somewhat more easily accepted than would seem to be true on the surface.

3. *Ingrates:* "I'm only doing it for your own good, so don't be ungrateful." This turns out to be equally as elegant a double bind as the first variation; mother has, by definition, assumed that what she is doing is good for the other and only an ingrate would refuse her efforts. So the recipients of mother's elegant service can either refuse to have something done for their own good and be ungrateful or accept what is presumed to be for their own good and cheerfully continue to admire mother.

4. *Food for love:* "Here, take my last morsel, I don't need it." The basic feature of this ploy is to equate psychological nurturance with physical nurturance. Therefore, the recipients of mother's energetic nobility are continuously overstuffed with food. General obesity is not uncommon, but sagging self-esteem is the more basic issue. Love is measured in pounds of food consumed from the point of view of the giver; and the amount eaten indicates quite clearly whether the recipient really wants love or not. This ploy rarely occurs in families who live on a marginal subsistence level; rather, it occurs where food is substantially plentiful. Mother can only feel fulfilled if family members are filled full.

5. *The violin concerto:* "Let's play along with mom—and sweetly." Respect and adulation is substantially unilateral; these have not been acquired by mutual understanding but rather flow from the mistress of the manor to the peasants beneath her. Certainly, such nobility deserves to be accompanied by music. If the other members of

the family do "play along sweetly" with mother, they are aiding the perpetuation of such a pattern. They presume by doing so they may help her to feel worthwhile but only in the role of the martyr. Her basic feelings of unworthiness are never dealt with. And, in fact, their own simmering resentment may have its most "noble" achievement in their own perpetual acceptance of her sacrifices.

Dynamics: Perfection and Nobility

This pattern has a two-generation genesis and can be carried on through succeeding generations almost indefinitely. One must differentiate how an individual (mother) learned this in her own family of origin and then is able to continue it in her own family by perpetuating collaboration from her husband and children. The pattern is learned by her children and may be subsequently taken into their own families at a later date.

One possible point of origin is the *indispensable helper*. The self, to help younger siblings and to have value in the family, became very adept at feeding, supervising, and ordering. If she did not help in this way, she was treated as extra baggage. As the oldest, she not only ate more but cost more to maintain in every way without compensation to the struggling or lazy parents. She therefore became an indispensable helper in order to gain their acceptance. This is sometimes the fate of the oldest child in a large family; it may be the fate of a first child who is not as well accepted because she was a disappointment or outright surprise to the parents. This origin for the "Joan of Arc" pattern can occur when the pattern has not previously existed in the family. It does, however, require *perpetuating collaborators*, both in the family of origin and in this woman's marital family, persons who will take an active part in the disillusionment—resentment—denial—helpfulness—guilt—fear of abandonment—disillusionment cycle. The perpetuating collaborators will never comment openly on what goes on between them when they enact this negative and self-reinforcing circle; each will view all motives in the mutual relationships as derived from love and good will, rather than hurt and neurotic expectation.

A second possible genesis resides in the self's own parents' using guilt induction in the family of origin. The mother learned how to use seductive power to gain her ends, rather than to ride along with the give-and-take of a relationship. She was able to observe her own parents use various guilt-induction ploys as a way of getting what they wanted, while at the same time avoiding angry conflict over misunderstanding and outright confrontation of differentness. Her own family of origin emphasized goodness, de-emphasized conflict, but was overwhelmed with guilt and confusion. Imperfection and rejection were seen as synonymous; acceptance and perfection must then logically go hand in hand. This is basically an infantile and narcissistic assumption based upon how the self has interpreted past experiences that were laden with hurt and anger or that seemed overwhelming at the time because of the self's fear to ask for help. These experiences were also viewed as unique and without precedent and directed specifically at the self as the price of her existence. Only perfect behavior—to be absolutely good or completely worthy—was suitable penance. Characteristically, therefore, the "noble martyr" sees the present as a duplicate of her "interpreted" past. It may, in fact, not represent an accurate perception of the past at all. It represents, rather, a private and idiosyncratic understanding of her earlier difficulties.

A variation on the "anger is always bad and destructive" rule described in the previous chapter is present also in this pattern. Family members, especially the parents, subscribe to the dictum: "One is not to react to anything with anger." Since anger and resentment inevitably occur, a feeling of personal defectiveness arises. Both the anger and the subsequent self-label "bad" is repressed to avoid its discovery by others, because it is accompanied by the fantasy that others will retaliate if they discover one's own anger. This rule comes into play in family behavior whenever there is inherent conflict. Inherent conflict, on the other hand, will arise within family interaction when differentness between family members cannot be acknowledged. Such differences signal the call to war. Because the family operates on a basically pacifistic rule prohibiting the open manifestation of anger and hostility, situations that arouse resentment, critical questioning, or self–other evaluations must be suppressed. Not only must anger be controlled, the differences that lead to impasse must be diminished to resemble similarity.

In the initial relationship between husband and wife, a reciprocity is worked out between the dominator and the dominated. The children soon learn this fundamental way in which humans relate to one another. The dominator, in short, says "If I am worthless, then I must be indispensable to balance this out." She accrues self-value by behaving in an indispensable manner. This is fundamentally a very self-centered position and does not reveal any basic altruism. The dominated, on the other hand, allows himself to be dependent on the dominator and thereby accrues value because of the noble treatment extended to him. Any accrued value is accompanied by diminished autonomy on the part of the dominated, which leads to gradually simmering, but suppressed, resentment.

Within the entire family a basic fear of mutual abandonment eventually arises. The dominators are only of value as long as they are permitted to dominate. The dominated can only feel worthwhile as long as they are given to. Because of the autonomy battle and the underlying resentment, this seems like a most precarious arrangement. The significant problem involved in such a pattern is that the relationship between mother and other members of the family becomes one of unilateral sacrifice and induced guilt rather than mutual growth and self-realization. A vicious cycle of hostility inevitably ensues because the other family members' need for autonomy conflicts with mother's need for dependent control. Everybody loses self-esteem in this system. Mother feels unworthy in the first place, and all her grand achievements cannot convince her otherwise.

The other members of the family have no place in its productivity, because mother does all. Contribution is limited only to the acceptance of mother's deeds and services, but the others are frustrated by the inability to contribute to mother's well-being in return. She will not hear of it! She is there to be a good mother to them, and, as everybody knows, she certainly would not be a good mother if she did not do everything for them. Not uncommonly, mother will even invoke God ("As God is my witness") to signify that not only is she goodhearted, but she has the privilege of divine guidance as well.

Should resentment over her domination break through abruptly, it will shatter mother's value in her own eyes and deny husband and children special treatment. They will then feel less well thought of by mother. This leads to a "fusion" rather than a differentiation policy in establishing relationships within the family; the self really does not make room for the other, but rather the other is seen as an extension of the self, and not as a separate unique being. The others who are dominated, while resentful, are loath to unfuse the relationship with mother or wife for fear that she will reject them. The members of the family, therefore, act as if there is only fusion and sameness accompanied by resentment and despair.

Resolution: Humanness and Responsibility

The delusion that one must be indispensable and lovable must be strongly countered with reasonable reality. If, in fact, we had to be indispensable, none of us would be acceptable. The condition that is presumed to be a requirement of relationship is a human impossibility. Anger, resentment, disappointment, and disillusionment with one another is not necessarily followed by abandonment and rejection. Only if these feelings cannot be openly commented on and joint negotation with more satisfactory joint outcome entered into, does withdrawal from one another usually result.

The switch must be made from guilt induction to personal responsibility. Each member of the family is not only responsible for how they feel but for how they act. Mother, not her husband or her children, is responsible for her low self-esteem and for her fears of abandonment and rejection. While this might have emerged from her earlier experience with her own family, it is now a part of her, and she is responsible for herself. No one else can assume this responsibility with any hope of altering her feelings and behavior. She is the only one with the power to do so. Similarly, those she dominates are responsible for their resentment and the many forms of passive–aggressive foot dragging that usually accompany this resentment. Only they can express their resentment and only through this expression will they be able to begin to change their subtle hostility into workable annoyance and exploration. As long as guilt induction is a part of relationship, the inevitable result is mutual resentment. If one has to induce guilt in order to obtain support, affection does not come voluntarily but rather from assuaging one's guilt. Whatever one gives out of guilt is not genuine and authentic but simply a relief of one's own anxiety. Mutual self-doubts lead to further anxiety, despair, and fear. Only if there is no dominator and no dominated, only if each is responsible for his own feelings and behavior, can genuine and authentic relationship grow between members so they may fully realize their selves in open and intimate exchange.

Everyone in various degrees and from time to time experiences a kind of existential misery, when nothing seems to turn out right (i.e., our way) or when we experience an immediate, but transitory, unhappy feeling over various outcomes of our relationships. This derives from our idealistic striving to obtain close intimate relationship in an easy and immediate manner. In reality, such relationships are imperfect and accompanied by disappointment, but we do not have to be in misery all the time, nor is it ennobling in any relationship to suffer together. The process of mutual negotiation toward satisfactory joint outcome is not the easy way out, but it is certainly the most rewarding. If we don't succeed the first time, we must try again; we must struggle; we must be anxious. We can indeed succeed through negotiation. To turn this human struggle into a rationale for defensive withdrawal or as a basis for exploitation and manipulation is patently unproductive. To work toward the negotiation of joint outcome is a noble struggle, because the mutual result enhances self-esteem and leads to personal growth.

Chapter 8

"It's Nothing—Just My Heart Again"

Theme: Value a Desperate Heart

When all other attempts to insure psychological survival fail, the physiology of the body and the desperate needs of the human personality combine in a last-ditch evasion of a dreaded fear of desertion and abandonment. The self has a basic conviction of "unlovability" and constantly fears that others in the family must feel similarly about him or her; rejection and abandonment are anticipated just around the corner. An attempt is therefore made to secure acceptance from the other by the plea disguised in physical symptoms: "If you don't care for me, I will surely die." The picture of sheer desperation in this pattern evolves from the distorted conviction that one can only survive emotionally within the family by controlling the affection-giving aspect of family relationships. In other words, each member of the family is to view the self as valuable and lovable even in the presence of mutual detachment, selfishness, and indifference. When others are made subservient to the self's ill condition, it is hoped that affectionate concern will be forthcoming. The most important thing is to be loved, even if one does not behave in an especially lovable manner. The other must love the self "even if it kills him." The main thing is not to kill the self. The expectation of "being loved and cared for" is largely unilateral, however.

To the outside observer, family life resembles a television hospital drama, complete with deadly seriousness, impending doom, and sudden and unpredictable physical symptoms. While heart palpitations are common, others can be equally as effective. These may include hot and cold flashes, severe low back pain, and splitting headaches. The point to be made is that the other's loveless avoidance is the cause of these severe and surely terminal symptoms. The symptoms only occur, however, after the self has tried to control others in the family by various means that have failed, been only minimally effective, or, even worse, begun the slow process that alienates others from self. The unlovable self may often be the purveyor of numerous good works designed to win another's eternal gratitude. This may be overdone (as in "Joan of Arc") and results in resentment, guilt, withdrawal, or depression.

The symptom-bearer is often the wife–mother, who, while feigning weakness and dependency on her family, really has a strong need to have things her way through subtle manipulation. This pattern may be a continuation of "Joan of Arc" or it may exist as a primary tactic in itself, when all other forms of giving and suffering have been utilized with only moderate success. The impending death ploy is used as the final trump card. Since some wife–mothers are especially keen on physical symptoms and have a tendency to somatize their anxiety and fear rather than just suffer in general, they will prefer to use heart or other organ ailments as their basic ploy. These heart palpitations, therefore, represent a cloaked and disguised emotional suffering (fear of love withdrawal).

While it is possible that some genuine heart disturbance may be present and used for all it is worth, more usually no organic basis of the symptomatology exists. In either case, however, it is important to be aware, first, of how much real heart trouble there is, as determined by a competent medical authority, and, second, how the symptoms, whether organically based or not, are utilized to manipulative advantage.

The ideal prototype for this pattern is a family in which the husband has an isolated and withdrawn relationship with his wife and the children include an attractive daughter and an unattractive son. The mother, who receives little affectionate concern from the father, attempts to receive a substitute reward from her son. The father, on the other hand, not wishing to be left empty-handed, seems extra sweet to his attractive daughter; in other words, a competent but unemotional man is married to a fearful and desperate woman. She most likely married him out of desperation, voluntarily entering a situation in which she had some relationship, however small, rather than no relationship at all. Over time, it became apparent that the relationship she had was, in itself, not enough to even minimally meet her survival need for intimacy. The children basically care for their parents but do not want to be left out in the cold. Each parent seems invested only in self and hardly involved with either spouse or children, who tend to align themselves in coalition with the parent of the opposite sex in mutual affection giving. The daughter will say, "If mom doesn't seem interested, I'll try with dad." Mother is then out in the cold, unless she enlists son in a coalition of exclusive relationship.

Examples: Oedipus Wrecks and Coronary Love

The family of Arthur, age forty-six, Mildred, age forty-four, Tim, a twenty-year-old son, and Mary, an eighteen-year-old daughter has reached a rather crucial situation. Tim has decided not to attend college and to leave the family home and live on his own. Mildred, in reaction, alternates between depression and heart failure; she is desperate because Tim's decision to leave home will mark the end of her feeding, clothing, nurturing, and nursing period with her son. The "let me do it for you" time is about to end. Tim has always appreciated his mother's good works but has also been, at times, annoyed and resentful about her rather overcontrolling manner. She has always decided what is best for him, stuffed his mouth full of food, and continuously found him sickly.

Mildred has been singularly unsuccessful in her relationship with Mary who is really her father's girl. Mother can tell her nothing and is only able to get the girl to help out if she makes her requests through the father. Mary adores and understands her father; Mildred, on the other hand, seems only continuously frustrated by his lack of attention to her. As the years have passed, the father has become increasingly involved in his work and spends more time away from home or in his study at home—where he does not want to be bothered. In reality, Mary does not have as much of a relationship with her father as she would like to think, she is more appealing to the father than her forty-four-year-old mother who only complains about his work. Mildred has shown more interest and done more for Tim than anyone else in the family, and Arthur feels more than a little resentful about this.

Over the years these relationships have grown to their present state. If Tim leaves home mother is threatened with being completely left alone emotionally. She is close neither to her husband Arthur nor her daughter Mary. In addition, they have rather persistently and successfully eluded, if not combatted, her attempts to get them to be dependent on her, so she can feel worthwhile.

Tim has chosen to leave home, not so much because he prefers it but because of the nagging criticism of his father, his sister, and his peers. These people have goaded Tim for several years over his status as a "mama's boy." At this point Tim is hardly able to do anything for himself—mother has always done it for him. Also he is faced with leaving a mother whose heart can hardly bear to see him go.

In some families the mother might be in the menopause and can get hot flashes as well as heart palpitations at crucial moments. Any reasonable person would immediately see that only a real ingrate could leave his mother under these conditions. Tim eventually resolves the dilemma by developing a rather considerable depression due to, in his words, "difficulties at work." This combination will both keep him at home where mother can serve him and, in turn, be reassured by his presence and focus the cause for the difficulties upon Tim's work, thereby disguising the fact it is the family system of relationships that is the problem. Father can go on with his work without being nagged by his wife. Mother, after all, has something to do in her care of Tim. Mary can be supportive and understanding of father since mother is busy with her brother. All would appear to have a meaningful place in the function of the family.

The resulting pattern, however, leaves a mother who must overpamper her son for fear of heart failure, a son who can only be depressed to keep his mother alive, a father who has no other value in his family but to provide them subsistence, and a daughter who is overattached to her father to the exclusion of other relationships with males. The family is unquestionably intact but severely crippled by their interlocking neurotic complex of relationships.

This pattern can be carried on with or without actual heart involvement. Another variation, however, is a much more conscious ploy with no real conviction of any cardiovascular involvement. Simply by trial and error, mother has discovered that when she suddenly experiences physical symptoms, the family members show her more attention and concern. She soon realizes it is possible to evoke concern with physical complaints. This device is less desperate and more consciously manipulative. It is more characteristic of people who tend to be unimaginative but fairly practical. While the use of physical symptoms to gain what you want is hardly subtle, if others in the family feel guilty over their lack of concern about you, it may be a very effective control device at the moment. The pattern also frequently comes from an identification with earlier family experience. This mother's own mother may have been somewhat prone to do the same. This pattern is a characteristic example of how people may take earlier and past experience and fit it into current situations. The present is seen in terms of the past and not for its immediate, unique qualities. Negotiation is impossible since unilateral manipulation is the aim. But unilateral manipulation only creates further frustration and resentment.

Agnes, for example, has just returned from a thorough physical examination with the family physician. This was prompted to some degree by symptoms of fatigue, depression, and some minor physical pains that accompanied her menopause. The result of the examination was completely negative, however, and she was pronounced to be in excellent physical condition. Because of her age she was cautioned, among other things, to have more frequent physical examinations, particularly in regard to her cardiovascular functioning. This is a typical, not unusual, procedure with persons over forty. When Agnes gets home however, she discusses the results of the examination:

> Husband: How did things turn out at the doctor's today, Agnes?
> Wife: Well, he's really not quite sure. He seemed to be kind of worried about my heart and said I ought to watch it carefully.
> Husband: Has it been giving you any trouble lately?
> Wife: Well—I didn't want to say anything, but lately it *has* seemed to give me some pain from time to time. I'll just have to watch it, I guess.
> Husband: Well now, Dear, this might be serious. You can't be too careful, you know.

Because of incomplete and vague communication, Agnes' basic physical condition has been rather thoroughly misunderstood by both her and her husband. The stage is now set to pull "It's nothing—just my heart again," whenever Agnes has been refused something she dearly wants, especially when her husband does not show her the amount and kind of affection she expects from him. In their further interaction, only his attention and concern, if not overconcern, will alleviate her symptoms. This is really the behavior of a desperate woman who feels she will be abandoned. She therefore attempts to reinstate a more affectionate (albeit forced) relationship between her and her husband. Not only time, but differing interests, have gradually pulled them apart. They no longer seem as emotionally close and positive about one another as they once were. Her fears of lessening interest and concern are exacerbated by the emerging distance between them. Panic begins to rise within her and her heart flutters. Again, Agnes' emotional suffering has been cloaked in supposed physical symptoms. As long as this continues, however, a unilateral manipulation will tend to provoke increasing resentment on the part of her husband, who feels he is now burdened with a chronically ill woman. Agnes appears to perform quite adequately in many other circumstances, nevertheless, much to his puzzlement.

Dynamics: Who Does Care About Whom?

The basic area that becomes dysfunctional and serves as the basis for this pattern is everyone's need to feel wanted and valued in their family relationships. Again, it is not the need that is dysfunctional, but the means the family uses to meet these needs. In the above pattern, once the wife–mother begins to feel she is not wanted and valued in the family, she hopes to manipulate relationships in such a manner as to make herself valuable to the others. The result, of course, is that she becomes overdependent on them, which they resent. Pity and frustration replace affection and concern in relationships as far as the wife–mother is concerned.

To feel wanted and valued by other human beings is a matter of psychological survival; without this sense and order lose their focus. What sense and meaning is there to family life if relationships are indifferent and valueless? How can one predict joint outcome or feel secure in simple responses to another who is detached and insensitive? A relationship cannot survive in an emotional purgatory. There is no motivation from which productivity can emerge; intimacy cannot derive where affectional reciprocity is absent. In such an emotional environment, persons become so preoccupied with preventing emotional death that they have no time to sustain growth by mutual nurturance.

When any relationship is perceived in terms of unilateral gratification, the person who has "lost out" (everyone in the family) responds invariably with a defensive retaliation. Mildred must manipulate her son to love her by feigning near-death. But she never gets anything spontaneously from her son except resentment and depression. Her son's overdependency costs him his confident autonomy in order to emotionally feed his "dying" mother. Her husband can only further withdraw into his study, after he and his wife allow their son to beat father out as a love object for Mildred. She assaults all of them with guilt accusations over her condition. Daughter feeds father's hurt esteem with solicitous, but inappropriate, reassurance; he, as parent, should be able to encourage her self-esteem. The daughter compensates for a self-centered, hypochondriacal mother in her romance with father. In reality, each is using the other to gain a compensation for their own despair and loneliness. They are users, not real givers, and that is essentially the unilateral manipulation in this pattern.

The beginning of this dysfunctional family system goes back again to the architects of the family—the parents, and how they became married. In this kind of marital pairing, the woman initially has very low self-esteem and sees herself as being basically unworthy of a good match. She, therefore, marries a man who, while competent, is rather undemonstrative. (While she wants to be physically provided for, her own low self-esteem makes it very difficult for her to accept affection spontaneously. The fear of eventual hurt looms too large.) Her commitment to the marriage is based on a last-chance hope. His commitment to the marriage is to have someone cook and darn his socks. The wife soon realizes an increasing detachment has taken place between the two of them. This eventually supports her earlier conclusion that she is undesirable and worthy only of eventual emotional abandonment. It is not that she fears the husband will leave but simply that he will have little or nothing to do with her emotionally. While the relationship is intact, a state of emotional divorce exists. The love and care the woman really wants from the relationship is denied. Her choice of husband gave her a man who was really unprepared to involve himself emotionally in the relationship. Giving emotional support and open affection in the relationship seemed beyond his experience.

The wife feels, "He really doesn't care," which, in fact, is almost true and subsequently turns to her son. Psychologically her relationship to the son implies, "Since your father does not care, will you come to my rescue?" She wants him to attend to her needs of attention and recognition and insure her psychological survival. This not only places a rather large burden on the son but begins to seal off any possibilities for negotiation with the husband for a different kind of relationship. All along, both in the marital and mother–son relationship, there has been little or no open communication of the needs, frustrations, hurts, burdens, and demands that have become paramount in their relationship to one another.

If the family does not contain an attractive daughter, the father is more likely to end up deriving his attention from a rather quiet and sedate affair. The missing partner (the attractive daughter) in the family pattern is supplied by an outsider. The paramour, in fact, is the unwitting dupe of a stubborn struggle for unilateral survival on the part of the father and a nagging, desperate manipulation on the part of the mother. If the family should not have a son, then the mother will take second best, at least in terms of her own needs, and pull the same kind of manipulation on an existing daughter. While she would rather have a man, any relationship within the family will do in a pinch. This may lead to rather masculine expectations toward the daughter on the part of the mother. Mother does not exactly devalue the female in the family; rather, she wishes for a more masculine type of attention and concern to complement her own femininity. This unquestionably presents a rather difficult relationship for the daughter. It is not uncommon for the daughter to become very confused in her own sexual identification or, in general frustration, leave home precipitiously as a runaway. The daughter may then proceed through part of her life with considerable guilt because she abandoned her mother.

Resolution: Uniqueness and Concern

The resolution of this pattern requires, first of all, a clear and appropriate understanding of mother's physical condition. If mother should have some basic heart difficulty, it is necessary for all members of the family to understand the actual medical implications of her disorder. Realistic limitations need to be clearly understood. Mother, therefore, should not go to the doctor alone; her husband should accompany her and discuss the implications and limitations of her condition directly with her physician. Only then can he understand what is reasonable medical limitation and what is outright manipulation. Unfortunately, some family physicians, while they recognize the emotional nature of symptoms when there is no organic involvement, tend to confirm the faulty picture by prescribing medication rather than psychotherapeutic intervention. Increasingly, however, physicians recognize psychological symptoms masquerading as physical complaints and also recognize when genuine but mild physical disorders are used as a basis for relationship manipulation.

The basic approach to "It's Nothing—Just My Heart Again" is to see that something better than coronary symptoms can be mother's lot in life. Since the pattern has usually emerged from extremely poor communication between mother and father and unilateral communication between mother and son, the focus must be on opening channels of meaningful communication. It is the fears, needs, and aspirations underneath the symptoms that need to be communicated. Resolution depends on reawakening everyone's awareness to *needs* rather than fears and to provoking open communication by a direct and frank confrontation of what occurs in the family system.

The husband–father possesses an ignorance of emotional relationships that must be stimulated by awareness and confrontation. The mother's fears need to be quieted either by real attention or actual abandonment. More often than not, the husband is really concerned, and his ability to express affection is the real medicine the mother requires. In some relationships, the marital pairing has become so dysfunctional and disturbed that only separation or divorce is possible. Continuing to remain together only geometrically increases the despair, the detachment, and the hurt within the relationship. Each has by then become so defensive and so fearful of the other that he cannot risk any kind of negotiation.

To grow up safely is to be convinced that we may express our unique selves, communicate our needs, and reasonably expect our family members to consciously cooperate in the satisfaction of these needs. But this family erroneously believes that expressing oneself openly is only risking inevitable rejection and abandonment. In other words, should mother communicate her need for open and visible affection by the father, she fears either he will not or cannot do it. It may well be that the kind of man who marries this kind of woman is not particularly demonstrative. Since he obviously learned not to be, then he can also learn, through collaborative negotiation with his wife, to be more demonstrative. Whatever happened to them in the past no longer applies to their present relationship. This is a unique system that must be uniquely evolved from mutual negotiation.

Each member of the family really needs to ask himself what is he getting out of the existing situation. The mother gets an emotionally sick son, the father gets a fearful wife, the daughter a hostile mother, and the son the crossfire between his mother's overattention and his father's bitter criticism.

Open communication must replace images with reality. What actually is, not what is hoped for, must be faced. What is feared is an anticipation, an expectation, not necessarily reality. Fear can only be diminished when there is a commitment to openly communicate, to be frank, to confront, become aware, and then to negotiate. The heart is not only the mythological seat of love and affection but the physiological receptacle of fear and anxiety.

PART IV

The Powers That Be

A basic policy evolves in all families in regard to the nature of power-role relations between members that involve decision making, who leads, who follows, and under what circumstances. The crucial aspect of any policy in regard to power-role relations is who has the power to decide what rules are to be followed in the conduct of the relationship. Power policy emerges from the inherent problem all families face in its members making room for one another. It is another manifestation of what has already been referred to as the continual dilemma of the self–other relationship. Self and other simply do not exist idyllically. They must communicate, they must perform certain jobs in the family, and, more important, they must work out a way of dealing with affection and joy as well as disappointment and sadness.

Power policy may resemble a kind of "corporate structure"; each member of the family needs to know who has the power to decide, and under what circumstances, in order to minimize inherent conflicts. This kind of power policy relies on clear and open communication. Each person is able to manifest him or herself openly and clearly to each other in the structure. A power policy may also resemble labor–management negotiations in which each side attempts to obtain what they wish at the expense of the other and, if necessary, to use force, issue threats, or use various kinds of coercion to bring about the desired results.

In the early years of a family, the relationships between parents and children are more complementary in nature and therefore there is a disproportionate power relationship between parents and child. Nevertheless, if decisions for the child are not made upon the basis of what fits but largely on the premise of "I am going to control you," enormous amounts of resentment will result. It is the nature of early parent–child relations that resentment on the part of the child will accumulate to some degree, because he cannot always have his way. Similarly, resentment will accumulate on the part of the parents whose child-rearing ideals are frequently shattered by the uniqueness of their child. But this disappointment and resentment can be openly talked about and worked through.

The crucial issue in evolving power-role-relationship policy for the family resides upon whether decision making is based upon who's boss or on what fits. The first form is basically dysfunctional and results in either passive resentment or open rebellion. The reaction to the "who's boss" policy is a reaction to the improper use of power, rather than to the issue of deciding joint outcome. It becomes a matter of "who is to have their way" instead of "what is to be done." The pattern is dysfunctional because nothing is worked out, decisions are not made, and a struggle for power ensues. Functional role performance in this family may falter badly. The broken screen door may not be fixed, meals may be badly prepared, the children's rooms may become more and more disordered. Personal vendettas replace problem solving, and family members try to even the score and vindicate themselves rather than find ways of living together more satisfactorily.

Chapter 9

"Now Hear This: This Is Mother Talking!"

When the Captain on a ship wishes to have the undivided attention of his crew, he states clearly and firmly, "Now hear this: This is the Captain speaking." Anyone who might be unfortunate enough to miss the significance of what is said will find himself in serious trouble. It is not uncommon for various kinds of human organizations, including the family, to be referred to as "running like a taut ship." The following family pattern is similar, with mother in command.

Theme: Follow Me, Men!

Life in this type of family is approached on the premise that women are all-powerful and men are weak. Motherhood is divine; fatherhood is necessary. Children are seen as extensions of self, especially for the mother. Family life is a combat patrol with mother as platoon leader. Everybody is fearful of almost everything, especially attack (what is attacking is unclear). The world is seen as a dangerous place, but mother, who knows all and who sees all (has she *ever* been wrong?), is there to protect everything. While a state of war appears to exist between the family and the world outside, an assertive if not frantic commander-in-chief appears to be firmly in charge of the situation. It is, in fact, the danger from the outside that makes necessary mother's firm leadership imperative within the family. If anyone should presume for a moment that there is no external danger, there would be no need for militant leadership.

Such a family pattern requires a domineering woman; a beaten, withdrawn man; and docile, obedient children. Any other combination of people within the family would make the acceptance of the outside danger myth and mother's infallible direction very difficult to accept and, least of all, to act on. In such a family, it is not cleanliness but motherhood that is next to godliness. Such a combination would indeed be rather difficult to oppose. An aggressive and confident man would be an unlikely mate for such a woman; he would be left with the alternatives of (a) conquering her domination directly and openly achieving a more symmetrical balance to the relationship, (b) leaving her to her own devices, abandoning home, and beginning a new life, or (c) turning the relationship into an Alfred Hitchcock type plot, which would inevitably end up in either the morgue or the jail. The children of such a pattern learn very early not to oppose overwhelming strength.

Respect for mother is more important than anything else, especially uniqueness. Autonomy is taken as anarchy and will not be tolerated. Respect, like everything else she does, is a unilateral process to support her, and implies subjugation to her rather than awareness of her respectable qualities. When lack of "respect" should occasionally occur toward the mother, it is taken by her to be tantamount to matricide. At times, mother seems to be frightened, even in spite of her power and divinity. She can only be worthwhile if she is all-powerful and can control the lives of others and their response to her. To do otherwise, she feels, deprives her of all worthiness.

Example: Whistling in the Dark Is Better Than Fainting

Tom, an ineffectual man with needs to be dependent on another, married Jean, a dominant woman. Tom can evidently depend on Jean and therefore feel secure, while Jean is able to give direction and guidance to Tom and validate her need to be strong. In such a relationship Jean fills a power vacuum by mutual consent; Tom is willing to let her be dominant because he fears his own inadequacies. Underneath, Jean is really as fearful as Tom, but she minimizes her anxieties as she takes the part of the leading light and source of power in the relationship. She decides what rules are to be followed. But her selection of Tom as a mate assures her of significant passive collaboration.

What is easily overlooked in this kind of relationship is that Jean's need to be fearlessly dominant is really a method of protection against the anxiety of her own perceived inadequacies. It is a "whistle in the dark" method that covers a basic fear with an opposite, overt behavior. Her behavior (domination) convinces herself, in spite of her insecurity, and others, in spite of their autonomy, that she is confident and powerful.

On the surface, Jean appears to give something to a weak and dependent Tom. The collusion seems to meet his dependency needs, which really represent a lack of self-esteem on Tom's part. It is Tom's low opinion of himself that allows, in part, her generous gift of universal guidance. Intimacy between them is avoided, since her need to dominate emasculates him. In effect, the relationship makes room for Jean and not for Tom. His autonomy is thwarted; his growth into responsible manhood is put aside for the sake of the relationship. Ostensibly, they can only remain together as long as she dominates and he is ineffectual, a premise that assumes relationships are built on complementary weaknesses.

When children are added to the family, even more trouble will emerge from this dysfunctional system. If the child is passive, that is, rather placid and easygoing by nature, he or she will fit into the pattern comfortably. Like father, he will be ineffectual. He will not complain but will listen when mother talks. However, any functional performance of duties will be poor. The child will resent the "boss" tactics of the mother, and with passive resistance, will perform tasks in a most inadequate manner, slippery-fingered shoe tying, muscle-fatigue boot removal, etc. This further plays into mother's hands—her omniscient power is truly needed to guide this "helpless" little one.

If a child in this relationship has an aggressive constitution, that is, assertive and outgoing, noticeable difficulty both within and without the family will be apparent. An autonomy battle will emerge between mother and the aggressive child. This child will not easily accept the rule that mother is all-powerful and the only way to relate to her is through weakness and passivity. Since this child breaks this family rule, pressure will be brought on the child not only by the mother but by the father and any other passive siblings. Eventually, one might very well see such an assertive child become the scapegoat for family anger and hostility, developing a symptom pattern that gives him the family label of "bad."

Marie, for example, was the first-born daughter of Tom and Jean. She is a somewhat assertive, loud, aggressive, and, at times, obstreperous youngster. Mother finds it difficult to control her within the limits of her own expectation. While Marie's constitution cannot be changed, she eventually learns to regard herself as a rather "bad" person. Jean constantly restricts Marie in regard to what she should not do and how bad she is. Jean expects Marie to conform, to obey, and to be a "good" child (that is to regard mother as supreme and everyone else as subservient to mother).

By the fifth grade Marie's behavior in school has become somewhat intolerable to the teacher and principal. Mother is at a loss to understand her behavior since, at home, Marie has gradually been more conforming, or so it would appear. In fact the energy Marie has had to suppress at home has burst forth in school, creating a problem in the classroom. At home she must suppress and deny herself and school is her only outlet. On the surface then, it would appear that Marie is the problem rather than the family relationship system that has perpetuated at a dysfunctional level by marital collaboration and family collusion.

The most common variation of this same type of tactical manipulation within a family relationship is the long-suffering quiet talker who always has the last word. Mother is not necessarily loud and bossy, but oh how she suffers, and how she talks about how she suffers. While she may not talk loudly, it seems as if she is forever talking with heart-rending supplication. Her point is always the same: Mother has suffered so long that she knows best. The children cannot think fast enough to outtalk her, and even if they do, she may resort to hard-line "Joan of Arc" or "Heart Trouble" tactics. The husband gets a similar treatment.

The manipulation here, while it is more subtle, is just as effective. Domination and control lie squarely in the hands of the mother with only the passive cooperation of her husband and children. If other members of the family are not immediately subject to mother's control, the hint of overt matricide will enter both mother's thinking and talking. "No matter what I try to do, nothing ever works out (my way). Sometimes I don't know whether I can go on. It's (you are) just killing me." Her message has the elegant dysfunctional quality of vagueness plus comprehensive suggestibility.

Dynamics: Domination Is the Mask of Fear

While it does require a complementary behavior match in the marriage, the genesis of this dysfunctional pattern actually begins before the husband and wife marry. Both partners usually come from families where there was female domination and this has resulted in both Tom and Jean having very low self-esteem. They developed opposite reactions, however, when their autonomy was crushed and their needs for nurturance and dependence overridden. Jean tends to identify with her strong mother in terms of behavior and becomes dominant herself. Tom, on the other hand, had a weak father and therefore can only imitate the weakness he has observed. The pair have developed complementary defenses to manage their low self-esteem. She feels safe from attack with him. The threat of personal involvement (domination) she experienced with her mother, she can avoid by controlling the relationship with Tom. He can let her take further responsibility in hopes of avoiding further failure experiences.

In actuality, the relationship is based upon interlocking unilateral fantasies. He hopes to have his dependency met without giving much in return. She hopes to validate the myth of her personal strength. The inherent mutuality of their relationship is nevertheless avoided and undermined. If she is to dominate and control, any needs she has for dependency will go unmet. Since he must be weak and helpless before her power, his self-esteem is even further diminished. In particular, the mutual nurturance and dependency needs inherent in any relationship go unmet here. Each acts in a manner that is ostensibly to gain supplies for self-esteem, while they instead provoke further detachment and resentment. They "give" from perceived weakness and inadequacy, rather than confident strength.

Tom and Jean's relationship is also based on the mutual avoidance of intimacy. She is too powerful to be close to; he is too weak to respect. They mutually deny responsibility for what happens to them. Since she is infallible, she is never wrong; and since he is weak and ineffectual he can never be right. Therefore, she is right even when wrong; he lets her have it her way and can blame her when things do go awry. The relationship is based upon who is boss, not what fits the people involved. Needs are not met, only who is right or most powerful is decided. Afterwards, resentment arises in the power loser and various things do not get done. This, in turn, arouses the anger of the more power-fed person, with resultant orders more firmly, but now somewhat desperately, given. The circular process continues until both sides give up in mutual frustration. Their mutual legacy is frustration rather than realization.

The male children end up like father; they feel weak and lack responsibility. The female children can only feel safe if they, too, dominate, but they have difficulty in identifying with confident womanliness in such a powerful mother. Power, as they view it, is always accompanied by anxiety, and the result is either frantic domination or calculated martyrdom.

Mother maintains her power by constantly keeping all members of the family anxious about the dangerous world, and she determines how they relate to the outside. Both parents and children have few, if any, social friends. Mother says, "They're not the proper kind of people." This is really an expression, however, of the mother's own anxiety about being able to deal with other people, men and women, who may not accept the premise that women are all-powerful and men are weak. Relationships with outside persons must be minimized so the family system is not threatened by any external influences.

The pathology of strength paired with weakness that began the relationship between mother and father is picked up by the children and perpetuated; it is enhanced by the fact that no external or new experience is allowed to enter the family system. The family exists as a closed system and functions like a small secret society. Mother, in essence, keeps everyone else off balance so she can stabilize the system in her own way. She has at all times, however, the active collaboration of her husband and usually the passive children in the family. They all subscribe to the same myth of mother's strength and their weakness.

The eventual joint outcome in such a family is that dependency is overextended for all. The father assumes little or no responsibility since he can depend on mother's power. Mother depends on maintaining her self-esteem at the expense of everyone else in the family, and they usually collaborate. The children are over-dependent on mother and have little opportunity for autonomous growth. Autonomy is poorly developed and self-esteem is diminished for all. Intimacy is avoided, and the identity of any self in the family is very poorly developed, since distinctions between the self and others are very vaguely defined. Self is usually seen as a part of another rather than as a separate being. Children and the father are extensions of mother; similarly, the father and the children are nothing without her presence. Therefore, there is little room for self but only room for the other. Self–other operations allow only for sameness and likeness, not realization of uniqueness. In very desperate forms of this pattern, suicide by any member is possible.

Resolution: How Do You Read Me?

Everyone in the family may listen to mother's commands, but the family members, including mother, may not listen to what each of them wants and needs in their mutual relationships. Mother needs to shift from "Now hear this" to "How do you read me?" She must listen to what she says and develop an awareness of how it feels to be commanded and dominated. Her own domination by her mother has been repressed from her consciousness. What tends to go unnoticed by all is the simmering and repressed resentment that domination always arouses. This must be recognized. In her attempts to have a "happy" family and to hope to receive the love of her children, mother has, in essence, further perpetuated the repressed resentment system she brought from her own family.

The other members of the family, and father especially, keep the pattern in operation by going along with the mother. Thus, they have no responsibility for any relationship consequences between the self and others. It takes collusion to keep a dysfunctional family system in operation, and only mutual enlightenment will redirect it toward more functional outcome. Mother can only accomplish her domination if the others go along. This relationship is reciprocal and can be broken from any point on the circle of causality of domination—resentment—cop-out—domination, etc. Only when this sequence is disrupted can the whole cycle of behavior reciprocity be altered.

The basic element of resolution in this pattern depends on each member of the family's developing an awareness of how he or she uses the pattern dysfunctionally. Each one hopes to attain his or her needs; in reality, they almost always fail to do so. The weak and ineffectual father hopes to have his dependency met by a strong woman. But any possibility for autonomous growth, which can only come from experiencing and trying his strength, is minimized in such a relationship. Mother, on the other hand, cannot deal with her fear of being overpowered without using power to protect herself. Any need she has for dependence and nurturance is covered over by her own dominance. If she can become aware that she does not give strength but provokes resentment, she might rather have her family's affection and respect instead of their fear and anger. She also cannot grow without being dependent and nurtured, but this cannot occur without the other members of her family. The children, in their hopes to obtain mother's love, have knuckled under; in so doing they too have given up their opportunity for autonomous growth. For them, acceptance of mother's domination is acceptance of their own worthlessness.

In terms of meeting human need for survival, this type of family falters badly. While sense and order may be rather clear and direct, it is unilateral. Productivity is poor because self-esteem is so low. Continued domination, debasement, knuckling under, and giving in lead only to further diminution of self-esteem. People cannot produce anything but despair in such an environment; intimacy is a completely lost cause. One cannot really know another without manifesting the self openly and clearly, yet everybody in this family wears a mask. Mother is fearful but appears powerful; father appears ineffectual but is seething with resentment and retaliation; the children appear to be helpless and dependent but feel worthless and are rebellious.

A basic approach to this family would be to expose the underlying resentment that stems from the frustration of autonomous development and to allow this resentment and anger to be ventilated. This will make clear the destructive properties of their reciprocity that have, heretofore, been overlooked but most certainly experienced. The futility of continuing such a dysfunctional pattern opens the exploration of new ways of relating, ways that focus on needs and subsequently, what solution most fits the family members. Conflict is inherent in the multifaceted uniqueness of parents and children.

Hurt is not final; it is the beginning point of negotiation. There is little hope when they can look forward only to separation and loneliness. They could have reciprocal growth toward responsible adulthood.

Chapter 10

"Might Makes Right"

Theme: Only Squares Sit at a Round Table

In this behavior pattern to be male is to be right, dominant, power-ful, and fearless. Women are necessary, children subservient. Family life resembles an autocratic medieval court, with an absolute ruler and with much court intrigue. Father's word is to be taken as law. Personal feelings of other family members are seldom, if ever, taken into account. What is right is more important than what fits the situation. This reign of terror is, however, only accepted on the surface. While the court is presided over by the despot, the queen, princes, and princesses plot, sometimes together and some-times separately, to undermine the king. In other words, while everybody is terrified of (psychological) annihilation, all plot to overthrow. Yet they hope that the dictatorial despot will reform his ways and treat them with more kindness.

Such a family system requires an anxious, brutal, and perhaps somewhat sadistic father; a helpless, anxious mother; and frightened, rebellious children. Cloaked in father's brutal autocracy, however, is anxiety over his acceptance and virility within the family. Only a helpless, anxious woman would marry such a man. (One more confident would not have the neurotic need to be dominated.)

Her helplessness is the perfect foil for his domination and helps to perpetuate the pattern indefinitely. Difficulties are more likely to arise with the children. Their natural strivings for autonomy may take the form of subtle, and at times open, rebellion.

Absolute obedience to father is more important than growth and autonomy, choice and cooperation. The message is rather clear: Not to obey him is not to love him; and in that case, the father's infantile hurt turns to wrath. He acts as if he needs to destroy them before they desert him, mistakenly interpreting rebellion not as a sign of the children's autonomy but as an attempt to destroy his identity.

The most consistent emotion in this family is anger; affection seems largely absent, denied, or concealed. In fact, anger seems to be equated with love, so that mutual destruction and hurt get confused with affection. Demanding, shouting, and hitting are signs that one cares. Under such circumstances, it is not unusual to see resentful confusion in the recipients of such "love." They find it hard to accept the duality of hurt and love in the same act. Suspicion, hostility, and angry panic are the order of the day.

Examples: Bully for Daddy and Who's Got the Highest IQ?

Al and Betty married somewhat late in life in their early thirties. Prior to the marriage Al had trouble in high school and at his various subsequent jobs. In both situations he was sulking, resentful, and at times openly hostile. He had great difficulty in taking directions or getting along with his fellows; when he did not get his way, he would become angry and frequently abusive. His perception that others did not seem to like him was in general correct, for his peers saw him as a bully.

After his third job Al met Betty who was a shy, retiring, unsure woman evidently needing and wanting direction. She admired a "strong" man; her father was the strong, silent type. (This meant he hadn't talked much to his wife in fifteen years). Her father's silence was equated with strength of character, rather than fearful withdrawal. While Betty admired her father's strength, his withdrawal left a directional vacuum in the family. She hoped to find direction in her husband and thought she had succeeded when she met Al. Because Betty felt weak and helpless and needed the strength and direction of another and Al felt unliked and uncared for by his peers, they hopefully exchanged protection for nurturance. He could protect (if not control) her; at the same time he could rule with righteous domination and receive her love and adulation.

Al and Betty soon had children to prove his virility and her fertility; this ostensibly would raise the self-esteem of each. After the children came, and during their childhood, Al continued to rule with an iron fist. While she was a rather experienced doormat, Betty eventually had more than even she could take. Her resentment over Al's dictatorial policies began to build. He decided what they were to eat, he decided on the family car, her clothes were subject to Al's approval.

As Betty's resentment began to build, her favorite passive tactic was cold sexual responsiveness to Al, though she herself experienced little gratification. He would not openly admit his lack of satisfaction, but inside he was very much aware of her unresponsiveness and interpreted this as a smear on his masculinity. If questioned in any way, Betty could claim with innocent righteousness that she was sorry for their lack of sexual success; but, after all, even though she tried, nothing really seemed to happen. This was the beginning of a spiraling mutual frustration in the marital relationship.

The children's reaction to Al was to obey the letter, never the spirit, of his law. As they got older this came to mean many things. When "ordered" to clear the driveway, they left the sidewalks piled with snow. Infractions of the rules would lead to rather violent courtroom scenes, in which the children, in innocent stupidity, would plead their defense. After all, they had done only what father had told them to do. When told to get out of the house and stop bothering him, they didn't come home for supper. When he demanded their complete attention to his words, they were always standing next to him or hovering over him.

The mutual frustration in the family led to angry outbursts, violence, and eventual depressive fear and disillusionment. The emotional nurtuance Al wanted so badly in the form of affection and admiration was only spoken of, never present in the behavior of his wife or children. Keeping pieces of furniture intact was difficult at best. In the father's absence, the male children in the family would destroy things, much to the continual dismay of the mother. Even though father wanted them to perform well in school, they always seemed to fail. Like mother, they had tried hard, but nothing seemed to happen.

One could briefly summarize dysfunctional behavior in this family: The children failed in school, the mother failed in the home, and the father failed in the bedroom. Betty is depressed, the children are anxious and fearful, and Al rages in panic. Violent family rage may become homicidal.

There is an intellectual's variation to the "Might Makes Right" pattern, dependent on having higher educational degrees. Here the autocracy is cloaked in logical rationale. The degree-laden "genius," by logical deduction, will invoke the call of "stupid" and "unintelligent" if his logic is not adhered to. Violence is replaced by icy intellectual debate and punishment by elegant name calling, for example, "That's absolutely irrational." Within the intellectual's realm, to be illogical or nonrational is akin to being unhuman.

The wife and children's self-esteem is constantly and persistently undermined by the father's superior intellect. In this variation of the pattern, the children are still likely to fail in school, the mother to be unresponsive, but the father will spend most of his time at the office, or lab. (He may avoid the bedroom altogether.) The frustration and disillusionment remain, while the depression increases significantly. Violence and shouting are poor form to the intellectual; therefore, the ultimate solution to such desperate frustration is self-destruction, suicide.

Both of the examples given above illustrate the same process. They are not really opposites of the same coin, but variations on the same theme. The extreme solutions of homicide and suicide, while infrequent, do indeed happen. This need not be expected, but in situations of extreme frustration and insolubility, desperation and irrationality, rather than negotiation, determine joint outcome.

Dynamics: Hurt Is the Hang-Up

Again, it is necessary to go back to the beginning of the marriage to see how the family architects established the rules of the system. A man whose individuality has been previously crushed, and who is furious about it, marries a woman of similar low self-esteem who has reconciled herself to this (or so she thinks). The husband had as brutally despotic a father as himself. As a result his won autonomy and identity were crushed and self-esteem became dependent on power tactics rather than his unique worth as an individual. The "who is boss" policy defined the relationship between family members. Since father was always an object of power manipulation, he came to feel weak, powerless, and inadequate, but covers this, as did his father, with a power bluff. The husband is furious at these early experiences in his life, and his only retaliation is to treat others similarly which, in most circumstances, alienates him from people.

When he meets a woman who also had her autonomy crushed and suffers from low self-esteem, the possibility for unconsciously shared feelings emerges. What they see in one another, what, in part, draws them together, is a common feeling of intense hurt over past injustices. To complete the reciprocity, however, this pattern requires a woman who has also consciously reconciled herself to her low self-esteem. She is convinced that she is inadequate, bad, and ineffectual. The resentment her husband expresses openly in his despotism, she represses in her innocent helplessness. She can be nothing without his direction, but this leaves her as nothing more than an extension of him. Her dependency is overdetermined, and her identity becomes obliterated.

When the marital relationship originally formed, a dysfunctional rule was established that hurt was never to be admitted directly and openly. It could only be expressed in anger or in depression. The wife therefore must compensate her hurt by vicarious identification with his power. In turn, when she accepts his power, he feels strong, overcoming his earlier defeated and inadequate self-image. Realistically, however, because his power continues to deny her autonomy and identity, as it did within her family, she must eventually begin to resent it. Her acceptance of the passive role in the relationship leads her to passive resentment, for example, wooden sexual responsiveness. Her early admiration of his power degenerates into a series of passive undermining ploys as a means of defense against her self-esteem system depletion by him.

The unconscious behavioral purpose for this relationship is quite different than their conscious assumptions about it when they met and later married. She is to serve as a foil for his disillusioned anger. He can beat her down as his father did to him; he can turn his inadequacy into strength at her expense. On the other hand, he serves as the embodiment of her accepted fate, namely, the repressed and unexpressed resentment over her own crushed autonomy that is vicariously enjoyed in his despotism with others. When his despotism becomes part of their own marital mutuality her hurt is only increased; her earlier admiration of his power changes to passive resistance; the nurturance he had hoped to obtain from her, which was never really there, appears to vanish. They had hoped to mutually manipulate one another to compensate for their own negative self-concepts. Both are disappointed and disillusioned. Her compliance to his despotism is emotionally empty and without nurturance; the care and admiration he hoped to obtain is frustrated.

As the couple continues to live together, reciprocal reinforcement in their relationship perpetuates the following serial transactions—despotism—compliance—frustration—resentment—despotism. This unending circle continues to repeat itself. (See Figure 6.)

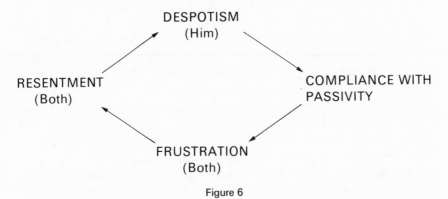

DESPOTISM
(Him)

RESENTMENT
(Both)

COMPLIANCE WITH
PASSIVITY

FRUSTRATION
(Both)

Figure 6

When children are added to the family, they become a working part of this same dysfunctional system. The natural autonomous strivings for unique identity in the children only produce another generation of tyrants and weaklings. The male children seek the best of a bad situation and identify with the father's aggression and hostility. They hope to gain something over the females in the family. The females, on the other hand, have a despairing but passively resistant mother as a model. Their only choice is the same passive undermining tactics she uses to foil the dominant male. The ultimate result for all members of the family is that self-esteem is further diminished and crippled.

The "Might Is Right" family myth is besieged by perpetual rebellious intrusion. As long as basic strivings for autonomy and identity are prevented either by despotic control or passive resistance, attempts will be made to overthrow these roadblocks. These important needs, if not met in the family, will either become a part of a continuous conflict in the family or will be acted out in behavior outside of the family. The mother, for example, if she cannot receive kind consideration from her husband, may attempt to find it from another man. Usually any affairs she becomes involved in are relatively short-lived. By now, unilateral manipulation has become a way of life for her; she seeks to obtain rather than to give in all relationships. What her paramours really offer is sterile sexuality, appealing at first perhaps, but shortly offering nothing to really develop a relationship.

The children in the family, because of their size and lack of mental maturity, can neither outfox nor overpower the father. They may in time express their resentment, as did the father, by bullying behavior in school or with their peers in general. They may even become involved with hostile, angry gangs. This eventually runs them afoul of the law, and the family problem then appears to reside in the delinquent child rather than the despotism—frustration—panic sequence that channels family life.

Identity awareness and intimacy realization are diverted into a desperate survival struggle: Attack and defend yourself at all times before you are relegated to a nothingness that consists of a subservience to another's needs without mutual reward. Mutuality is nonexistent. Who is right is more important than what fits the people involved. Creative productivity is hardly possible under despotic control. Sense and order are determined by one at the expense of the others and do not allow for feelings or individuality. Intimacy is not possible under a system where one is alternately attacking and defending. Only physical survival is insured; psychological survival becomes distorted and crippled by the spiraling battle between despotism and retaliation.

Resolution: Enlightened Leadership

The resolution of this pattern must begin with the recognition that the misuse of interpersonal power and authority in a family leads to generalized rebellion and meets nobody's needs. The focus must be frankly and openly placed on unmet needs, on personal values of mutual significance, and on the state of psychological ill-being in family relationships. Sense and order, productivity, and intimacy have become confused and unpredictable in the power struggle for dominance; and power and domination alternate with retaliation and rebellion. The needs themselves continue to be unmet.

Sense and order must be clear and firmly delineated, but not unilaterally determined by power tactics, lest they are accompanied with fear and anger, leading only to disillusionment and despair. Sense and order from mutual negotiation lead to consistent expectations that give a feeling of security in mutual relationships. It must be established that something more mutually gratifying can be worked out, nothing perfect or completely compensatory of earlier hurts but workable enough to enhance the self-esteem of all family members. Productivity that is forced by power is joyless, sluggish, and full of vindictive and undermining traps. Productivity that derives from mutual exploration and responsibility for joint outcome can be both joyful and creative. The third basic psychological survival need, intimacy, cannot be legislated or forced; it can only evolve from mutual nurturing, sharing, and exploring.

When the focus of family awareness is shifted away from the vicious cycle of interaction toward these unmet needs, a new awareness can emerge. The autocrat is in reality a fearful child who receives no support and affection. He is boisterous and threatening but lonely and afraid. Nevertheless, it's very difficult indeed to support and show affection toward somebody who beats you. The father who acts the role of the autocrat needs support and assurance of his value not reinforcement that his powers are absolute. This requires awareness and change by all—not just him.

The family must begin to see itself as rather unhappy. The rebellion that constantly plagues its functioning is, in reality, identity-seeking fulfillment. This phenomenon should be examined more closely. When autonomy is thwarted, denied, even smashed, we seek some other method of establishing our identity. Rebellion is the natural result of the purposeful, even though unconscious, seizure of another's autonomous responsibility. It is the attempt, at times misdirected, to establish identity and to seek meaning in order to raise self-esteem. Unruly behavior in the family must be seen as such, not as a plot to rob father and deprive him of his identity.

The primary task of the family will be to unmask the hurt underlying the anger and rebellion in the family, for this is what motivates both the despotism and the rebellion. As long as the hurt goes unlabeled and unrecognized, dysfunctional defensiveness will predominate in their interaction.

Mutuality must replace fearful defensiveness. This requires the open manifestation of self and the willingness to negotiate joint outcome. Enlightened leadership is more productive than autocratic dictatorship.

Chapter 11

"Blackmail, Children's Style"

Theme: The Family Protection Racket

This family pattern results in some behavior reversals among family members: Father acts like a child, mother seems helpless with her child's wishes, and the child, with supreme confidence, appears to be in charge of the family. This behavior begins from the assumption that parents are weak and indecisive and children are really smarter—or at least cuter—than their parents. The apparent advantage within a family in the parents' weakness and indecision is that they may shift responsibility elsewhere. However, the only place left is with the children. This is something like putting a lighted stick of dynamite in the hands of a child and later wondering why things didn't turn out better. The parents' ability to shift responsibility for family direction to the children is a basic evasion tactic. If they both act helpless and inept, what goes wrong within the family is not really their fault. Instead they plead, "Look how hard we try to be good (all-giving) parents."

This type of family meets needs largely by tactical manipulation and guilt induction; the more the parents feel weak and indecisive, the more room for manipulation exists with the children, who can get what they want but "innocently" refuse responsibility for their behavior. If the parents protest too much, the children can imply the parents are inadequate, fools, unloving, or all three. If the parent eventually gives in, the result is chaotic and thoroughly unpredictable behavior within the family. Nobody appears to be in charge of direction and regulation of family tasks (when do we wake up, eat, wash, leave for outside responsibilities like school, and go to bed). The children are unsure but aggressively brazen. They are not stupid; their initial successes in outmaneuvering a larger but not particularly formidable opponent leads only to further demands and manipulations. The parents are guilty and repentant, always making up for what they did wrong. They accept the blame whenever things go wrong, which leaves who and what is to be responsible for the direction of the family life unfinished. The parents feel guilty, frustrated, and disillusioned and turn to evasive and withdrawal tactics to avoid further disappointment within the family. Their abdication of responsibility, direction, and discipline leads to anarchistic chaos. The children are deprived of confident autonomy; what they all end up with is impulsive, frightened, and frantic leadership.

Certain kinds of parents and children and active collaboration between them are necessary for this pattern to evolve. The parents must be guilty, uncertain, and lack confidence. The husband felt inadequate and married his wife for her supposed strength; she, in fact, did the same. The result is mutual inability to nurture, support, and direct, with tragic results not only to their own self-realization as adults but to the eventual lack of growth in their offspring.

In the parents' relationships with the children, various forms of bribery are the basis for intergenerational negotiation. Mother and father specialize in appeasement and, in general, hope the children will raise themselves without fuss. The children are quick to learn that the parents view the family as a rather unstable boat nobody must rock; they accept the parental bribes, but such blackmail is obviously unending. Whenever the children want something, they merely issue a threat to misbehave. This, in turn, arouses the parents' anxiety, and they give in to the children's demands. The sequence is capable of indefinite repetition.

Self-discipline is virtually unknown and the idea itself smacks of coercion. "Being accepted" is a focal value for the parents, "making the haul" without responsibility a focal value for the children. Because the parents feel very little value in themselves or from one another, they hope the children will love and adore them. One way to ensure this is to give them what they want. The children accept the generosity of the parents, but since their ability to postpone satisfaction is poorly developed, they ask and demand more and more with threats of family disruption to barter for further goodies.

Lasting and mutual independence and responsible identity, hopefully one of the outcomes of functional family living, is rendered inoperative by this "protection racket." As long as the parents pay off, the children will protect them from the awareness of their inadequate parenting. The parents can do nothing with the children. (Mainly, they never really try.) One-up-manship predominates through bribery: The parents would seem in control of the family, while the children, from the cradle to college, obtain all that they want—and much more—by the constant threat of potential trouble.

Example: The Good Ship Lollipop

When Don and Bonnie were married they looked forward to the time when there would be children in the family. There had been some mutual disappointments in the first two years of the marriage. Both were rather shy and retiring persons; each had hoped to receive significant support and encouragement from the other. Their own inhibited way of relating, however, made it difficult to expand themselves in the relationship and to feel close and confident with one another. In addition, Don was not satisfied with his work, primarily because of a lack of appropriate aggressive involvement. Bonnie was unsatisfied with homemaker tasks but was too anxious to work outside of the home. She saw herself as plodding on a treadmill. Unable to experiment and be creative in her own homemaking, she preferred a "feel sorry for me" fantasy life.

Giving their children everything they didn't have was their philosophy. Feeling like underdogs in their self-perceptions and disappointed in how they were raised, they felt they would "do it right" when they were parents. Their own parents, each in somewhat different ways, had provided them only with a rather dull and mediocre family life. Both Don and Bonnie felt their parents should have made them happier. It is curious to note they accept little of that responsibility themselves. Rather, they are convinced their parents had failed them. Because they had not gotten from each other the support they wanted, they were convinced that their marriage was a failure too. This was never verbalized, however; it was a well-kept, but mutual, family secret.

Children psychologically represented another hoped-for happiness that life had thus far not provided them. The children's achievements were also expected to compensate for the parents' vocational failures. The children's hedonistic and infantile nature was taken as evidence of strong personality—because the parents perceived themselves as insipid, this offered some vicarious self-realization —but it often frustrated the parents' attempt to bring about the behavior they desired. They thought these innocent little lambs would, out of sheer gratitude for the privilege of birth, behave exactly as the parents wished. Certainly, the children were expected to be clairvoyant in fulfilling the parents' expectations of adoration and respect.

Unsure of themselves, and of relationships with others outside the family, Don and Bonnie doubted their success as parents, especially when their unverbalized expectations and hopes for their children collided head on with the autonomous strivings of the children themselves. The fantasy of two loving and adoring children first disappeared in the era of the terrible twos, only to be followed by the exploiting fours, fives, and sixes.

The children quickly learned the "you're a lousy, unfair, mean, unloving parent" ploy. Faced with that the parents shortly rescinded their directive and gave in to the child's demands. The children then liked them again and their guilt over hurting the child was assuaged. The temper tantrum, or even the threat of it, became valuable barter in attaining a bribe.

The children, who entered the family essentially emotionally healthy, soon learned to make the best of their initially unexpected successes until exploitation became a way of life. By the time they reached ten they had an awesome array of manipulative devices, both versatile and calculated: The sulk, the temper tantrum, the hunger strike, to name a few.

1. *The hurt sulk.* "You'll be the death of me yet, mother!" The implication of this ploy is that mother seeks only to destroy the child. She certainly doesn't understand and therefore couldn't possibly care. No mother who really wanted to be "good" could

possibly wish to hurt her child's feelings "intentionally," could she?

2. *The outright temper tantrum.* "I'll show you *and* the neighbors." This ploy works because the parents are embarrassed enough with the problems they have with the children without further vociferous and visible evidence provided to the neighbors. Since the parents' management of the children evolves around their success with the children's not rocking the boat, socially obnoxious behavior threatens to tip the boat over.

3. *The hunger strike. "You've made me unable to even eat."* The idea here is to convince the parents that they and not the child are responsible for their child's eating behavior. Horses, as well as children, will only drink if they choose to if they are led to water. Therefore, this choice, while basically the child's, is distorted to make it look like the parents' responsibility. Again, only "wicked" parents would want to starve their child to death.

Once exploitation has become a way of life with children, they tend to utilize it, not only within the family, but outside as well. In fact, "Blackmail, Children's Style" was recently very popular on college campuses, with the college administration substituting for parents. If temper tantrums work at home, why not against the administration? Some students' wishes are interfered with by college regulations, and frustration is likely to occur. Obviously, not having everything your way is a patent violation of your "rights." The students shift from a lousy, unfair, mean, and uncaring parent to a lousy, unfair, mean, and uncaring "establishment" and "administration." After all, their parents were weak and ineffectual, why shouldn't *in loco parentis* college administrators be likewise susceptible to such magnificent ploys. While it is clear that not all current student disturbances are a manifestation of this behavior pattern, it is also apparent that the successful realization of "Blackmail, Children's Style" within the family may have rather far-reaching complications. These power ploys are not used only by chronological children but by emotional children as well.

Dynamics: Guilt—The Lever of Pint-Sized Tyranny

This manipulative family system rests on mutual collaboration derived from the current parents' own unhappiness with their own parents. Don and Bonnie, "unlike" their own parents, seek perfection in parenthood, which they measure by child compliance and child "love." This system implies that the child must accept the parent as all-giving, all-loving, all-resourceful, and all-protective. Only then may the parent feel worthwhile. Since such a relationship is patently impossible, the parents soon experience the very failure they hoped to avoid. This is only the failure of not being perfect, but since they equate imperfection with inadequacy, Don and Bonnie then play out a failure drama with consistently inadequate behavior in relation to their children. They try to make the world the children's oyster, since they themselves couldn't have it.

The feelings of failure and inadequacy, however, linger on, and once the children learn this and sense the parents' guilt, the stage is set for a familywide elaboration of the pattern. The children use guilt induction to manipulate the parents, which ties in with the parents' own guilt over their fantasied and real failures. "You and I are not perfect, which is my fault" would represent the unconscious dialogue between the parents and the child. This, of course, is consistent with the parents' own conviction that their feelings of failure are the result of the years with their parents and not the result of the adult years they have wasted, self-hospitalized with a bad case of "ain't I just wretched."

In addition, the parents' disappointment in one another results in a rather low-key marital conflict. As the children become aware of this they can separate the parents further and play one off against the other, implying that Daddy is really more loving than Mommy or vice versa. In this way they can escalate the bribe to a rather significant degree, catching the parents in a one-upmanship contest of outdoing one another in loving consideration for their children. The process is perpetuated by a cycle of reciprocal reinforcement as in Figure 7.

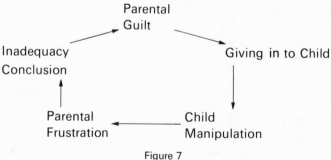

Figure 7

Parental guilt, the cornerstone of the process, permits the child's manipulation in order to assuage the parents' guilt, resulting in escalation of the child's unmanageable behavior. This further frustrates the parents' expectations of perfection and idyllic family life, leading to greater parental guilt perpetuating the cycle.

The parents find themselves in a bind: To allow the child his way in return for love eventually leads to an obstreperous, demanding, and obnoxious child. Not to give in to the child is to have to withstand his loveless criticism and withdrawal (e.g., the sulk and hunger strike maneuvers). Any attempt on the parents' part to alter the nature of the system will result in the call of inconsistency on the part of the child. This may be true, but it is still another manipulation variation. Often the parent will feel that to be loved by the child is better than to be loved by nobody.

Parental capitulation to the child's demands sets up the child's expectation that all people will be like his parents, making no use of their adult experience with confidence and direction. Since this is not true of a great many others, the child finds himself progressively in trouble with adults. The older he becomes, the more pronounced this will be. Eventually, even his peers become adults while he, by contrast, is a physically large child. The "child" then comes to the same conclusion as did his parents about their parents: His unhappiness is their responsibility, and not his.

Parents who feel unworthy and guilty have difficulty in providing a confident, predictable, and secure family atmosphere. Their children question, therefore, whether the parents care. Secondarily, the exclusive protection from interpersonal reality (mutual give and take) that the parents offered the children, has, in the long run, led the children to become involved in considerable difficulty outside the home. Who else will always give in as did their parents? Consequently they end up blaming the parents for their problems with others; they will assume no responsibility for it themselves. This pattern, unchecked, may repeat itself for numerous generations. At this point in its development, the parents, if they have not already given up in sheer desperation and frustration, almost disown the child.

Resolution: Who Is Socking It to Whom?

It is imperative for the parents to recognize that blackmail is unending. They must principally receive love from one another in their marital relationship and not from their children. The children will learn to love and respect and to become involved in mutual relationship negotiation when they observe this in the parents— when they are taught by example and by firm guidance. The parents will need to realize that children are basically rather uncivilized and desperate in their need attainment until guided toward responsible growth by their parents. As long as the blackmail situation continues, all members of the family are losers. The parents continue to feel inadequate, and the children never learn how to be responsible adults (which takes much time and patience). This failure increases difficulty for the children later on in their lives when they become chronological adults. When exploitation is a way of life, mutual negotiation goes out the window, for basic human and survival needs can only be met through mutual negotiation. If this is not learned in the family, it will be absent in their later relationships, which will be sterile, unilateral, and manipulative rather than rewarding and mutually enhancing of self-esteem. The children foster the parents' feelings of inadequacy, and the parents foster self-centered manipulation and narcissistic self-gratification in the children. The rather persistent concern on the part of both the parents and the children over who loves them has no small connection with their rather unlovable behavior. There is no mutuality in attempts to exchange affection. The parents unilaterally expect it as their just due for the act of infant creation; they furthermore confuse giving in with giving love. The children's own progressively obnoxious behavior alienates the parents' affection by its very nature.

Parents are not only smarter than their children, they are more experienced. While it is unfair to the child's evolving autonomy to allow the parents' experiences to serve as the exclusive prototype of the child's life, it is also patently absurd to allow the child to blunder headlong into hurtful situations without guidance and, if necessary, firm prohibition. Allowing a two-year-old child to play in the street does not help him develop his own awareness of traffic hazards but aids him in his own extermination. The potential for a certain amount of human failure is quite obvious to the experienced adult. Permitting the child to engage in rather overwhelming situations does not enlarge his self-esteem but allows him to experience the world as continuously threatening.

Both parents and children have needs. Unless both the marriage and the family meet the needs of the parent couple, their effective parenting will be diminished. When affection and support are missing in the marital situation, the couple will seek it in the parent–child relationship, which is distorted to a grotesque degree. Only the honest expression of needs for all can lead to negotiation of joint outcome. The family must assume the attitude that "we are in this together." They must focus on working out mutuality in their common existence, not on who manipulates whom for what ends. Need satisfaction is never unilateral, it is mutual. Frustration and imperfection are things we must all learn to struggle with; we can do it much better together than separately. Guilt and blame accomplish nothing, except to foster more feelings of inadequacy. Joint responsibility means that each person accepts responsibility for his behavior and its consequences to each other member in the family. Each, therefore, has a mandate to negotiate conflict toward more satisfactory joint outcome.

PART V

The Marital Blitz

The chapters in this section are devoted to an analysis and description of the psychological features of marital relationship, including those exclusive aspects of the marital relationship that do not involve children directly, such as sexual adjustment. The focus is on those aspects of marital relationship that represent an exclusive dyadic system either in itself or as a subsystem within a larger family including children. In the latter case the children do not participate directly in the marital pair relationship, but may, by displacement of conflict, bear the consequences of marriage difficulties.

The marital pair relationship in many ways is a double-edged sword. It has the potential for the maximum amount of growth, enjoyment, and intimacy as well as the greatest potential for conflict, pain, and desolation. The problems that arise can and do take on very lethal proportions.

The marital relationship probably functions best as an exclusive dyad, without children or inlaws involved in any way. The presence of either of these presents a natural disruption to the unique rewards of the marital pair, as the single-generation dyad is the basic element of human relationship. When room must be made for a two-generation triad, the inherent reciprocity of behavior influence in the family has tripled. (See Figure 8.)

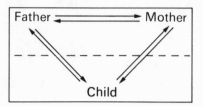

Single-Generation Dyad   Two-Generation Triad

Figure 8

In addition, the husband also takes on a father role, and the wife, a mother role. With the addition of a single individual to the initial marital pair, three emotionally significant changes occur:

1. Roles for the adults multiply.
2. A two-generational system develops.
3. Interactional complexity triples.

These developments destroy the highly valued exclusive pair relationship and substitute an inclusive familial system complete with built-in generation gap. The exclusive pair relationship is the most potentially need satisfying (who doesn't like exclusive loving?) and presents the least "reality" problems. (Remember what dinner was like before the children were born?) The same disruption of this ideal pair arrangement is present if one substitutes "in-law" for "children." The generation gap simply appears at the other end of the age continuum. Dependency, autonomy, and responsibility are all affected by this shift. Of course, some dysfunctional pairs prefer children, whom they use as displacement and mediator objects in the relationship. The children "hold the marriage together," and without them, a deadly elimination game would ensue.

The consequences of the original marital choice are one of the basic dilemmas that emerge in the marital pair relationship. All married couples unconsciously marry one another for various healthy and neurotic needs that they have and that they feel the relationship will satisfy. The degree to which their expectation for need satisfaction matches the actuality of the transactional relationship is a measure of functional outcome. A man who looks for a lost mother in his wife will be disappointed to find that the unique qualities of his spouse will defeat the ultimate attainment of his hoped-for image. The woman who, in apparent weakness, seeks a strong protective man will find difficulty in fulfilling the complementarity of needs that is required in any pair relationship. Where mutuality and reciprocity fail, conflict and manipulation appear.

In spite of our defensive cover-ups, the most hidden portions of our self will appear in the marital relationship. Spouses will reveal despair and joy, affection and hostility, concern and disinterest—if not openly, then nonverbally—even when mutual trust is minimal, because of the close and inescapable proximity of the spouses in the home. It is difficult, if not impossible, to escape from the *meaning* of a continuous relationship; this may be enjoyment or disillusionment, but it is an inescapable part of marital existence to be lived with and dealt with. If the marital relationship reaches proportions of conflict or indifference (opposite sides of the same coin) that eventually result in its dissolution, whatever degree of trust was characteristic of their relationship is carried by each into their next dyadic association.

In essence, marriage is a relationship between unique persons with varying degrees of friendship, acquaintanceship, intimacy, and neurotic redundancy. In its origin, it resembles an attempt on the part of the two parties to achieve in their relationship to one another something very similar to the exclusive love and protection that existed between the young child and the parent. If the current marital relationship must be a recapitulation of earlier relationship successes, intimacy in the current relationship becomes hard to achieve. If spouse must be like parent or previous partner in meeting needs, the present spouse's uniqueness will be denied. If one expects nearly the same things from uniquely different people, one cannot really get to know them—only use them; this is not intimacy but manipulation.

In our country marriage is based on a prior romantic love relationship that works against and defeats the real attainment of intimacy. Romantic love is built upon an expectation, a projection of an image, a hoped-for relationship. The other must be something that self wishes, rather than what other actually is. At times, the idealization of the person we marry precludes our genuinely responding to their unique qualities and, in turn, inhibits their genuine responses for fear of displeasing us. The ideal images that grow up between engaged couples or young marrieds interfere with really knowing the other they are married to. Conflict is minimized to enhance togetherness and closeness, but these rest on ignorance of unique difference. It is only years after the marriage that they really get to know one another.

The unique qualities—values, ways of doing, expectation of results—of each person in the marital relationship are also the basis of conflict in the relationship. Hopefully these two very different people will come to know one another and to negotiate those differences into a satisfying mutual relationship. They need not allow the relationship to drift into a kind of dyadic impasse but can work out a kind of need-satisfying complementarity that allows for individual identity as well as mutual support and nurturance.

The marriage relationship can therefore be seen as a joint struggle for psychological survival that requires the negotiation of joint outcome. Two people live together, share together, and experience pain together when there is not a satisfying fit to the outcome. Since they share the consequences with their spouse, the outcome must be purposely negotiated; any decision arrived at or any consequence of behavior affects both. They must reveal their needs to themselves enough to see what solution fits the reality of the situation. It is imperative that the couple talk out their wants, needs, conditions, and alternatives. When there is disagreement, and there inevitably will be, the use of any ploy or tactic is essentially dysfunctional, for it leads to a power struggle.

Compromise, for example, may be an effective solution to a business conflict; it does not work in the intimate relationship of marriage. This must be qualified with a consistent-pattern provision. How often and under what conditions does the couple compromise? Is it a redundant pattern? Most couples will reveal a particular style in their relationship, which is rather consistent and manifest in all facets of their relationship. If the pattern involves negotiation, the relationship will become functional; if it involves compromise consistently, it will eventually acquire dysfunctional properties. In a marriage, self-realization is denied in a compromise. For example, if one spouse wishes to live in New York and the other in San Francisco, and they compromise by moving to St. Louis, neither one of them will be satisfied. Compromise leads to residual resentment, which is eventually covertly acted out in the relationship. The opportunity for retaliation, though it is "not nice," is too available within the marital relationship.

The process of negotiation allows each person in the pair to label, for self and for other, the needs that lie behind preferred choices in a hoped-for achievement. The preconceived and often romantic delusions each spouse has about the other must give way to a negotiated structured reality. They must inform one another, so they can plan ahead; they can operate together and apart from one another as their needs require; they can relate both to the demands of the relationship and to outside obligations. The fantasy of an all-loving and protecting, ideal parent is replaced by an awareness of differentness, conflict, and of a potential for joint resolution. The mutual sharing of experience and responsibility toward each other replaces infantile wishes for continuous, unilateral nurturance. Neurotic hang-ups place guilt and blame ahead of responsibility, self-aggrandizement ahead of self-realization. The spouses' nurturance of one another is a reciprocal process that evolves over time from an open communication of needs, feelings, and perceptions. It is an emotional feeding of crucial survival needs. The couple's ability to understand how and when to be helpful, supportive, and comfortable with one another is a negotiated achievement of many years' duration; the failure to achieve this is the failure of many years of self-centered conflict and desperate manipulation.

Complementarity or Competition?

The marital relationship requires a complementarity of need satisfaction for its most functional realization. Competition, a unilateral achievement orientation, is especially destructive because of its potential, in a close relationship, to perpetuate hostile defensiveness. It bypasses mutual attainment and denies the reciprocity of influence in the relationship. The pair will either emotionally survive together or emotionally degenerate together. Since differentness is inherent in human uniqueness, each marital pair can either negotiate the differentness to satisfactory joint outcome, or they can compete for the title of "best loved, most accomplished" and deny joint outcome as crucial to emotional survival. The outcome hinges on what the persons will do with the differences, not the presence of differences per se.

If one looks at marriages that work out and those that do not work out, one is struck in the first instance by how hard the spouses work at negotiation. In a functional marriage human needs do not have to dovetail all the time, but the way these needs are met must be complementary to each spouse. There is no competition, a greater problem than one might suppose in marriage, for who is best and who is most valuable.

Time is both the enlightener and the destroyer of marriages. It allows a period in which to work out negotiations that will guarantee mutual survival. It also allows for phantom battles of the past to creep into the present relationship, bringing neurotic manipulation and eventual disillusionment.

Marital Relationship and Family Consequences

While there are numerous aspects of marital relationship that are private and peculiar to the couple, apart from their children, the emotional consequences of the marriage relationship are familywide. The nature, content, and extent of the heterosexual relationship of the couple, for example, is not a part of the child's life, but the feelings and attitudes derived from the sexual satisfaction or dissatisfaction in the marital relationship can most certainly be displaced to other areas of family functioning outside the exclusive marital relationship. Sexual satisfaction in marriage can either raise or lower self-esteem and subsequently affect one s mood in general. The disappointments of mutual sexuality in the marriage also very subtly affect the way in which sexual matters are discussed in the family. How sex education is handled emotionally depends to an extent on whether the parents relate touching to affection or touching to exploitation. Marital sexuality reflects the way in which the family deals with the proper place of the physical body. What happens in the bedroom also affects what happens in the kitchen, the living room, the family room, and even further, in the laboratory, the office, and the classroom.

There are also noticeable emotional consequences within the family related to occupational satisfaction on the part of the parents. If the father is dissatisfied with his job and this cannot be compensated for, to some degree, in the satisfactions in the marital union, his dissatisfaction becomes total. For a wife who is a homemaker, unending demands and the boredom of household tasks cannot, in and of themselves, be worthwhile, unless there is meaningful human relationship with the husband; the wife's mood and outlook can become totally negative and depressed. While his job satisfaction and her homemaker satisfaction are rather unique experiences in the roles of husband–father and wife–mother, they may become easily displaced onto the children.

In spite of its private and peculiar properties, the marital relationship represents the foundation for the development of the family system. Parents are the architects of the family; the soundness of the design lies in their hands. There must first be a negotiated policy for the marital dyad before the triads in the family relationship can be satisfactorily dealt with. Basic human psychological survival is involved; the stakes are not only high, they are total and ultimate. True negotiation is difficult and very painstaking, but perpetuated neuroticism can only eventually result in disillusionment and despair.

Chapter 12

"Love Is a Many-Splintered Thing"

Theme: I'll Be Angry If You Care About Me

A self who feels chronically rejected will create a marriage relationship in which he will provoke rejection outright or interpret other's behavior as always rejecting, no matter what other does. Each spouse in the relationship acts as if no alternative exists but to further validate the conviction of worthlessness that arose from his or her earlier experiences in relationships. Everyone is seen as dangerous, nobody can be trusted, but loneliness is too much to tolerate. Such spouses keep one another company, while fending each other off. Emotional closeness is dangerous, because it represents vulnerability to rejection.

Love in this kind of relationship is actually a kind of interpersonal detachment that provides safeness: The couple cannot hurt one another because the detachment prevents the relationship from being meaningful enough to take any ensuing hurt seriously. Their love does not involve the exchange of mutual affection and need meeting; there is an agreement not to openly comment on the actual lack of intimacy in the relationship. Their relationship is guided by this primary rule, which may take the form, behaviorally, of either openly detached and sullen withdrawal or, more often, hostile, rejection-provoking actions.

With such pairs the decision to marry after a period of dating is often arrived at in a most casual and uncommitted way. Neither really makes a proposal, but neither has anything better to do, so they get married. Their rationale might be (a) we were over 21, (b) it was raining on Saturday and there was nothing else to do, or (c) it seemed like "the thing" to do. In no instance do they voluntarily commit themselves to a mutual relationship. They might say, for example:

He: I suppose we could get married sometime.
She: I suppose we could.
He: Maybe I could get a license.
She: That's not a bad idea. I guess there would be enough time today.
He: Well, I'll call you if I can get one.
She: All right. In the meantime, I'll wash my hair.

They share a common conviction that risking exposure of self is worse than taking the chance on self-growth and self-expansion that could potentially derive from an open statement of needs and feelings. They do not arrive at marriage by negotiating a beginning relationship with a feeling of commitment for one another. Any feeling of commitment is disguised, because they fundamentally see human relationship as a threat, though less so than loneliness, to self-esteem. The chance to grow and expand in a relationship is viewed as unattainable. Self-revelation is seen as self-exposure and has acquired a defensive value for the individual. (Exposure indicates vulnerability to attack, revelation a willingness to reach out in mutual exchange. It matters a great deal whether a person sees relationship as an exposure or a revelation experience.)

If self marries a detached and withdrawn other, a mutual rejection pattern is easily achieved; each may then interpret the other's detachment as rejection in itself. If either member of the relationship should accidentally comment on the detachment, two basic moves keep the original theme intact.

1. Self abruptly assaults other in a hostile, rejecting manner, which causes other to withdraw. This restores the original detached balance to the relationship.

2. Self can say to other, "If you really cared, you would come to me." This invites the other to make the first move, to stick one's

neck out in order to define the relationship as more close or more caring. Since the previous relationship has often been both hostile and detached, this invitation looks like all risk and no gain.

If, however, self should err in his initial choice (which includes the fantasy and the hope of complete self-fulfillment in the relationship) and end up marrying a fundamentally accepting person, he will hope for the best but look for the worst so as not to be disappointed. The more accepting spouse will need to be provoked extensively for the detachment–rejection pattern to emerge. Even if self does not choose a hostile, detached person as a mate, he may choose someone who is easily provoked. In time the more accepting spouse, becomes, if not schizophrenic, "gun-shy." This leads to defensive withdrawal and helps to perpetuate the detachment–rejection pattern between self and other.

Marital relationship in this pattern is based on the principle that something is better than nothing; that is, any relationship, that prevents total loneliness, even if dysfunctional, is better than no relationship at all. The choice seems to be between nothing and almost nothing rather than between something tolerable and something mutually gratifying. In this case, self can control the amount of detachment and rejection by adroit provocation and thereby keep the "almost nothing" state, which is least threatening, intact. The basic principle in this type of relationship is to keep self and other at a distance that will make deeply felt hurt impossible. At the same time, it is apparent that such maneuvers will make any kind of mutually gratifying relationship impossible.

Example: Fire When Ready, Gridley!

Dick, who is hostile and withdrawn, marries Barbara, who is anxious and self-deprecatory. Each is convinced that no one else would have married them. From the beginning the relationship has been stormy, argumentative, and at times violent, but neither person has made any move to separate. There are threats of leaving, suicide, beating, and lengthy loud arguments over the basic themes of "You don't understand me," "You don't care about me," "You don't ever consider me." Accusation is followed by counteraccusation. While Dick is usually the aggressor in their battles, this sometimes alternates. When Dick seems rather depressed and more silent, Barbara will rise to the occasion and become vitriolically critical. An alternating dysfunctional complementarity is present. The pairing must always consist of an "attacking spouse" and a "depressed spouse" in combination. Either person can assume the roles, however. If at any time the relationship should not manifest an attack of self by other or other by self, someone might end up revealing concern, which would break down the previous "safe" distance in the relationship.

For brief periods of a day or two peace and tranquillity reign in the home, only to be abruptly interrupted by more of the same old story. All that is required is a slight misunderstanding of needs. After a successful day together in the country on an outing, for example, Dick sits down in the living room to begin reading. Barbara sits near him, and as she attempts to engage him in conversation she is met with a tirade of criticism that might include: "Why are you always hounding me? I can never have any peace and quiet without you butting in." Each mistakes compassion for pity and affection for strangulation of individuality. Affection is not a mutual aspect of the relationship but a bribe to be repaid. ("You only like me because you want something.") If other accepts self's affection, he must "pay off" in some way. He cannot himself accept other's affection as a response to his cherished uniqueness. Because he views himself as unlovable, he sees other's affection as phony. The relationship, therefore, is not manifest by spontaneity but by a set game in which each battles for an acceptable degree of autonomous loneliness. Each time one moves to be more affectionate or understanding of the other, a truculent suspicion on the part of the other ensues. Amid much shouting, virtually no one listens. There is only a continual verbal defensiveness on the part of each to protect their rather selfish individuality from what they perceive as outright violation.

Barbara, who still shows more open affection than Dick, learns to protect herself by the use of alcohol. Her drinking is a form of "dipsomanic immunity." She can always say, "After all, I was stoned," when she does express her genuine hurt and despair over the relationship. Her hurt, despair, and need for support are denied with the arrival of sobriety. By rejecting her need for Dick she protects herself from his hurtful attacks. As long as he attacks, she must protect herself; and as long as she protects herself, the detachment is maximized. The alcohol gives her a way of expressing her underlying feelings of concern, while it provides an excuse for doing so.

Dick and Barbara cling to one another in their relationship with almost bulldog tenacity. While it is basically a hostile, detached relationship, it is, nevertheless, a stable one for them. There is little threat of divorce. They might, in fact, have a hard time finding somebody else to put up with their behavior or to preserve their own conviction of worthlessness. Having once found so "unworthy" a partner, they may continue to live in perpetual, safe isolation from one another.

The relationship between Frank and Alice represents a silent variation of the "I'll Be Angry If You Love Me" theme. Each time Frank acts withdrawn, Alice assumes that he does not "love her" and is rejecting her. She, in turn, withdraws and is silent. It is then Frank's turn to make the same interpretation as Alice. This sort of reciprocity is really based on a hurt reaction that derives from a false perception of "loveless withdrawal" on the part of the other. Their own mutual unconscious fears of abandonment lead them to conclude that all withdrawal by other is a rejection of self. What is a defensive maneuver to prevent further hurt is perceived as an insult to self. Defense is mistaken for offense.

In this variation, the accusation–counteraccusation sequence goes on within the thinking and feeling of each person rather than being externalized in the form of arguments as in the relationship between Dick and Barbara. Eventually, Alice has a symptomatic extramarital affair and Frank begins drinking. Frank's drinking in this relationship is of a somewhat different nature than was Barbara's drinking in her relationship with Dick. For Frank alcohol is no "dipsomanic immunity maneuver" but a "denial solace" for the most intense hurt of all—Alice's infidelity. No consideration is allowed for the hurt Alice must have sustained to prompt her to the affair. His own battered self-esteem (not very high prior to the affair) is all that matters.

In her affair Alice hoped she could find love without responsibility, the responsibility involved in living with someone daily—as well as the exchange of affection and sexuality. It is, of course, far easier to love and adore from a distance (as in dating) than to live with the emotional ups and downs of a continuous marital relationship. Extramarital sexuality serves essentially the same role for Alice as does alcohol for Frank. It soothes ravaged self-esteem. Alice's affair, however, was conducted in such a manner as to leave substantial hints, indiscretions, and visual clues for Frank, including several devices to arouse suspicion or convey guilt: the unexplained absence accompanied by a self-satisfied grin, the extramarital meetings held in the couple's favorite haunts; the presence of some items of a second adult male's clothing in the home. A shy, inhibited, but imaginative, hurt wife could utilize the first and last of these without the actual affair.

The combination of Frank's natural suspiciousness and Alice's rather bumbling peccadillos eventually brought the relationship into redress. When the affair was exposed, Alice began to talk more openly about her hurt and where it got her. Frank could likewise confess his own concerns more easily because they had led to his drinking. The underlying purpose of a mutual confession, however, only further validates the conviction of worthlessness each possesses. Alice has her moment in "guilt court" over her unforgivable and evil affair. Frank can further cement his depraved self-image in place with his admitted alcohol use. The focus is on guilt and blame and how "bad" they are, rather than what it was that resulted in mutual hurt. If they are able to kiss and make up without developing an awareness of the underlying dysfunctional assumptions in their relationship, one can expect a future repetition of the same events.

Dynamics: Declare War Before You're Attacked

In this pattern, differentness is seen as "you don't love me." The perception of unique qualities between spouses leads only to defensive anxiety. To feel unloved is to experience a conviction of meaninglessness in human existence—to feel a very real threat to psychological survival. Therefore, it becomes a survival necessity to defend against any such awareness of threat. This defensive posture is all-pervasive since the spouses are inherently different and these differences sooner or later lead to conflict. When the presence of conflict is taken to indicate the absence of loving, then a reaction of regard, or engaging in active rejection, provoking as a means of of either interpreting all differentness and conflict as loveless disregard, or engaging in active rejection provoking as a means of self-protection (based on the premise that the best defense is a good offense).

Both spouses came from families where differentness was regarded as a hostile challenge to do battle. Destructive family "wars" resulted in either serially perpetuated arguments or sullen withdrawals. In either case, the atmosphere was in no way conducive to mutual exploration and growth but only to continual guerrilla warfare. The only basis for acceptance was sameness, and difference was at all times tantamount to a declaration of war. The home was fraught with perpetual abandonment and rejection for being unique. A person could only survive if he kept his existence rigidly intact. While sense and order in such a family is clear in its meaning, that meaning is dangerous and threatening and therefore gives no security. Rejection is inevitable. Productivity is very minimal since most of the energy of the persons in the family is sapped by continuous battles for existence. Intimacy is completely impossible, because getting close means risking annihilation.

When a man or a woman from such a family come together into a relationship, they anticipate that their being together will result in hurt, rather than pleasure. A couple relationship is seen as a potential to make war, not love. Affection is continuously contaminated by hostility and threat, by self-vindication rather than support.

To these people any relationship, such as marriage, that holds the promise of self-fulfillment to any degree must be accepted with suspicion. Each spouse anticipates that any such hopefulness would be inevitably followed by betrayal, rejection, and emotional abandonment. The defense of choice when such a dilemma presents itself is to "beat the other to the punch" by provoking hostility in order to control the other's anticipated rejection. Such a defense, however, by its very nature, provokes rejection and perpetuates a circularly reinforced despair that, unless interrupted, may continue unabated indefinitely. The need for continual "defending" is imperative in such a system. The other spouse, even if initially to some degree accepting, soon learns to defend self against other's hostile and aggressive onslaught by angry counterattack. How else is one to react to hostile provocation and attack? The prophecy that relationships are threatening and dangerous is, therefore, self-fulfilling. (See Figure 9 below.)

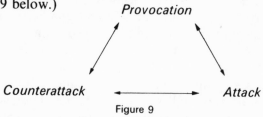

Figure 9

Provocation relieves the anxious uncertainty of anticipated rejection and leads to attack behavior (e.g., hostile criticism, sullen withdrawal, or outright invective attack). The attack is responded to by defensive counterattack, which serves to provoke the original attacker to more of the same. The relationship becomes a paradoxical dilemma of safeness and detachment or rejection and relationship. At all times hurt is completely concealed and justified as legitimate defense under attack. To let up at all in one's own defense is to run the risk of total annihilation by the other. On the other hand, the only value for self-survival is in having fought a good battle. The couple is able neither to give up mutual hostility or to, even when badly hurt, leave the relationship. It is medieval jousting transposed to contemporary relationships. To charge on your horse without using the lance is to surely be injured by the onrush of the other. At least one can say that there is some nobility and fairness in the game because each runs the same risk of being injured and each agrees that no quarter is to be given or taken. The fight is the reason for surviving at all. This is, however, mere existence and not living.

Resolution: Up to Your Old Tricks Again?

Since the continuance of any reciprocal behavior in the relationship is dependent on perpetuating mechanisms the couple have built into the relationship, these perpetuating mechanisms must be dissolved. In the pattern described in this chapter, the couple must develop an awareness of the anticipation—provocation—rejection—hurt—anticipation sequence. What perpetuates this pattern over and over is the couple's unconscious acceptance that each step in this sequence must be followed by the subsequent step. Circular causality is reinforced by the unconscious need for the vindication of a negative self-image ("See how terrible I really am").

Since the pattern is circularly causal, it does not matter who interrupts the pattern or where the pattern is interrupted, only that the pattern be interrupted. A productive place to begin is for the spouses to comment or ask, "Up to your old tricks again?" The old tricks are the words, phrases, and gestures that in the past have triggered off another aspect of the dysfunctional sequence. These are "red flags," similar to those used to enrage a bull in the arena. Wave a flag in the right way and the bull will be stimulated to charge. Spouses often know very well how to enrage one another with certain key phrases and behaviors that are sure-fire provocation devices. This often involves a certain amount of "bull."

To block the sequence from developing, each partner must feel free to comment on the presence of provocation, the anticipation of rejection, or feelings of hurt. The open awareness of the cycle and the process of calling the other partner on it tends to discourage the use of ploys and thereby prevents the perpetuation of the pattern. In essence, if we can keep each other "honest" (keep interaction openly labeled), we can survive the neurotic need to provoke and misinterpret.

A diagrammatic device often helps couples who are caught up in this repetitious mutual provocation. These diagrams try to accurately represent each of the spouses' primary contributing role to the perpetuating sequence; the labels of "prohibiting father," "innocent princess," and "silent martyr" characterize the way either husband or wife continually add fuel to the fire. The transactional interchange is represented by the relationship vectors and is labeled by the phrase or word that keeps the sequence going. This illustrates briefly and schematically how the sequence develops and is perpetuated.

Figure 10 illustrates the repetitiously provoking nature of the relationship between a husband and wife. The husband's behavior toward his wife is generally characteristic of a prohibiting father; the wife, on the other hand, acts very much the part of a dependent child. One of the features of their mutually provoking relationship occurs when the wife, very dependently asks husband, "should I?" in regard to a multitude of activities she knows he disapproves of.

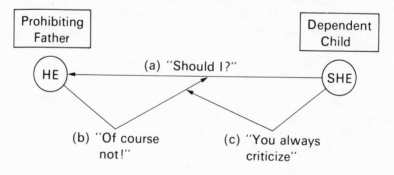

Figure 10

Naturally he always says, "Of course not." Her response then is to claim that he "always criticizes her." This represents the initial sequence that can eventually escalate into a first-class father–daughter tirade with a "weeping daughter" and a father with a "strong upper lip." Seeing the pattern visually will make it easier for them to spot its recurrence in the future, and the pattern will certainly repeat itself. This is one way they can become aware of a pattern in which they are enmeshed but not consciously aware of. The consequences are apparent, but the sequence of behavioral steps which leads to the consequences is unknown to them. Once they know these steps it is easier for each to block the moves of the other and, therefore, to prevent the sequence from its complete elaboration.

One couple took a diagram similar to Figure 10 home. He taped a copy on the mirror so he could see it when he shaved. She taped a copy of the diagram on her vanity, visible as she fixed her hair. As a result whenever he acted the part of the prohibiting father, she would say "Yes, daddy," and whenever she acted the part of the dependent child he responded with "Let's see now, my little child." This effectively blocked the other's attempt to maneuver the other to provoking positions. When this occurred the nature of their more underlying needs came to the surface and these then could be openly and mutually negotiated. The result was quite surprising to the pair. It also gave them a device they could continue to use.

A more dysfunctional pattern may be represented by the diagram in Figure 11.

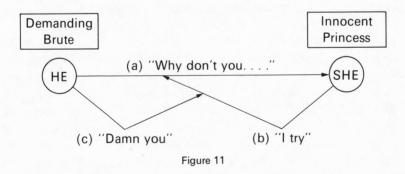

Figure 11

In this sequence a rather harsh domineering husband who acts like a demanding brute is married to a woman whose innocent "stupidity" is almost beyond human understanding. When she becomes fed up and annoyed with his demands, she simply begins to take poor care of the home. At this point the demanding brute enters and states, "Why didn't you," which may be followed by "take care of the house better?" "prepare a better meal," or "make sure we weren't overdrawn at the bank?" The innocent princess, of course, always replies by stating, "I try" and, if necessary, accompanies her response by tears, hurt looks, or whatever mechanism will reveal her innocence and his brutishness. The demanding brute, true to form, replies, "Damn you." This usually means (a) he realizes she hasn't tried and (b) even if she did try, he'd let her have it anyhow.

Diagrams can also be used to illustrate nonverbal patterns of mutual provocation as seen in Figure 12.

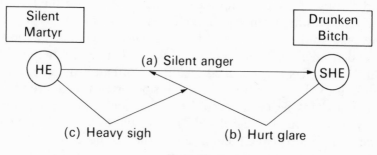

Figure 12

In this pattern, the husband initiates interaction by silent anger. The wife, usually a complaining alcoholic, comes on very much like a "drunken bitch." However, she complains only about emotionally unimportant things, never about her real pain and fear. When she drinks, he can treat her with self-vindicative but patronizing good will. When she drinks heavily, she is often too depressed to complain at all. (Her satisfaction does not come from simply railing at him endlessly, but from stimulating him to some response besides silent nobility.) At the point of her greatest despair, she falls silent. With the absence of her nagging provocation, he feels "uncared for" and responds with an angry expression but no words. She comes back with a hurt glare, and husband answers by a heavy sigh. This pattern can go on indefinitely. Concealed in the overt silence is the despair and disillusionment of mutual isolation. These nonverbal expressions need to be replaced by open verbal manifestations of perception and feeling.

Such diagrams appear to help develop awareness in situations of marital distress where severe pathology is not present. Some couples are able to do this by themselves with some brief instructions. In many other instances, however, conjoint marital therapy is required, with the use of the diagrams as part of the therapy. Either way, the question, "Up to your old tricks again?" takes on new meaning and significance for the pair.

Chapter 13

"'Til Death Do Us Part"

Within the marriage ceremony is an exhortation to maintain one's commitment to the relationship "until death do us part." While some couples take this statement to imply the necessity of negotiated commitment to maintain the relationship in good times and bad, other couples seem to view it as a justification for a commitment to progressive homicidal conflict. ("I'll show you whose best, even if it kills you and me.") These dysfunctional couples perceive the inherent conflict in the marital relationship as a significant threat to self-survival. The unspoken question arises: "How can I live with your differentness and still value myself?" The awareness, however dim, that self and other are different identities always results in a question of which is right, best or most valuable of the pair. This in turn leads to the constant need for proof that one or the other is, indeed, superior. The threat to each partner's tenuous and questionable superiority is quite clear to them.

These couples deal with this "threat" by developing an amazing array of "do or die" guerrilla tactics, a constant series of undermining ploys that, if not successful, soon lead to outright attack to discredit the other partner as worthwhile at all. Conflicts over decision making are especially focal to their dysfunction and may arise over almost any aspect of differentness between husband and wife. Each views the result of conflict that comes from differentness as either ultimate success (the winner) or ultimate failure (the loser). There is no negotiation of their marital conflict: To win is to survive and to lose is to die. This extreme view of conflict makes it absolutely essential to win in order to survive psychologically. The winner's victory is presumed to represent *prima facie* evidence of worthiness.

This type of pattern arises when other is seen as different than self, and may be revealed in various ways—from attitudes about furniture arrangement to the timing of sexual response to one another. Differentness is viewed as other's not fulfilling all of self's needs. Of course, everybody understands that the purpose of marriage is to have all our needs and fondest hopes realized in total ecstasy. Self had hoped from the beginning that other would be the ideal companion for self's own aggrandizement. But because this leaves unsettled the matter of who is to aggrandize other, eventual resentment arises over the lack of mutuality in the relationship. Each views the other in the marriage as a unilateral self-esteem "sugar daddy."

As a result, no one's self-esteem is enhanced; this disillusionment leads to anger and retaliation for this disappointment. The marriage becomes a right-or-wrong struggle to raise self-esteem; each wants to decide the rules of relationship conduct between them. To do so would allow self to guarantee that other would always act in such a manner to meet self's needs. It becomes an exclusive directorship battle; who is boss is more important than what fits the two of them.

This mutual marital disillusionment results in mutual bitterness and projected blame. No matter who is "wrong" (different than me), it is always the other guy who was "wrongly" different. The marriage soon becomes a series of hostile ambushes and numerous "search and destroy" missions. It becomes so neurotically vital for self to be 100 percent correct that the only way to realize this is to eliminate the competition by constant harassment of self-esteem. The relationship, therefore, is a competitive one and lacks any kind of mutual and productive complementarity. Since all is fair in love or war, all kinds of hostile maneuvering tactics are used but eloquently denied. Obviously, since one is always right, he can't be wrong. Any tactic that is used to subjugate the other in order to prove self right, is merely the vehicle of "inherent truth."

Mutual attack and defense become the vehicle of the relationship. Self always feels that other is responsible for his happiness. When complete happiness is not manifest in the relationship, this becomes other's failure. The refusal of other to believe and accept self as perfect is evidence of ignorance or stupidity, if not both.

Such a pattern requires a couple with a refined sadomasochistic interchange capacity; that is, each must be able to dish it out as well as take it. At times, they will wait patiently through the attack of the other, hardly hearing a word but, as soon as the other is finished, will launch into an immediate counterattack. The relationship continues because of the mutual hostility and alternating retaliation. While they are hostile, they are relatively fair. Each has his innings and each has his strikeouts. Some people, it must be remembered, make a career out of walking over a bed of hot coals without pain or complaint. Behaviorally, this is not to show they enjoy pain but to demonstrate that they are impervious to it.

Usually when the couple reaches a relationship impasse (nobody gets his way), they engage in a verbal and physical battle to psychological death. Such fatalistic hostility runs the risk of placing one or both partners in the morgue, the jail, or the mental hospital. This might also lead to losing their "worthy adversary," however, and every attempt is made not to reach that point. Since fundamental psychological survival is at stake, this can by no means be guaranteed.

The kind of sadomasochistic interchange that is characteristic of this relationship is basically different from the "Joan of Arc" or the "Might Makes Right" patterns. There is a similarity of underlying anxiety, but a complementarity of ways to it. The "Joan of Arc" woman can only succeed with a downtrodden husband and the "Might Is Right" husband can only succeed with a downtrodden wife. In this pattern nobody is consciously downtrodden. The couple shares a symmetrical pattern of defenses that is assertive and often attacking. Their slogan is not "If you can't beat 'em, join 'em" but rather "If you can't beat 'em, annihilate 'em." This pattern does represent a more pathological and unconscious refinement of "I'll Be Angry If You Love Me." In "'Til Death Do Us Part" the character defenses of the persons are deeply ignored and rigid. Feeling about self's esteem is deeply unconscious and denied. Only a hardened "superiority complex" is evident.

Example: Don't Shoot Until You See
the Whites of Their Eyes

Prior to their marriage, Glenn saw Ruth as the ideal woman. Ruth, in very much the same way, saw Glenn as the ideal man. There were a great many things they enjoyed doing in common. They were a physically attractive couple, who preferred activities where they participated with other people. Long walks, quiet talks, and other such exclusive pair activities were generally not to their liking. They preferred loud, large, and boisterous gatherings. Although they were often together, they were seldom alone with one another. In their premarital relationship, mutual adulation was their most obvious behavior. They were fashionable dressers, popular and admired by "the crowd." They admired one another's participation in their group activities, the "mutual admiration society" personified.

Since they obviously had so much in common and enjoyed so many things together, it was natural that they should think of marriage. The wedding ceremony was like many other of their enjoyable activities and was conducted as if it were the social event of the decade. In the early months of marriage, flush with their independence and freedom (from responsibility), economically well off, and with no familial responsibilities, there was a long romantic period of pleasure seeking. There were trips, parties, and sexual pleasures. In essence, they had a "big blast" and enjoyed it immensely. In viewing their relationship, however, one got the impression that they did not so much do things together as they did the same thing at the same time, somewhat like preschoolers before they have had the experience of nursery school or kindergarten. They did not actually collaborate or cooperate but tended to have the same interests at the same time, carrying on parallel but basically personally isolated activity.

As joint decision making gradually entered the marital relationship between Glenn and Ruth, differences of opinion began to lead to rather violent quarrels, and as the months stretched into years in their married life, this became more pronounced. In time their sexual relationship became a barter weapon in the struggle for interpersonal supremacy. When and how sexual relations were to be had became a matter of right and wrong rather than what they might actually work out. Sex became primarily a means of exploitation, of gaining an advantage, and only very secondarily for mutually shared pleasure. The withholding of it either openly or through a subsequent lack of response led to many arguments over whose obligation was what.

The couple argued not only over sex but over their finances and any other decision that affected joint outcome. Their relationship was like a country managed by two presidents. These fights were at times physically violent and became more frequent with the passage of time. Even though Glenn was physically stronger than Ruth, her agility at avoiding his blows and her accuracy in hurling objects evened up the odds. There was name calling, insults, swearing, and all varieties of direct ego assault on one another. At all times each had a stubborn conviction of rightness, and there was no backing down. They likewise acted as if they had little responsibility to one another. There was difficulty in scheduling mealtimes—sometimes Ruth would not even be home. Glenn would work late and not let her know. Many "bluffs" were attempted to dominate the relationship. For example, Ruth would insist that Glenn wear a particular-type suit for a jazz concert they had planned to attend, or else she would not go with him. In order to save face he refused. ("No woman is going to tell me what to wear!") Ruth then countered by storming out of the house, only to return ten minutes later. In the interim Glenn left for the concert, and she felt she had to remain home alone to carry through her promise. Even though he would have enjoyed discussing the music with her, he felt he had no other choice but to go alone, and thereby signal only he would decide what he would wear, that he was in control, not she. In this situation, whenever the bluff was called, each had to go through with it or else lose their own valued esteem by "giving in."

Within this pattern there are two rather common variations, both clearly projecting blame for what went wrong on to the other and giving a picture of self's basic righteousness.

The first type is preferred by intellectuals and clearly involves a double bind; self clearly insinuates that other is really to blame, even though self ostensibly accepts blame. "Of course, now I see how stupid I was not to have caught on to that sooner." For self to claim that he is stupid and yet see through other is really not possible. That would be like insisting that one is naive and insightful at the same time. However, the implication is quite clear that other has purposefully and intentionally duped the spouse. For example, he might have "just caught on" that his spouse always wants things her way. This, in itself, is hardly anything new, since it has been going on for years. If other admits that self is right, then she comes off as bad and, husband comes off as stupid but good-hearted—not a bad compromise, they may feel. If, however, she refuses "to be caught," then he is making a rather nasty insinuation but still is not stupid. This puts the shoe on the other foot; he is "calling names" while she remains innocent. He is nasty; she is offended but "pure"—again, perhaps, a suitable compromise.

The second maneuver ("I'm only living with you for the sake of the children") can be utilized by either husband or wife. (So can the first variation.) It amounts to an insinuation that I am right and good and you are bad and selfish. The most damaging implication is that self really doesn't care for other but out of the goodness of his heart will condescend to continue their association.

Both variations usually set the stage for the name calling, swearing, and the throwing portions of the battle. What began as a righteousness debate, soon escalates into total relationship war.

Dynamics: Righteous Wars for Self-Esteem

The origins of this marital system can again be more clearly understood if we go back to each of the spouses as personalities prior to the marriage. With each spouse, one finds that their selfhood has always been very much in doubt in their mind. To them, to be worthwhile is to be perfect, always acceptable, adorable, and desirable. In their families of origin, there was considerable dissatisfaction, criticism, and selfish exploitation in regard to almost everything. "Having it your way," and grabbing for impulsive enjoyment became the cornerstone of personal existence. (Family survival was considered hopeless.) This pleasure-bent and narcissistic attitude toward life became characteristic of their premarital adjustment and was carried into the marital relationship as well. It broke down however, when the essential mutuality of the relationship required negotiation, not unilateral or mutually exploitative enjoyment. Like most of the patterns discussed in this book, the basic ingredient of underlying low self-esteem is still common to both of them; in this instance it has been very deeply repressed. Any awareness they may have of their basically exploitative attitude in life or of their poor self-image is not obvious in their thinking. To all appearances, they both, in supreme confidence, regard any relationship as a one-up-manship exhibition. There is a desperate assertiveness of their unique rightness, however. Each behaves as if his whole survival depended on being in the right. When certain mutual aspects in dating, partying, etc., do not work out toward satisfying joint outcome, there is a displacement of responsibility for dysfunctional outcome in the form of blame of the other. Self can remain guileless and innocent, while other is tabbed as the trouble-maker.

When these people marry, it involves the selection by self of an other who appears to be not only similar but almost identical. Self's own identity (which is only marginally accepted) will hopefully, therefore, not be challenged. While they are alike in terms of their self-doubts, this is wholly unconscious. But the characterological and latent sensitivity they share is the impetus for their relationship. They are more aware of their similar manner of handling relationships. They are, in action, outright manipulators for their own gain. However, since they both act similarly in terms of how they manipulate, they give the impression of having "identical" personalities. What this behavior really represents is their common symmetrical defense system. But the very nature of their defense patterns brings them to a head-on clash with one another.

Prior to the marriage, each had hoped for support of views on life; this was the basic unconscious wish. In actuality, self and other were unique and therefore different in a great many ways, and these only emerged as they lived together. The hedonistic pursuits they had prior to marriage represented only a superficial overlay of their real emotional needs. They had hoped their relationship would give them more value; instead it gave them less and their inherent differentness, which was equated with rejection, threatened the self-protective defenses they had erected. Because the symmetrical nature of their defenses leads them to a violent and immediate head-on clash with one another, these relationships tend to be relatively short-lived and end either in the morgue, the divorce court, the jail, or the hospital.

What is actually established, is a dyad of mutual threat, in which survival is attacked and not enhanced. The peril of loss of identity and esteem is immediate, and defense against this, imperative. The result is a variety of hostile–aggressive and unilateral manipulations to keep self "one-up," over other. Since both engage in the same tactic, their behavior only further escalates the marital war. (See Figure 13.)

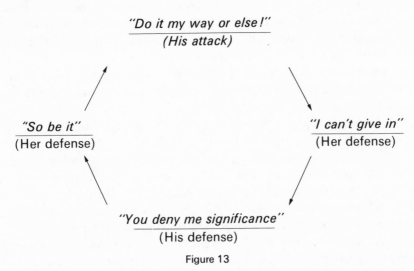

"Do it my way or else!"
(His attack)

"So be it"
(Her defense)

"I can't give in"
(Her defense)

"You deny me significance"
(His defense)

Figure 13

As long as each plays into the other's hands in this reciprocally reinforcing manner, the theme of "better dead than led" emerges. To give in to the other's demands in regard to decisions is to give up one's own identity and to cease to exist psychologically. Perfection is taken to be essential, negotiation as a sign of weakness, and absolute control the only acceptable kind of personal strength. Whatever needs exist for affection, attention, mutual support, and nurturance are completely lost in the personal battle for supremacy over the other. These needs exist, but are not expressed openly, and are certainly not met in this type of relationship. Prior to the marriage, the awareness of these crucial needs has already been deeply repressed; what emerges in the marriage is a "righteous war."

Resolution: Put Away the Red Flag

In the previous chapter, reference was made to the idea of the red flag in a transactional relationship, key words or phrases that can always be counted upon to provoke other. In the pattern here there is also a prevalence of red flag interactions between the partners, but these come from the absolute necessity on the part of each to be 100 percent correct. Their self-esteem can only be maintained by the myth of perfection, and it is this constant arrogant striving to be perfect that is so provoking to the other. This behavior in its various manifestations represents, therefore, a continuous stream of provocative red flags. The difference in this pattern is that the red flag emerges from the desperate strivings of each to maintain self-esteem by attempts to fulfill a picture of perfectness at the expense of the spouse; the result is the same—disillusionment and despair.

The escalating conflict and violence in this type of relationship are perpetuated by mutual use of red flags, and the only way to begin to counter this pattern is to stop the enraged bull's charge. The provocation cycle must be revealed, recognized, and then broken up so that a truce can be arranged, thus the use of the white flag to negotiate a settlement. Before this can be accomplished, however, the distorted rule of relationship must be faced up to between the pair: Any conflict in the relationship has been seen as a threat to the survival of one's identity. While conflict is inherent in all close relationships, these couples appear not to be able to tolerate inherent differentness without vicious and hostile counterattacks. To resolve this pattern, the threat of attack must be divested from the inherent conflict in marital relations. The basic differentness of the people involved in any marital relationship must be reinterpreted as uniqueness, rather than as "I can't stand you." Perfection must be seen as obviously unattainable and unnecessary to survival. What persons in a relationship need for emotional survival is a feeling of adequate personal identity as well as adequate trust and faith in the marital relationship. This can only come from a more basic mutuality of relationship, which, in turn, results in more satisfying joint outcome. Without this there is, in the end, a much greater threat to the survival of personal identity and to the relationship. Adequacy carries no implication of perfectness, either of self or of a relationship; it does imply comfortableness and satisfaction in one's self and the self–other relationship. This can only be attained through joint negotiation to develop mutuality.

As children, these marital partners may have been adept participants in "Blackmail, Children's Style." If so, they have grown up to expect their wants to be supplied from the outside without effort on their own part. They have difficulty accepting responsibility and are unable to view their participation in a relationship as a mutual aspect of its joint outcome. The value of negotiating joint outcome is that it may result in more satisfactory joint outcome; the red flag must be put away and the white flag brought out. Negotiation can then begin.

Acceptance of one another in the relationship must evolve from an acceptance and understanding of the self–other dilemma in the marriage, a dilemma that is naturally replete with differentness, conflict, irrational expectation, and pain, as well as pleasure, hopefulness, and mutual attainment. There will be confusion and despair, joy and enthusiasm. Our human, paradoxical nature needs to be accepted as a workable base for a mutually satisfying relationship. This requires hard work, humility, and patience—not arrogant aggression. The outcome can only be functional and rewarding if enough blood, sweat, tears, and toil accompany the couple's mutual hopes for attainment. Honesty, openness, and self-responsibility must take precedence over ploys, self-deception, and projected blame.

The basically rigid and self-righteous foundation of "'Til Death Do Us Part" relationships leaves the prognosis for change in question. Marriage therapy in the hands of a skilled and experienced practitioner is usually indicated. Even then, any significant resolution of the pattern is only occasional.

Chapter 14

"After You, My Dear Sweet"

Theme: Killing Them with Kindness

The primary assumption in this marital dyad is that a relationship can be maintained only by disguising hostility and hurt with self-recrimination and overconsideration of the other. As in any close pair relationship, the inherent differences between the people lead to a conflict of self-interests. If this is viewed as a threat to self-esteem, it will be responded to by hurt or hostility. However, to openly admit to or label one's feelings as hurt or anger is considered to be extremely poor form; each spouse will feel they allow vulnerability to the other's lack of real concern, a conviction that stems from the distorted interpretation that not having all your needs met equals rejection. The usual tactic, therefore, is to grin and bear it but never let the other really know how you feel. This artful and apparently noble dodge succeeds only in preventing adequate self-manifestation. Each marital partner only emerges as a shadowy and vague personality in the joint relationship. Their commitment to a mutual relationship remains forever obscure and unpredictable.

The marriage, rather than resembling a needs—conflict—negotiation sequence, resembles a hurt—distance—detachment sequence. The behavior of the spouses toward one another is an

146

Alphonse and Gaston routine, punctuated by subtle blackmail. ("If you don't let me be good in my way, you will be guilty of obstructing goodness.") The basic goal of the marriage appears to be aspiration to the "nice guy" award by unanimous acclaim. The one with the most goodness, kindness, and understanding is the winner. These terms, however, take on a rather different meaning in this kind of relationship. The phony niceness serves only as a disguse for hostile and hurt feelings and defensively functions as a means of protecting one's personality from self-esteem depletion; each spouse has an underlying and continuous conviction of the danger of open commitment with resultant hurt.

In actuality, both spouses in this type of relationship have thin skins and rich fantasy lives. In other words, while they "bleed" easily, each hopes the compensation for this psychological hemophilia will be a relationship paradise without conflict, frustration, or disappointment. Anger is forbidden (even when it is present), and kindness is the rule (even when unwanted). Self-abasement presides over self-awareness. When self gets hurt, he reacts in a rather insincere and gushy overkindness that, it is hoped, will cover up the more underlying hurt and anger.

Acceptance of "blame" has considerable upstaging value in the relationship; that is, self will always attempt to accept blame when something goes wrong, not because he really believes it but because he hopes other will feel guilty and therefore be in a manipulatable condition. It is assumed other will feel so bad over self's accepting blame, he will naturally wish to accept it himself. This, self will usually let other do. This bathetic performance will occur even when nobody believes a word of it; neither self nor other feels to blame for anything. Their mutual underlying feelings of hurt and anger are disguised by the contest for "the most selfless scapegoat" award.

Such a dysfunctional relationship requires a couple with the adroit ability to alternate between being the "victim of injustice," a condition to be borne bravely, and the "noble critic," who only finds fault for the good of the other. Both roles can be exhibited by either spouse. The "goodhearted nobleness" tactic is most effective when: (a) there appears to be little hope for getting even for being hurt by other without being caught at it; (b) self has obviously been betrayed by other, and this is a good way to emphasize other's cruelty; and (c) when it is well known that other will always give in if self appears to be helpless and beaten. On the other hand, there is some advantage to be gained in the relationship if you are the "victim of injustice." This tactic helps when: (a) you chronically feel sorry for yourself and need reassurance you have reason to feel sorry; (b) your spouse can have "value" to you because he gives you something you can feel sorry about; (c) everybody backs the underdog. An innocent victim will either provoke guilt and penance in the wrongdoer spouse or be able to enlist the solace, if not the direct aid, of neighbors, children, relatives, etc., in the cause of righteousness. Either way avoids negotiation.

While one partner may be better at one side of this pattern than the other, either can handle both tactics when conditions encourage it. It is a very difficult reciprocity for the participants to untangle, because self-deception is at a premium in the relationship. Each assumes the intent of the other is basically bad, while their own intent is always labeled as noble. The consequences are always seen as the result of such intent.

The spouses are both fearful, suspicious, hostile, but naive to a fault. They are weary of being let-down. Because they act innocent to provoke guilt or cloak anger in helpful faultfinding, the spouses each appear to relate to the other's ploys with unbelievable neurotic gullibleness.

Decisions are almost impossible. Joint outcome is spurious rather than anticipated, much less negotiated. To decide is to accept responsibility for the consequences of one's actions—the last thing either partner wants to do. Relationship is a matter of calculated, but often unconscious, evasion of responsibility for what happens between them. Married life becomes a continuous morality play in which all acts have the same ending; namely, "See how noble I am and how hurtful you are."

Example: Promise Me You'll Be Perfect

Before their marriage, Bruce and Florence had a rather stiff and formal relationship—somewhat distant but very faithful. They could always count on one another to never do the unexpected or novel. Polite consideration was the hallmark of their behavior. Just before, as well as after, the marriage, there were frequent low-key arguments resulting in quiet but petulant sulks by one or both. If by one, there were pleading supplications by the other to be forgiven. If both sulked, the silent torment eventually and gradually lifted until they jointly forgave one another.

There were also off-again, on-again threats of divorce given with hurt resignation. These were interspersed between periods of blissful, almost idyllic, but rather distant, living together. While great discussions on the nature of the universe, weather formations, and arts are frequent, little is ever said about "how we are getting along." "Honey," "dear," and "sweet" are repetitive vocabulary, alternating with "you did that on purpose" and "you knew that would hurt."

Periodically, however, a rather intense relationship crisis develops. These occur every four to six years and are accompanied by a bribe followed by conciliation: "I simply cannot go on living with you" (she). "If you will only live with me, I'll never do it again" (he). A very elegant, but dysfunctional collusion is entered into by each of them in collaboration with the other. If she agrees to live with him only if he *never* does "it" again, most certainly the crisis will reappear in the future, since nobody can *never* do it again. If he accepts, he must succumb completely to her demands; in order to be "a good boy," he must behave in a manner approved by "mother" (wife). But his very abdication of self-responsibility to please her is tacit admission of his guilt, while she seems innocent. When, however, in the future he acts up again, she is betrayed once more. The repeat performance is inevitable. In fact, Bruce and Florence are capable of repeating this procedure every four to six years without fail, whenever their relationship becomes rocky. This is the point at which the underlying resentment and anger, which overlay the hurt, are most close to open and uncontrolled expression. The crisis accomplished, in a somewhat disguised manner, her manifestation of hurt, his manifestation of anger, and, after the confession, a loving reconciliation.

Neither, however, has really become any more aware of the needs and feelings of the other, and so the episode repeats itself whenever the emotional tension in their marital system requires an outlet. The relationship dialogue between them focuses only on hostile intention, never "look what this is doing to us" but always "look what you did to me." Part of this dialogue might be:

Florence: I found lipstick on your handkerchief. What have you been up to? (She already knows.)

Bruce: I don't know what came over me. I felt. . . so lonely. . .
            I don't know why I did it.
Florence: Oh Bruce! How could you!
Bruce: I'm so very sorry, my dear. I don't understand why I do
            such things.
Florence: (pause). . . I can't talk now. Let me be alone for a while.
Bruce: (pleadingly) I'd like to explain.
Florence: I couldn't bear it.
Bruce: Oh, what I have done! (His anguish is now equal to hers.)

Both dissolve in tears but go to separate rooms. Perhaps later that
night or in a day or two they will talk again. She claims she "can't go
on," he promises "never again," she accepts with righteous reluctance,
and they begin the pattern again.

There are several other tactical maneuvers in their relationship
that allow a partial expression of the underlying feelings, while
never quite clearly making these feelings manifest. It is more an
acting out of anxiety than the struggle for awareness. At the end
they are left no better off than when they started, somewhat less
tense and more relaxed, perhaps, but as ignorant of one another's
uniqueness as before. The same needs and feelings continue to be
disguised and therefore unmet. Frustration grows and eventually
the teakettle blows again. There are many manipulative variations:

"If you *really* loved me, you would ——." The blank space here
is filled in by whatever demand self wants of other. If it is not forthcoming, it can be labeled as overt evidence of "not loving." This is
one of Florence's favorite tactics, and it clearly leaves Bruce with
either giving in to her demand, which was to love her by her definition, or not giving in, and being accused of withholding *his* love.
Again, this involves both bribe and blackmail. The ploy is stated in
such a way as to initially imply that love must be proved. The
accuser places the accused in such a position that if he has any
capacity for guilt, he responds first of all as if he were guilty and
then attempts to make some conciliation.

One of Bruce's favorite ploys is, "You know, darling, I *really*
didn't mean it that way." This is intended to be utilized every time
he has insulted her. He only needs to couch his insults in either
carefully worded sarcasm or vague sentences so as not to be held
to an open and direct statement about her. He may say, "I'm sure

I love you, dear" or "I wish I only knew—but I feel so confused, at times, about how I feel about you." This is difficult to respond to since, if she claims insult, he can retort, "I didn't mean it." Florence then has made Bruce's point for him (that she is overly sensitive or quick to unjustly condemn). This ploy also leaves Bruce in the superior position, as she has dared to besmirch his good intentions with a rather suspect interpretation. She becomes the accuser and he the sufferer of unprovoked injustice.

A final example, though there could be many others, is, "We will (you will) get over it (the crisis) soon; our love has never failed!" In this collaborative ploy they both agree to berate one another at the same time or else take turns. Implicit is a restatement that they do love one another, so the pain must be tolerable. If the relationship should collapse (which is extremely unlikely), then this only means that "our love" did fail.

They are saying to each other, "If you will be my target, I will also be your target and we will call it love." Such a relationship, if not manifest by genuine affection, at least must be admired for its fairness.

Dynamics: Marriage as a Morality Play

In their relationship Florence and Bruce represent the acceptance of a basic dysfunctional rule: *Nobody* can *ever* be trusted. Thus, there is no viable basis for a mutual relationship in any marriage; it will be a pretense, an empty shell, but not a meaningful association. The couple are together because of mutual loneliness but without nurturance and a commitment to grow together. Their suspicion and unsureness in the marital relationship is covered over by a kind of glossy and rosecolored kindness, however. The apparent road to psychological survival lies in making self unassailable to other by a "Mr. Nice Guy" act. This is, nevertheless, a unilateral payoff to insure *self's*, not "their," survival.

This pattern too requires several generations of "kill 'em with kindness" to flourish. Both the husband and the wife learned this rule in almost identical fashion in their families of origin, and they share it in their present relationship. The second generation continues to solidify this very dysfunctional assumption of relationship, and, subsequently, the children of the current marriage learn the rule from both their parents. Should a child of Bruce and Florence have a spouse who has come from a similar family, this pattern will be perpetuated for the third generation.

Since the marital relationship is fraught with fear of hurt and mistrust but necessitated by human need, any emotional commitment the spouses have to one another must necessarily be perceived as psychologically dangerous. As long as each provokes, rather than reveals and discloses, commitment to intimacy is not possible. Obsequious appeasement and fawning niceness isolate true feeling from action and thereby prevent self–other negotiation. One can only negotiate differences that are actually perceived, which, in turn, rests on manifestation by self to other.

The basic dilemma of such a relationship is: "I never knew you cared, because I was really afraid you didn't care, and, therefore, I never asked you." This mutual dynamic is interlocking as far as the relationship is concerned and perpetuates both the fear of rejection and silent defensiveness or glossy cover-up to circumvent the rejection each feared from the beginning. (See Figure 14.)

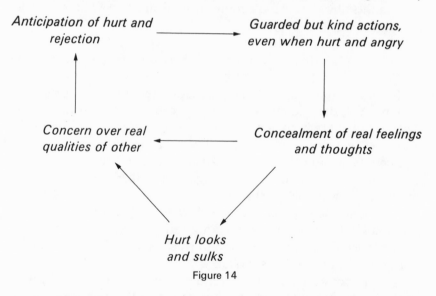

Figure 14

An alternating critic and injustice reciprocity helps to perpetuate the dilemma in a two-step process:

1. Each partner in the marriage defines love as existing only if neither is *ever* critical of the other. Since this is a human impossibility, the conviction of not being loved is continuously present. For the

most part this is covered up by glossy goodness and phony niceness. Before they were married, the couple reacted to their parents' admonishments and restrictions as evidence of loveless criticism and an angry denial of their own autonomy. Later on when they began to date, even before they met one another, the dating relationships could only persist as long as there was an idyllic romanticism, a fawning, but nevertheless "pushed," affection. When Bruce and Florence eventually met one another and married, the relationship they formed could only be continued as long as any evidence of criticalness, anger, or interpersonal difficulties were glossed over. The more they glossed these over—which they would convey by subtle and nonverbal forms of communication—the more the suspiciousness increased.

2. Since they basically built the relationship with the conviction that nobody has ever cared, they are really not surprised when nobody seems to care. Other, in actuality, is simply protecting himself by not revealing his feelings. But he therefore seems indifferent and distant. Very likely the reason it appears that no particular other has ever cared for self is because self has never committed himself intimately and honestly to another in a relationship. Nothing given only results in nothing returned. Self may then say, "Perhaps I deserve not to be cared for," in the hope of bringing about the reassurance that spouse *really does* care. Then the question arises, "Can the reassurance be real, if I had to provoke it by asking for it?" Very often other will respond to this pitying ploy by reassuring self that he, in fact, does not deserve to feel so badly. But it is other's guilt over his disappointment in his mate that provokes this response. Nothing is gained except further reinforcement that they tolerate, rather than really care for, one another.

Any time negativeness creeps up in the relationship, the instigator is labeled as the critic, while the recipient of the negativism becomes the injustice collector. Each partner in such a marital pair is quite capable of alternating in these roles. They reinforce one another and continually perpetuate the "After You, My Dear Sweet" pattern. After years of adroit but collaborative manipulation of one another, it is possible that the injustice collector will have collected enough "injustices" to trade them in on a "free" suicide. In a relationship where self-debasement presides over self-awareness, the press of despair may become the individual legacy of one of the partners.

Resolution: There Is Mad-ness in My Method

The suppressed or repressed anger in such a relationship is covered up by phony niceness, which serves as an evasive tactic for legitimate anger. The method, in fact, contains a huge reservoir of angry feelings; it is a method of mad-ness. In this pattern what is promoted is isolation, suspicion, and inevitable frustration of both idiosyncratic and survival needs.

To be human is to feel hurt, angry, and retaliatory at times, not necessarily all or none of the time. The closeness of marital relationship leads to feelings of hurt that, in turn, lead to feelings of anger and fantasies of retaliation. This, in itself, is not dangerous. What is dangerous is never to express these feelings at all or to viciously, physically attack one another in violent anger. The second possibility is the method of choice in the "Til Death Do Us Part" pattern.

Acceptance of our humanness in a relationship comes from honest self-disclosure, not vague and fearful, but nevertheless phony, niceness. Only when these feelings can be talked about openly can each of the spouses in the marital relationship understand and know one another. They may then live with their essential, albeit at times troublesome, humanness. Mutual self-deception not only destroys the awareness of this relationship reality but eventually results in mutual frustration and depressive despair.

Because there is so much repression of feeling involved in this pattern, it can often only be resolved with the professional help of a therapist trained in the conjoint marital approach. The therapist may be able to help the couple to reveal their fearfulness and gradually their underlying feelings, which will open up the avenue for functional intimacy between them. To be hurt, after all, is not to be unliked or not cared for but only to reveal the very human response that is the result of having one's toes stepped on in the mutual struggle for psychological survival. Anger and aggression, when appropriately felt, are one way to reveal oneself as a real person to our spouse. The dangers of too much anger and aggression come only when we allow ourselves no outlet. Then we permit, by our own doing, a dangerous reservoir of hostile feeling to consume our thoughts and direct our actions. Through mutual self-deception and fear we are party to our marital demise.

PART VI

The Functional Relationship

In reality any human relationship does not appear fully dysfunctional or fully functional. There are elements of both functional and dysfunctional outcome in all relationships. However, it is possible to distinguish between functional and dysfunctional patterns, and, subsequently, to distinguish families that are basically dysfunctional and those that are basically functional in their joint outcome. At times even a functional family, under certain situational stresses (e.g., family business failures, death or severe injury in the family, or wartime) may behave more dysfunctionally than usual. However, a basically functional family will be able, because of its flexibility, to recover much more rapidly from such stresses than the dysfunctional family that tends to plunge even deeper into dysfunction with accumulating situational stresses.

The most easily observable distinction of the family with a functional relationship is not the absence of problems but the presence of an ability to deal with problems—to resolve them to satisfactory joint outcome for all involved. One of the basic premises that characterizes functional relationships is that intention is divorced from outcome. What counts is, in fact, what actually happens, not what each person hopes will happen. If outcome does not meet the human needs of the family members, then it is seen as dysfunctional and discarded or renegotiated. Redundant neuroticism is minimized, and negotiated joint outcome is maximized.

The functional relationship differs both in quality (evasiveness largely absent and commitment largely present) and very often in quantity (they spend more time with one another). Thus, functional relationships look different to an outside observer and feel different to the members of the family. Basically there is less discrepancy between what each member of the family feels inside and what he is willing to reveal openly in his words and behavior to other family members.

In the functional family the majority of interaction is relatively free from the threat of psychological annihilation. The members can say: "I am O.K., he or she is O.K., we can together search and struggle, share and enjoy, grow and expand ourselves. We can survive better together than either one of us alone. Neither of us individually needs to fear catastrophic loss of self-esteem. In functional relationships there will be disappointment, hurt, and misunderstanding, but there will be no desperate fear or continuous defensive anxiety with one another.

Functional relationships are characterized by the ability of the members of a family system:

1. To report what they hear, feel, see, and think both about themselves and others; to admit these thoughts and feelings to themselves and to be able to openly manifest them in words and gestures. This is seen as valuable and necessary to a relationship, regardless of the positiveness or negativeness in the perceptions, feelings, and thoughts.

2. To ask for clarification, if they don't understand what is happening in the family as a whole or in any dyadic relationship between self and another. This means that when something doesn't seem to be going well, it is first admitted and every effort is made to ascertain why and how it has gone wrong.

3. To experience differentness as uniqueness. Differentness is not seen as a threat to the identity and integrity of another; it is a manifestation of their human qualities as a distinct and separate person, but one who is part of the family. Uniqueness is seen as a potential for growth and expansion by being able to experience something new and to learn from it.

4. To actively work toward better joint outcome by being specific,

clear, and congruent in communication with one another. They can feel freedom to criticize, to experiment, and to give and receive affection.

5. To say: This is what I am under these circumstances. This is where I am going. This is how I hope to get there. This is what I eventually hope to be. I am this kind of man. I am this kind of woman. I am comfortable in what and who I am, and I intend to grow and to enlarge myself to be different, to change, and feel secure in doing so. There is mutual feeling on the part of each member of the family that he possesses a firm and committed identity.

Chapter 15

"Speak for Yourself, John!"

Joint outcome can only be negotiated if each spouse reveals himself to the point where differentness clearly emerges. This is the functional aspect of what Virginia Satir refers to as the process of "manifesting self." The question is not whether you manifest yourself but how clearly. The realities of relationship dictate that each person in his relationship to another is responsible to make clear what he sees, feels, thinks, and hears about himself and about the other, including what is pleasant and unpleasant. Support and encouragement are as freely given as are critical concern and frustrated annoyance. We reveal our feelings—not only what is inside of us but what the other person outside of us has stimulated in us—to another in words, in gestures, and in our overall behavior. Self-righteous martyrdom can be replaced with responsible awareness.

If we are obscure, tangential, and evasive in our communication, we can only build a relationship that is obscure, tangential, and evasive. We must take risks as we reveal our feelings, reactions, and thoughts, and depend on overall trust in the relationship. It is a matter of how far one can go in revealing himself to the other. The risk is to make clear our most vulnerable self—our most cherished thoughts, our most tender and angry feelings, our most crazy and absurd convictions—and in so doing to chance altering the illusions and expectations in the relationship. What will inevitably develop is a more realistic appraisal and less of a fantasy expectation. Disillusionment of preconceived hopes based on unilateral self-aggrandizement will give way to the realization of a negotiated relationship.

The fact that we communicate verbally as well as nonverbally means it is difficult, if not impossible, not to reveal ourselves to another in some form or fashion. But the more openly and clearly this is done, the less confusion, guesswork, and apprehension exist in the relationship. Because we often deceive ourselves, we may reveal an aspect of our feeling about self, other, or the relationship that we deny to ourself. When such a malfunction of self-responsibility occurs, negotiation of joint outcome is hindered. When differentness is denied, it cannot be used for growth. Growth is related to our awareness of self "as is" and our willingness to accept responsibility for who and what we are to the other person—not what we think we are but, in fact, what we are. To a large degree, in a functional relationship there is a strong belief in each of the partners that together they will survive the conflict of their inherent differentness. When this conviction is present, then, indeed, John can speak for himself. Differentness is apparent, uniqueness is valued, and negotiation can be realistic.

Because we must assume some risk as we reveal ourselves to another, it is clear we must put our identity on the line with the other person, who may affirm or contradict it. This is an opportunity for the relationship to grow. Emotional growth comes when illusions of perfectness and completeness can be put aside in favor of an acceptance of human difference and conflict as a mandate to negotiate for realistic joint outcome. The relationship and the persons will change and alter their moods, manners, and attitudes. This alteration is mutual and derives from open self-reports from which relationship reality is ascertained. What is really possible? Together, how much are the couple *willing and able* to act differently for what mutual goals? Only if this is determined can they work out what fits rather than who is right. It is a shallow victory when personal vindication hinders and diminishes joint emotional survival.

To risk self openly with another, however, requires a level of *emotional nurturance* between the persons in the relationship, whether this be husband—wife or parent—child. This emotional nurturance comes from not only the give and take of visible affection between the persons in the relationship—but the prior shared, mutual struggle from differentness and conflict to negotiation and growth. Not all of this shared experience is positive, but it has been mutually valued and survived, with the result that such shared experience enhances the person's conviction to deal with human reality. The realities of human life not only rest on such questions as "When will the bomb be dropped?" or "Will overpopulation snuff us out?" but more mundanely and much more persistently on whether our existence is worthwhile and meaningful through a mutually nurtured relationship.

The Three-Party System and Whistling a Happy Tune

All families really represent a three-generational system. It is quite obvious the parents and their children constitute two generations that are always present. However, there is the third generation, the parents' parents, who are usually present in spirit if not in person. Such absent in-laws often represent a "ghost count" of psychological influence in the family, in which parents act as if they were their own parents, rather than as autonomous adults. What is reenacted is a repeat of prior parenting without regard to the uniqueness of present generations.

The picture may be no different in the true three-generational family, where the in-laws are actually present. What needs can be met in that system? Who is to speak up for whose needs? Who is responsible for parenting, decision making, and overall policy? Will generational links be observed and enforced, or will there be a power tactic free-for-all? It is appropriate, of course, for the children's wants and nurturance to be largely supplied by their own parents and for the parents themselves to supply these needs for one another. This is a clear distinction between a parent generation and a child generation. However, the parents' parents represent another adult generation. If the relationship between the grandparents and the parents comes to represent another parent–child system, then the parenting function within the family may be significantly altered. What may result are grandparents who really act the part of parents over two generations of children, one large, one small. (See Table 1.)

The emotional needs that may have been a part of the parent–child relationship as the current parents grew up can no longer be appropriately a part of the present three-generational system. The

TABLE 1

Actual Status	Status in Relationship	Psychological Needs Status
Adult (dependent)	Grandparent	"Who do I nurture? (Am I valuable?)
Adult (independent)	Parents	"Do I nurture or am I nurtured?" (How do I realize value?)
Child (dependent)	Children	"Who is primary nurturer?" (Who helps me to grow to be valuable?)

parents usually do not wish to, and certainly should not, be treated as children, since they are not. An adult–adult relationship between the grandparents and the parents is a much more appropriate and suitable point of departure for negotiation. Children who have grown up to become parents themselves often are financial resources for their own parents. They cannot, however, be an emotional resource for them in the same way as when they were children. It is often questionable in terms of differing experience and education, especially these days, whether grandparents and parents have a significant communality between them to make the relationship emotionally viable. This is basically the bind of the three-generational family. Matters of autonomy, authority, and sexuality can become a three-way conflict unless wants are manifested openly and negotiation mutually accepted without power ploys ("Remember, I'm still your parent"). Yet there must be an ultimate policy of direction from the architects of the family (the parents of the current children).

If sense and order and productivity are to exist in a family, there must be a very clear-cut understanding of who, in fact, the responsible parenting people are in the family. A competition or a conflict between the parents and grandparents only serves to undermine the consistency and order the children require for their security. A conflict of direction and authority may require that the parents will have to be rather blunt, direct, and honest with the grandparents regarding "the powers that be" in this family.

If the parents should deal with the conflict between them and the grandparents by abdication, then a power vacuum will be filled by the grandparents, much to the confusion and consternation of the children. The children may well grow up to view "parents" as somebody who are controlled and manipulated by their own parents, dependent and undirected, and not very reliable. In all three-generational family relationships, some differences may be so large as to be unnegotiable and too laden with conflict to live with. In that case all three generations are better off if the grandparental generation is separated from the parent–child family system.

Even in families where the grandparents do not live in but have frequent contact with the parent–child system, they may exert considerable influence on its functioning. If the grandparent has based his own life entirely on the relationships with his children, he may be unable to let them grow up and be parents within their own family. The direction and support of a family under these conditions tends to become fuzzy, confused, perhaps at times unpredictable. Only if John, the father in the family, will stand up and speak for himself, will the helm of the family ship be restored to the hands of a single, directive, and confident captain.

A man must leave his mother and father and cleave to his wife and, as a result of this union, become a nurturing parent to his children. In order to grow and mature in his own responsibilities, a rather irrevocable disruption and separation from his own parents must occur. It remains his responsibility to do this.

A basically functional example of the pattern described in this chapter is the mutual self-help system that must evolve within the relationship dyads in the family. When Matt notices that Helen acts withdrawn or depressed without any accompanying comment as to what is bothering her, he will ask her about her mood. If he should be met with an "it's nothing" answer, he will not accept this but, in essence, will ask her to speak for herself rather than forcing him into a position where he must guess and estimate. He can observe her obvious mood. He knows something is wrong but not what.

Helen: (goes about her supper preparations with little conversation, but with a somewhat bedraggled and tired appearance)

Matt: (notices her actions) Helen, you look tired. Do you feel all right?

Helen: Oh yes (sigh), everything is okay.

Matt: Is something bothering you?

Helen: No (pause), it's nothing.

Matt: Well you really don't look like nothing is bothering you. You look tired but you say you're not. Something seems to be wrong. It's really hard for me to believe that it really isn't anything. I'm really no good at guessing, why can't you tell me.

Helen: Well, I feel sort of upset about something.

Matt: Why don't we take the time to talk about it now.

Their ensuing conversation may then evolve into an exploration of what was really underlying the rather "bedraggled appearance message" she was giving to Matt. Together they can begin to explore what may be going on between the two of them that resulted in non-verbal communication to Matt that something was wrong. Before this is possible, however, Helen must reveal herself to Matt—her perceptions, thoughts, and feelings that underlie her appearance. One can see the same sort of behavior in a relationship where one of the spouses engages in the "whistle while you work" syndrome. On the surface this relationship appears to express happiness and contentment, but it is accompanied with little or wooden affection between the spouses. Clearly there is a patent discrepancy between expressed mood and relationship behavior.

   Tiredness or depression or a "whistle a happy tune" attitude are good indicators of unexpressed hurt and anger that needs to be uncovered and talked about. Spouses must really help one another to do this. They must, in a sense, unpry or unfreeze one another's affect. At the same time, each must be responsible to speak for himself, to make his contribution to the openness and clarity in the communication of the relationship between them. To a certain extent, individual human defensiveness will hinder a person from doing this alone. Mutuality offers a way of maneuvering around this. If Helen will not speak for herself, then she is responsible for fostering dysfunctional outcome. If together, however, she and Matt can get to the point the dialogue illustrates, it is then possible to move into mutual negotiation and more satisfactory joint outcome.

   In general, the expression of concern with direct words and actions is much better than a policy of tolerant forbearance with discrepant behavior. The latter may be "noble," but it gradually enlarges emotional distance in the relationship between persons.

Happiness Is an Error-Activated System

In any marital or family pattern where the members of a human system are able to manifest themselves openly and clearly, one will notice certain rules that govern the outcome behavior of that system. In the functional relationship, these rules may be seen as the following sequence:

1. There exists a basic conviction on the part of the persons involved in their ability to survive unpleasant realizations that may have to do with unexpected traits or characteristics of persons in the family and natural feelings of hurt. The closeness of the family living situation and the inherent conflict of differentness is bound to produce a rather persistent day-to-day supply of this type of situation—the sandpaper of family existence. However, if the persons view their relationships with one another as revealing, rather than exposing, oneself, these difficulties will be dealt with directly and worked through. Conflict need not be denied, evaded, or avoided; it can be grappled with, struggled with, and pushed through to a mutually understandable conclusion.

2. The repeated survival of conflict among family members enhances their confidence in the relationships. There is a joy, not a fear, of being with one another. This is based on reality that has emerged from their actual mutual experience, which tends to circularly reinforce confidence in the relationship. Circular reinforcement is the same in any system—functional or dysfunctional. Figure 15 is one way of visualizing functional reciprocity and reinforcement. Manifesting self openly permits greater trust in the relationship and in the person with whom negotiation must necessarily take place. Such repeated experiences of trust build a reservoir of confidence in the relationship, which, in turn, leads to a willingness to continue to reveal self openly. This process, therefore, feeds upon itself in a functional way. It enhances self-esteem in two primary ways: One feels secure in the knowledge that what he sees, hears, feels, and thinks can be validated openly and without evasion; mutual outcome becomes more predictable, because outcome can be openly negotiated rather than evasively defended against. This makes it possible to evolve working relationships that are both secure and predictable.

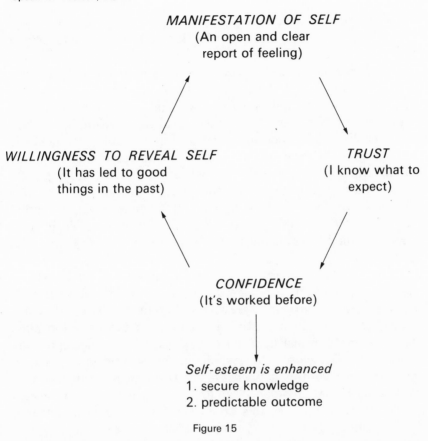

MANIFESTATION OF SELF
(An open and clear
report of feeling)

WILLINGNESS TO REVEAL SELF
(It has led to good
things in the past)

TRUST
(I know what to
expect)

CONFIDENCE
(It's worked before)

Self-esteem is enhanced
1. secure knowledge
2. predictable outcome

Figure 15

3. In system terminology, the functional family is an open, error-activated system. The inner feelings and behavior of the individual members of the family are reported in the form of constant "condition reports." People not only say what is going on inside of them but what they see going on outside of them. This represents, in essence, a report of both the internal state of the parts of the system and a report on the integrative functioning of the system as a whole. An open system is a viable set of relationships in which joint outcome can be negotiated, where trust and confidence build self-esteem, and where the realization of self is possible through the affirmation of one's identity in relationship with others.

Why Isn't There an Easier Way?

Functional outcome is the result of consciously directed processes of negotiation that are based upon an open system of communication and that can only continue with incessant repetition. It is neither glamorous, easy, romantic, or always self-fulfilling, but, once established, a functional relationship will eliminate neurotic repetition and replace it with negotiated outcome. Then we can truly live in the present without duplicating the past or, hopefully but unrealistically, anticipating the future. We can live with one another in the here and now, making the fullest use of mutual experience to deal with the rather obvious frustrations, disillusionments, and embarrassments that are the lot of people living with people.

If we don't speak up, if we don't manifest ourself clearly, if John or Jane or Matt or Helen do not stand up and make it clear who they are and how they see and feel about the others they live with, we are basically accepting a unilateral myth in relationships: "She hurt me. I'm just licking the wounds, but that doesn't really affect her." This closes the system to any awareness of its own dysfunction; when this happens, repair is not possible. It has been blocked by denial, avoidance, and evasion. This, as we have seen in the earlier sections of this book, bears the seed of destruction of the relationship and of the people. There is no easy way, at least in the arena of human relationships, to accomplish mutual gratification and enjoyment without negotiating joint outcome.

Chapter 16

"What's That Again?"

In order to communicate needs, wants, and feelings within a family, each member must check out meaning with other members. He must be free to ask, "What do you mean?" even, "What the hell are you talking about?" Family members must have a basic conviction that:

1. Openness in revealing oneself is both safe and rewarding.
2. Meaningfulness between people only comes from clear and congruent self-revelation.
3. Meaning in a relationship is mutually negotiated for joint satisfaction.

What is meaningful and worthwhile for one person is not necessarily the same to others. How persons within the family communicate with one another is accepted as critical to the awareness of uniqueness and the subsequent negotiation of joint outcome. Discrepancies between words and nonverbal signs can be reported and clarification sought. The conflict and hurt that *may* ensue from open communication is accepted not as something that is either good or bad but simply as something that is, that exists and is present, in fact, is routine in close relationships. You don't have to like the fact that conflict and hurt may be present, but you must deal with it in order to survive psychologically. With differentness there is inherent conflict, and with conflict there may be some ruptured self-deceptions. But satisfying mutuality implies some common awareness that is clear and congruent and therefore reliable and predictable. Such a base to a relationship gives the security and trust that makes being together worthwhile and meaningful.

Meaning that is not consistent with some mutual frame of reference between members of the family can, and often does, become obscure and potentially threatening—too much is unknown or must be guessed at. If a common frame of reference is negotiated, meaning can be mutual and can enhance joint outcome. Sense and order is insured, productivity is possible, and because there is a lack of communicational hangups, intimacy is promoted by the experiential awareness of the other's real, and at times blunt, qualities. Self-deception is minimized, and reality becomes secure and predictable. This results not in idyllic romanticism or perfect "compatibility" but in a workable relationship. There are conflicts and problems to solve, but there is also a commitment to struggle together in a planned way. Glossy hopefulness is absent, and confident, conscious collaboration is present.

The type of functional relationship pattern described above gives security and confidence to the relationship. This security is necessary in order to provide the motivation for family members to go back over and complete an unclear message until it is clear. There is no unknown vagueness to threaten a relationship. What is understandable can be used and predicted; it thereby loses its power to lower self-esteem. Insecurity in a relationship that diminishes self-esteem comes from vagueness, overgeneralization, and fantasied expectations.

A functional pattern of relationship also requires patience with disappointment, which may be a way of saying, "I have not gotten my way." Such disappointment is inevitable. There is no need, however, to tolerate continuous disappointment. Most importantly, one must not let it simmer; one cannot say, "Oh well, that's what I expected." It is crucial not to withdraw, but to struggle together, to understand the nature of the disappointment, and hopefully to negotiate a less disappointing joint outcome. Without clarifying the communication between members in a relationship, there is no opportunity to deal with disappointment; it remains accepted as our lot in life. This need not occur.

Let Me Know How You Feel

Three kinds of examples illustrate this pattern. The first has to do with a rather typical dilemma in marriage and the pattern of renegotiation that can emerge to effect more satisfactory joint outcome. The second example illustrates intergenerational communication between parent and children. The third example is an excerpted dialogue between members of the family as they negotiate a specific task they have been given.

Al and Jenny, prior to their marriage, would be described as a couple "in love." (They hoped each would ideally meet the other's needs.) After they married and lived with one another for awhile, they became aware that some of the supposed understandings they had agreed on prior to marriage did not in actuality work out. For example, when they became upset and angry with one another while dating, they could each go to their own apartment and be alone for a while to gain some perspective on the argument. After they were married, however, there were no separate places for each of them to go to. When Al was especially upset and needed to be alone, his period of "required aloneness" left Jenny feeling quite isolated. His withdrawal was hard for her to tolerate. Al often felt trapped in his own withdrawal, unable to come out, sensing that her immediate presence was either prohibiting or threatening—mainly to his infantile omniscience.

Since Jenny was more affected by the temporary isolation than was Al, she began to go to him and say, "This just isn't working out very well. I feel let down and deserted. You seem too much apart from me." Al would respond in a pout, "I don't really feel that much apart from you." Desperately, he continued, "It's best to remain alone for a while." Jennie would answer, "I don't get it. You seem to wish to remain alone, yet you sound rather desperate and look somewhat depressed." At this point the discrepancy became unveiled. Al would usually begin to report his underlying feelings of hurt and disappointment. It then became apparent to each of them how this incident had come about and how they, in their own idiosyncratic way, had reacted to it. It became possible to deal with the disappointment, the isolation, and the resultant broken communication.

If Jenny had not reported the discrepancy in her perceptions of Al, they might have gone on indefinitely playing a game of mutual self-deception. When two people really care for one another, they often hurt one another's feelings. This is not always intentional, it often comes from irritability with peers, imperfect understanding, and unconsciously projected past experiences. Sometimes, out of retaliation, it is intentional. However, the most important issue is discovering how to stop a dysfunctional and vicious cycle of communication between spouses. The perpetuating interchange must be stopped first. Only then is it possible to find out how it came about and to establish a more functional relationship between the two. Obviously what has meaning to Al does not have meaning to Jenny. She did not have the same requirement to be removed and alone from him as he did from her. It is necessary, therefore, that they check out the differential meaning in the relationship that led up to such an impasse.

Since the parents are the architects of the family, the children will follow the patterns of relationship and communication that have been established by them. This is probably no more clearly illustrated than in the area of respect for one another. Respect is gained where respect is given; one learns how to respect by being respected. I once observed a mother and her two preschool children just prior to the children's bedtime. The living room of the home was somewhat littered with toys, both broken and intact, as well as some scattered pieces of battered cardboard. When it came to pick-up time, they all worked together. Mother helped, but she certainly did not do all of it. It became something they did together, and pleasantly so, rather than something authoritatively dictated with the threat of punishment hanging over the children's heads.

I noted that the mother came upon several pieces of cardboard, roughly four by six inches in size. They were somewhat shredded and rather dirty. One would certainly assume they had little or no value. However, when she came to them, the mother asked each of the children if they wanted to keep them. They enthusiastically replied they did, so she put them in a box with some other obviously valuable (expensive) toys. The important thing was not whether the mother thought they were valuable or useful, but what the child thought of them.

In this instance, respect on the part of the mother would lead to respect, in turn, on the part of the children. This was borne out by later observation of this family. The meaning of the pieces of cardboard was, in fact, negotiated to some degree, however briefly. On the other hand, phony survival issues could have been made over whether the pieces of cardboard constituted: (a) a public health hazard for the family, and thereby should have been discarded for the sake of good sanitation practices, or (b) a clear-cut insult to mother because their pieces of cardboard were preferred to her expensive toys.

It was interesting that this mother hesitated for a moment when she first picked up the cardboard. She realized they were not of much value to her, but on the other hand, they might be to the children. When she proceeded to check this out with them, she discovered this indeed was so. This kind of negotiation led to what any observer could actually see was mutual and satisfactory joint outcome. She was not hurt by having to keep the cardboard, and the children were pleased to have her see their point of view.

The third example points up rather vividly how persons in an open family system communicate. The family described below—a father, mother, and one child—had come together to enter into a joint family decision task. They were given three games and were to discuss which one of these three games they would like to keep. They would in fact keep the chosen game and take it home with them. In this family task they had to learn to live with the consequences of their negotiation.

Mother: All right now, if we chose this one (X) . . . (she is interrupted by father)
Father: You're going to try to sell us on that one?
Child: (laughs)
Mother: (continuing) If we choose this one (X), it's very difficult with our three schedules to find time to sit down and get through a game as complicated as this. The second thing is I'll (laughing) lose my temper when you land on me.
Father: You're trying to tell me you don't like to lose.
Mother: (laughing, while nodding in agreement) Another thing is that one player can play this game (Y) and the others can sit there and look on. For instance, you can do this while you watch TV.

Father: You can't do anything while you watch TV (referring to the collective family)!

Mother: But you especially can't sit and spell while you're watching television (referring to the first game, X).

Child: (to mother) You can't sit and watch the game (Y) and watch television too.

Mother: But it (X) takes too much time.

Father: How do you know what I can do?

Mother: (She laughs and nods her understanding of the father's request that she not talk for him.)

Father: Well, two of these games (X and Y) seem to be essentially the same. You just use marbles instead of men.

Mother: Well, another thing would be if Y game could be placed on a table it would be a real decorative thing that could stay there.

Child: I suppose so.

Father: You've got some weird criteria for making a decision.

Mother: Well, that could be somewhat of a factor.

Father: All right (to the other two members of the family), if we would rule out the X game, which is just like the Y game in essence, which of the remaining two games would you prefer, the Y or the Z?

Child: I can get in trouble (laughingly).

Mother: No, you're not (smiles in confident reassurance).

Child: Well, I guess I'll pick Z.

The members of this family are able to communicate rather openly and clearly about their feelings, not only toward the task at hand but about one another. The father is able to comment on what he perceives as "weird criteria" on the part of the mother. This is clearly a point of differentness between the two of them and is taken into account in their ensuing discussion. The child, on the other hand, at the point of decision, seems to feel she may get into trouble if she decides on one of the two games, one of which was father's favorite and the other of which was mother's, but she can report this openly. Mother assures her immediately, clearly, and succinctly that trouble will not happen. As you read over this dialogue carefully, you see they are not only completing the task, they are negotiating joint outcome through a continuous awareness of one another's feelings, thoughts, and perceptions. The mother is the most unclear when she disguises her concern over "losing" in schedule concerns. Father makes the literal clarification.

Their communication and negotiation is, at times, struggling and imperfect, but there is relative openness in reporting feelings and thoughts. They help one another to clarify and use feedback of prior messages. This example is a kind of emotionalized problem solving that is person–uniqueness focused. Compare this dialogue with the dialogue on page 39 that is emotionalized self-vindication. In the latter nothing can be solved, because each is caught up in a self-centered desperation that is never openly commented upon. The dysfunctional cycle is perpetuated by the lack of feedback in the message exchanges.

Negotiation by Commitment and Clarity

The observer of a functional system of relationships in which the members can comment would be aware of several cardinal assumptions that govern that system. In the first place, survival appears to be enhanced by clear and congruent meaning among the members. Only messages that are clear and congruent actually make sense. Since nobody can be clear and congruent all, or even most, of the time, communication between family members is guided by constant feedback. Requests are frequently made for clarification, restatement, and reports of discrepant messages (verbal and nonverbal mismatch). Meaningfulness of communication is insured, not through perfectness but through the direct and confident use of observations about imperfect communication. Sense and order are enhanced because predictability is possible. Each party knows where he stands and where he is going. Expectations derive not from fantasies and wishes but from negotiated understanding of experiences. Over time, the persons gradually come to know one another better in terms of personal and practical realities. The intimacy of the relationship is, therefore, enhanced, supported, and perpetuated. Self-esteem in the relationship can derive from a negotiated outcome that is predictable and reliable.

Another aspect of this type of relationship system is the safeness to comment openly and clearly to one another. Without this confidence, family members would not be able to use feedback to clarify and specify messages. There is no fear of punishment or risk of vulnerability, which is debilitating to the dysfunctional family.

Concerns and doubts can be openly voiced, and the meaning of these can be checked out. It is accepted that everything that occurs in the family relationship is joint outcome. The question then becomes, "How is such *inherent* joint outcome to be more functionally achieved?" While outcome eventually derives from negotiation, no negotiation is possible without prior clarification of the conditions and the feelings at hand.

The vital conviction the members of this functional system share can be stated as follows: If our relationships (actions, words, crises, problems, disappointments, and frustrations) have mutual meaning, then we can live more comfortably with each other. Each member of the family accepts that eventual satisfying joint outcome requires a struggle with both inner needs and how others can help us satisfy these needs. These may range from planning a family vacation to the negotiation of the frequency of sexual intercourse between husband and wife.

It Seems Like We Have Done This Before!

Human relationship problems within the family are kaleidoscopic in their variation. *Problems,* in this sense, does not define a major crisis area by content but the inherent conflict of differentness. Each new problem therefore requires a renegotiation toward solution and a constant repetition of checking out meaning with one another. Difficulties with discipline, money, furniture arrangement, sexuality, etc., are really symptomatic of a more basic difficulty in living with differentness within the family. The focus of problem solving is how to live with differentness and conflict without sacrificing someone's identity and diminishing self-esteem. Before persons can begin to consider an emergent solution by mutual exploration of relationship differentness, clear and congruent messages about self and other must convey accurately and plainly what the exact nature of such inherent differentness is.

While this message checking may appear tedious and contrived, it only seems so because of the amazing degree to which we have come to accept inappropriate repetition of past experience and expectations. To project the past onto current dilemmas only deprives persons from utilizing the here and now, the immediate encounter, as the basis for open and relevant negotiation. Nobody is always or entirely able to check out meaning or to persistently use feedback comment on incongruences. As humans we must get used to making mistakes. Again, it is not a matter of perfection but of characteristic and habitual usage. Becoming accustomed to making mistakes is not the same as accepting that we must make the same ones over and over again simply to prove we are human. We can separate humanness from neurotic repetition. Humanness implies awareness and planning as well as imperfection.

The functional pattern described in this chapter can reverse itself if communication is not checked out among family members. Misunderstandings then will multiply and redirect the system in a dysfunctional direction:

1. If an unclear or incongruent message is accepted as clear and meaningful, the sender proceeds erroneously on the basis that you are on the same wavelength with him.

2. When the receiver does not respond in keeping with the sender's expectation, the sender will be confused.

3. If the sequence is not checked out, further confusion, false expectation, and threat of hurt will escalate because of the unclarity in the situation.

The spiral of pathogenic relationship that emerges from this type of situation has already been described in Chapter 4.

It can also be said with some assurance that once the rules of functional communication have been established, the members of the family aid one another in practicing them. If each person is aware of the typical evasion ploys and manipulating tactics of the other, they are much less likely to play an active, but unconscious, part in the perpetuation of dysfunctional cycles. In moments of regression, other can point out his ploy to self and thereby redirect communication in a more functional way. When feedback is expected, the system continually reinforces itself in a functional direction. The results of functional communication, which lead to the negotiation of more satisfying joint outcome, are considerably more rewarding than the hurt caused by misunderstanding, which derives from unclear and incongruent communication. Perhaps functional communication, like genius, is 1 percent inspiration and 99 percent perspiration.

Chapter 17

"Let's Both Be Adults"

Functionality from Responsibility

Joint outcome will be more functional if each member of the family accepts responsibility for self in what goes on among family members. Each will then report openly what he feels and thinks, sees, and hears and use this as the basis for negotiation. This applies to children as well as adults. What goes on in a family is all of the behavior that occurs between them. The sighs and the grimaces, the words and the gestures are all reacted to as significant communication about relationship between people.

To be adult is to be responsible for the consequences of one's behavior with another. What might have been intended is divorced from the consequences of what actually happened. "I didn't mean it" doesn't really matter; "What's going to be done about it" does. Who is at fault is irrelevant, but who can help change the situation into a more mutually satisfying experience is not. If one is responsible, then one can possibly do something functional about what has happened. Doing must be preferred to moaning; action is preferred to guilt.

The focus of behavior between various self–other combinations in the family is directed toward finding emergent solutions to conflicts. Emergent solutions come from (a) a manifestation of self needs by each involved person, and (b) a choice of realistic, available alternatives to best meet these divergent needs. Each party assumes equal responsibility in the mutual search for the emergent solution. Who's right or who's wrong is superseded by what fits the persons involved.

The accomplishment of this theme in family relationships requires persons to accept themselves first and foremost. If self is seen as worthy and significant, it can allow room for other in a mutual relationship. This is not a unilateral acceptance in a self-centered way but the intrinsic value to reciprocally give and receive. Persons who are comfortable with who and what they are do not view self as complete, or flawless. They see it at a point from which growth can occur—the point from which self can be expanded and enlarged in confidence. Spontaneity, flexibility, and genuine self manifestation can then become the basic core of relationship with another. Self-growth requires persons who accept what they do: Behavior is not good or bad, it simply is. What may not work out the first time will be examined, refined, and attempted again. Enthusiasm and the search for satisfaction will override despair and disillusionment.

What fits the persons involved will not destroy personal and relationship identity. We can both gain together, enjoy the relationship mutually and support one another when inevitable disappointments occur. One does not give up or give in to anything; rather, one gains an expansion of self from mutual experience. Both the individual and the relationship are facets of our existence; childhood (impulsive arrogance) is over, and adulthood (mutual awareness) has begun.

Reciprocity Rides Again

Robert and Beverly argued over how the family income was to be managed. This, however, was simply one prominent area in which differences between Bob and Beverly were manifest. Each of them had been brought up in a different family. They acquired meaningful but different convictions as to how money should be managed for the benefit of a family. They are newly married, and their income is limited, so they wish to make the best out of the resources they have. Beverly has accepted responsibility for keeping accounts, but Bob persistently wants to decide how the accounts ought to be kept. Each time he makes a suggestion, Beverly has a better way "for her." As they discuss this, however, their voices begin to rise. Suddenly they confront one another with anger and hurt determination.

The issue at hand fundamentally has to do with *who shall decide* what rules are to be followed in their relationship. It is inevitable that such conflicts will arise in a marital relationship, as it evolves around the apparent dilemma of maintaining individuality while at the same time maintaining a pair–relationship identity. There may be some hurt feelings if it is presumed that who is to decide has to do with who is worth more; it could prevent mutual negotiation. What makes the difference in their conversation is that in spite of the conflict they can comment openly and directly on the conflict and the feelings it arouses in them. For example:

Beverly: Look, Bob, if it's so upsetting to you for me to keep the accounts my way, why don't you keep the accounts?

Bob: We agreed earlier you would have more time to do this than me.

Beverly: Well, I'll go along with that. But then it seems to me I ought to do it in a way I'm comfortable with. I know you're better at figures, but as long as I can keep track of things financially with my methods, why not let me be comfortable?

Bob: But it is somewhat inefficient, you know.

Beverly: It's worked out for me in the past, Bob. Why can't you accept that? Does it really matter how it's done as long as it's done adequately?

Bob: I guess it really grinds me, Bev, that you won't let me decide this. I feel hurt because you won't accept my judgment on this.

Beverly: I wonder if you're hurt because of what I've said or because of something inside you that what I've said runs counter to.

Bob: Probably the latter, I guess, because you're really not being unreasonable.

Beverly: I'd like to have us work out a way that we can both be comfortable with, Bob, but I don't see that either one of us has to lose. The main thing is to get the job done.

Bob: You know, I can feel more clearly now that in my

family, Dad always made these decisions. I guess I'm not accustomed to having them done another way. I suppose in the end I would rather have us manage our income well than to always harangue over who's going to be boss.

In their discussion, the inevitable question arises, "Am I angry because there is hurt inside me that has been tapped or has your behavior been hurtful per se?" Without intending to, Beverly and Bob discover more than once that they have acted in ways that arouse hurtful feelings in the other. This feeling, however, emanates from within the affected person. It may represent a reaction to careless, if not hostile, treatment by another. It may also represent a self-vindicated maneuver to maintain self-centeredness. If the latter occurs, there is a tendency to attribute blame or guilt to the other person for disruption of one's favorite myths and illusions. Again, it is necessary to say, "Those are my toes, friend."

In the above conversation it can be seen that each accepts responsibility for his action and his thoughts as they work toward the emergent solution that will fit their need to manage family income. This is a problem-solving policy that derives from the encounter of differentness in the here and now. It is a policy of relationship that does not fall into the pitfall of interpreting the present in terms of the past. Rather it overcomes the use of the past to justify the present. It places the present in the frame of an experience with different people, and therefore calls for a negotiated, not repetitious and stereotyped, responsiveness.

A second example of this type of functional behavior can be seen in the way in which children acquire a sense of responsibility within the family. The process involved in learning responsibility for a child is made easier if he lives with parents who are responsible in their behavior toward one another; that is, the parents assume responsibility for what they do in their mutual relationship. Solutions are sought, pain is not denied, and consideration is mutually practiced. The child is able to experience and to witness a satisfactory model in parents who focus on evaluation and action instead of on blame or guilt.

Children also appear to acquire a more confident and consistent attitude of responsibility for their behavior if they have had to deal with the consequences of their own behavior. It is questionable whether a child learns responsibility if he is only given tasks for which he is held responsible. He learns to please the adult, rather than to have any inner conviction about the necessity of responsibility. Responsibility is derived from experience in which one bears the consequences of actions directed toward a *meaningful* goal. If a young child is *told* to dry dishes seven days a week so he will learn responsibility, he learns either performance to please or performance to avoid punishment. If he is *asked* to help out because mother is tired on certain days, he can become a part of the mutual responsibility that involves requests she fulfills for him.

Even more important, the everyday life of a child, especially during the school years, is full of a great many experiences that are directly important to him. Deleterious consequences that may emerge from these experiences are, therefore, much more meaningful to him than those that may be ascribed by parents. For example, children continuously come into conflict with their peers because of impulsive comments and behavior. The more the parent interferes with this process for the sake of "justice," the less likely are the children to benefit from their own mutual learning. Direct experiential learning gradually begins to circumscribe the kinds of behavior and comments that can be lived with and those that cannot. The only necessary intervention need be when imminent physical harm is present. This, in actuality, rarely occurs. However, injustice situations are often set up by the child when he knows mother or father will join him in a power coalition against sibling or peer.

It is not at all unlikely that, when allowed to experience conflict and differentness in their own child relations, the child will gradually learn it is not wishes and images but consequences of behavior that affect relationship. When they are allowed to work it out for themselves at their own level of experience, they learn that the most satisfying solution is the one that emerges from what fits, rather than who is boss. Parents who would interrupt this basic learning experience, tend to deprive the child of accepting responsibility for his own behavior; the child learns that he can rely and depend upon a higher authority to settle such matters. Adulthood does not provide such protection.

Children also have their own possessions, which, although given to them, they often cherish. Care and responsibility for these possessions can be and should be entirely their own. Their loss, destruction, or misuse should be borne by them. The same applies to their use of money, which a small child sometimes spends with lack of judgment for what might seem to be entirely foolish things. It is far better, however, to make these mistakes when young than when older. Parents cannot make a "mistake-proof" environment for their child. That is patently unrealistic. Parents can suggest, advise, and even exhort some age-appropriate thrift, but their own open management of family assets will be the most convincing influence. A child gains confidence and awareness when he can correct or compensate for misjudgments and inexperience in an appropriate way for his age. (For example, he pays for what he breaks in proportion to his income and savings, compared to the parents.)

It will naturally emerge from the mutuality of relationship between parent and child that each is able to help the other. At certain times in the life of the child, therefore, especially when he is older, he will be able to perform certain tasks that will be helpful to the parent. If son Jim uses the car two nights a week, he can bear the expense and effort on maintenance (washing, etc.) of this proportion of his use. If Jim cannot, because of financial or other limitations, contribute in this way, he may then do something for the parents of equivalent value to them. There is no reason why, if the child refuses to help the parent, the parent should be available to help the child when he requires it. Not to learn this essential mutuality in relationships is again to deprive the child of what is inevitable in his later adult relationships, emphasizing manipulation rather than reciprocity in relationship. It is not uncommon that parents and children can negotiate a contract that involves mutual assistance. If the child fails to live up to this contract, he will lose the help of the parent. The parent, likewise, should hold to the same responsibility in regard to the child.

Responsibility for Reality

With any given family system, the "Let's Be Adults" pattern evolves from one of the basic rules the family has accepted that governs its systematic behavior. We must inevitably *deal with actual behavior*. Two principal corollaries accompany this rule: Behavior within the family is reciprocal, and consequences of behavior are mutual in their influence. Any process that helps to determine what fits the needs of family members is central to family problem solving, which is focused on what actually happened rather than what we hoped for, wished for, or said happened. Reciprocal responsibility results in a way of dealing with problems, conflict, and differentness among family members that is predicated on what will work out. The focus can consistently remain on results that affect all. From this rule, the family develops a policy that psychological survival within the family group is easier if the members struggle together to clarify mutual meaning. This in no way hinders the uniqueness and individuality of the members; rather, it is their uniqueness and individuality that must at all times be taken into account—especially as these characteristics have mutual relationship significance. For each member of the family to make room for the others requires an awareness first of his own uniqueness and then, necessarily, the uniqueness of other family members as well. This assumes that one is responsible, first, for self and, second, aware of other's qualities.

A characteristic dynamic of this functional pattern is that a mutual struggle to achieve emergent solutions—coming from an awareness of the present—replaces interpersonal stereotyped maneuvering. The emergent solution should represent real alternatives to what went wrong in the past that are possible under the circumstances of (a) what has to be done, and (b) how the people involved feel about the task and one another. It may often turn out that these conditions limit the alternatives to one not very good, or that there is no real alternative at all. But in a functional family a decision is made to work it out in the best way available.

In the struggle for emergent solution, *reality* is both what one feels about a situation and what the situation appears to be. The reality of feelings (emotional response) is often the qualifier of what we will do with the objective situation. To be adult is to evaluate both of these accurately for the members of the family as a unit of persons. Neither the extremes of coldly logical deduction or random bursts of emotion exclusively structure the decision-making process. In the functional family, both one's ability to reason and one's emotional reaction are both given significant value; one does not rule the other. They must both be utilized and taken into account, and this is accomplished by open reporting of feelings and observations of the situation. Any reality can only become viable if its contents, limits, and implications are clear, apparent, and meaningful to the persons involved.

The culminating characteristic of this functional pattern is the safety the members of the family feel with one another. There is confidence and an expectation of concern and mutual regard. ("There will be no retaliation if I say what I think and express what I feel.") There is a conviction that they will grow, in the sense of expanding self, if they allow solutions, decisions, and relationships to emerge continuously from the experience of being with one another. The focus of their expectation is decidedly on growth through negotiation, rather than psychic dismemberment through unilateral manipulation.

Let's Get On with It

Personal as well as interpersonal responsibility has nothing to do with being right, only with doing what is required to be done. This emerges from the struggle between persons to define their relationship to one another in terms of thoughts, feelings, perceptions, and consequences. Little is to be gained in complaints about how things ought to be or should be.

One function of mutual living—with its many paradoxes and dilemmas—is hard work. Functional relationships require attention, awareness, and a willingness to put out effort. It is not a matter of how good we are, or how good our spouse or children are, but what we can do together to satisfactorily survive in a psychological sense.

It may well be that functional relationship, like democracy, is obtained at the price of eternal vigilance and hard work. Since we pay a price to have either functional or dysfunctional relationships, we might just as well direct our efforts toward a kind of relationship that ends up as worthwhile and meaningful. To be together in relationship with the family is to experience moods, feelings, hurts, desires, joy, grief, and satisfaction. Living with others is a process and not a stagnant state; the functionality or dysfunctionality of behavior within any family system therefore evolves from continuous change and the effects of new experience. The functional pattern that has been described in this chapter may, without the presence of eternal vigilance, resolve itself into dysfunction if:

1. Responsibility for self begins to shift to blame when things go wrong.

2. Everybody gets caught on what was intended, rather than what actually happened. "The road to hell is paved with good intentions."

3. Each person waits for the other guy to make the first negotiating move; rigor mortis may occur before functional outcome.

4. Everyone looks to sources outside of the family system for solutions (including experts who write books on family psychology) instead of going to one another. If this is done, family life may become a courtroom scene rather than a satisfying experience.

5. Everybody backs away from growth that derives from mutual confrontation, because it looks as if it may threaten cherished and precious illusions.

PART VII

The Future of Family Relationships

The future of any system of relationships depends on how well our survival needs and idiosyncratic needs are met. As long as the family, for the most part, meets our needs for sense and order, productivity and intimacy, and our unique constitutional needs, we would presume the family has a vital future. Such families can promote psychological growth. Its members are able to see present circumstances with the others in the family as unique moments and not as shadows of a painful past.

Yet any dysfunctional behavior when *commonly accepted* as a way of meeting needs will tend to persist. War, for example, has been accepted as a legitimate and needed way of resolving conflict through the centuries. Even though its results are dysfunctional—war is destructive, painful, and humanly disruptive—it persists nonetheless as a method of conflict resolution. If persons are convinced that no other alternative exists to a dysfunctional resolution, they continue it.

We know that, once established, the system of relationships we call the family tends to perpetuate itself. Innovation and change is difficult at best; at other times it appears to be nearly impossible. It is possible to think about future family relationships, therefore, on two different levels:

1. If we consider individual families, we are left with the rather obvious conclusion that some families have a future while other families do not. The concept of the individual family allows us to focus on the kind of functional pattern within its system of relationships that gives a positive and growth-oriented future. This is related to how survival and idiosyncratic needs are met within a particular family.

2. If we think of the family as being part of a larger social pattern of expectancy, we are able to see how the family as a cultural phenomenon has changed and continues to change over time. This gives us more of a generalized picture of how a family has met survival and idiosyncratic needs within a given society.

All systems of relationship have a future that may either be functional or dysfunctional. There are, however, more basic questions: Does the family of today threaten survival or enhance survival? Does the family provide the nurturance for emotional growth and personal expansion or the sterile soil for emotional attrition and meaningless existence? Is it possible to disrupt and alter the accepted perpetuation of dysfunctional patterns of family life?

Throughout this book an emphasis has been placed on the importance of the basic survival needs vital to all human beings and idiosyncratic needs particular to a given individual. The fundamental questions in regard to the future of family relationships must relate these two sets of needs to the following conditions:

1. The emotional nature of man
2. The emotional nature of family life
3. The effect of man's own material and social creations—his technology and his social expectations—on his identity and on his family life.

Seldom does anyone ask, "Why live in families?" Why is there not some other way of meeting these needs? Does the family as we know it represent the best way of meeting these crucial needs of man? And even if families are the best way we know to meet these needs, is the achievement of intimacy, so crucial to our psychological survival, a myth or a true possibility within the context of family living? Must we tolerate family dysfunction as a human necessity, or can families meet the human credibility gap with honest awareness and struggle?

Chapter 18

What Are Families For?

The history of the family has been to a large extent also the history of mankind, which as a species has a nature that has, in part, resulted in coming together in families in order to survive better. His nature has emphasized self-preservation as a basic instinct—to keep his physical self intact and alive. With an emotional aspect to his nature as well, he also needed meaning and purpose to survive. Initially, we presume very primitive man had no family organization at all. It was only when mutual survival was seen as valuable that man, woman, and child lived together with some commitment to mutual aid and protection. This was solely a matter, at first, of physical survival. That was man's absorbing and necessary purpose. As physical survival became more assured, the emotional aspects of his existence came more into prominence. The human instinct for survival has always represented, however, an admixture of physical and emotional components.

The rationale for coming together in family units is historically old and pragmatically purposeful. Over the centuries families have fulfilled both institutional and functional purposes and perhaps more basic, emotional–psychological purposes. The institutional purposes of families have to do with the social management of persons, with the ways in which persons mutually survive or exist in a larger society outside of a particular family. This involves not only biological continuance of the species through reproductive regulation and infant protection but also a social continuity over time, a continuity of experiential learning that enhances each future generation's ability to survive better physically and emotionally than the previous generation. This learning is passed on from person to person within families and, more formally, in our educational institutions (where you can get credit hours' worth of "canned experience"). In itself, this generation-to-generation learning has been an evolving process, with continuous change and increased complexity.

The learning of institutional and emotional purposes for living together, particularly in the American family, has been significantly related. Historically, there were institutional practices that basically fulfilled physical, social, and individual survival functions at the same time.

There are three fundamental and overlapping purposes to family life. These have been present in both historical and contemporary American families and have also served both institutional and emotional functions for family members:

1. Reproductive legitimacy (social regulation of reproduction)
2. Mutual caretaking (physical and emotional nurturance)
3. Protective child rearing (socialization and security)

The first of these, reproductive legitimacy, is multifaceted. It is a basic legal consideration in the family in regard to ownership and inheritance, defining, to an extent, the parents' responsibilities to one another, as well as to their children. These legal formulas represent a more or less "forced" commitment between family members. Their very presence suggests that commitment and responsibility in human relationship is more of a "sometime thing" than we would care to think. Reproductive legitimacy also has an emotional value in terms of affirmation of one's identity. The legally born child has an immediate and future link to a socially accepted familial system. He is part of and belongs to them (in the sense of belonging to a meaningful group) throughout his maturation; this is essential for identification with and differentiation from his parents, a process necessary to evolve a personal identity, a confident affirmation of who and what one is as a person. An illegitimate status not only has social implications but great personal and emotional implications as well. The illegitimate child who is or becomes aware of his status always questions his worth and his place in his family and society. This questioning of basic self-value is also frequently done by other persons inside and outside the family. Reproductive illegitimacy also represents an area of societal and familial sanctions for the unfortunate individuals who get caught. This castigation of social rule-breakers often involves considerable projection of guilt in the form of social indignation by the accusers. While the expectations of the societal group (one's peers) as well as the family prohibit sexual activity that may lead to pregnancy, the punitive behavior (scorn, shame, rejection) is directed not at the doers per se but at the evidence. (Since the Kinsey report, there has been accumulating evidence to indicate that what we say we do sexually and what we do is indeed quite different. Sexual morality appears to relate to who is caught than what is done.) These sanctions shame and undermine the self-esteem of persons who will need to give to the resultant child a sense of worthiness and identity in himself. The child and his parents are caught in a social vindication cycle that castigates the careless. Confident identity and self-affirmation is crippled when nineteenth-century thinking on reproductive legitimacy takes precedence over twentieth-century awareness. Guilt and shame overshadow responsibility.

Reproductive legitimacy also includes, under the rubric of human responsibility, the guarantee of mutual caretaking and protective child-rearing functions. The legitimate but unwanted child, however, receives a very different emotional quality of caretaking and protective rearing than does the wanted child. His parenting is emotionally poverty-stricken. Adequate emotional care cannot be prescribed by social expectation or carried out under a cloud of guilt. Psychologically, adequate emotional relationship between parent and child is a matter of reciprocal, intergenerational nurturance within a family system. Adequate physical care prescribed by statute will not, in itself, guarantee psychological survival.

The second purpose of family living, mutual caretaking, is becoming an exclusive nuclear family function. In the past such mutual caretaking might occur over as many as three to four generations simultaneously in an extended family system. It is in this area of interaction that families most visibly meet the physical as well as emotional needs for survival. While physical survival is much less a problem today than two hundred years ago, psychological survival has increased in significance as an aspect of mutual caretaking within the family. With physical survival more assured, greater leisure time is left in man's life space. What then becomes the focal point of his existence? He must fill time with meaning, which is related to how to live, rather than how to avoid death. Achieving meaning is a psychological survival necessity; without it, a person's orientation to survival becomes blurred and unimportant. Within family relationships meaning derives from the mutuality present. As long as psychological caretaking is mutual and based upon negotiated need awareness and need-satisfying policies, this purpose is functionally achieved. To the degree that such caretaking is unilateral, the members in the family, while they will suffer to varying degrees, will nevertheless as a unit be deprived to a certain extent of psychological growth.

The third purpose in family relationships, protective child rearing, has two basic facets. First, it provides the child with experiences on which to base his own behavior. He is socialized to fit into his own family and, presumably, given a base that has relationship application to persons from other families. It is a fundamental "learning how to get along with others" experience. Secondly, protective child rearing provides the child with safeguards from his own poorly controlled impulses as well as from the dangers of the environment around him, an environment that is both physical and emotional. If the child is able to gradually acquire a confident and usable style of relating, he will feel secure and be able to expand his self. If he is overprotected physically and underprotected emotionally, he will lack confidence and be fearful and rigid.

Whether the child is fearful or confident is related to whether he comes from a family where he learned to "prey" or from a family where he learned to "pray." In essence, this represents the difference between (a) exploitation as a way of life ("preying"), or (b) other-directedness as a way of life ("praying"). Other-directedness implies an involvement with others for mutual survival—not a denial of self to please others but an ability to be aware, to respond and to negotiate with others for mutual purposes.

While reproductive legitimacy and protective child rearing within any family are the legacies of the children, mutual caretaking is a facet that is the legacy of all family members. It is first the promise of the marriage, and later the result of the family. Either the degree of psychological survival gives the family members security, direction, and value or it undermines and delimits their emerging identities. Reproductive legitimacy emotionally implies a kind of direct, open, and negotiated commitment in the relationship between the parents before the child comes into the family. Man and woman *can* agree in a planful way, not by accident, to bring the child into a positive emotional and social climate. The child has legitimacy within their relationship, as well as in the larger society. Rebellion, self-vindication, and need desperation discolor such legitimacy with self-justifying manipulation. Likewise, protective child rearing requires a collaborative negotiation between wife–mother and husband–father. The three purposes for family living are, therefore, both institutional and emotional in nature.

Wither Goes the Family ?

Numerous writers in the field of marriage and the family have pointed to the evolving changes in our society in regard to the structure of the family. While these will not be elaborated in detail here, they will, in this chapter and the following ones, be interpreted from the point of view of their consequences for an emotional relationship system. Basically, persons who study the family have become alarmed over what seems to be the considerable evidence of the breakdown of traditional marital and family structure. This does not indicate that the family *per se* is dysfunctional. Rather, it may show that as environmental and technological influences on man have changed, he has not consequently redefined and reoriented himself in terms of a change in family structure and expectation. The more traditional family forms and expectations, some dating back a century or more, tend to persist, when, as such, they cannot really fulfill the emotional needs of the individuals in the family of today.

One bit of alarming evidence regarding family disruption derives from national divorce statistics, though these figures are very inconclusive. We know that approximately one divorce decree is granted for every four marriage licenses granted. This by no means logically leads one to the conclusion that one out of every four marriages ends in divorce. Those people who marry in any one year are only rarely the people who also become divorced in that year. (The figures, therefore, represent two entirely different populations.) At the present time there is little reliable information to indicate which of the people granted marriage licenses in a given year eventually end up with a divorce decree.

The divorce picture, even if it could be accurately known, really tells us only what the top one-tenth of the iceberg is like. There is no way of knowing with any certainty the number of marriages that continue intact but in abysmal despair. Family and marital clinicians have every reason to believe that this number is several times the number of divorces granted every year. Some marriages are entered into for the sake of reproductive legitimacy and other marriages are continued, even though dysfunctional, because of the responsibility for protective child rearing. The broken marriage or family represents almost universally, a failure in mutual caretaking. In most instances divorce indicates that the emotional needs of the couple are not being met to such a degree that all other considerations become secondary to what appears to be the impending psychological death of the marriage partners as identities. Desertions and separations, while they allow for the fulfillment of reproductive legitimacy (at least for the children born prior to the separation), represent a rather serious denial of the protective child-rearing and mutual caretaking facets of family life.

Divorce and its consequences may well be an increasing phenomenon. Does the increase of divorce as a method of relationship resolution indicate that marriage as we know it is outmoded as a means of meeting emotional and institutional needs? Perhaps divorce phenomena indicate our current difficulty in integrating basic emotional needs with rapid social, economic, and technological changes? One possible answer to these questions will become clear shortly.

Another change in family structure over the past five decades is the degree to which the family has become less and less of a significant economic and educational unit and much more of an emotional resource. Increasing amounts of the education and socialization of the child have been shifted to schools, churches, and activity groups such as the scouts. In addition, with the widespread use of reliable oral contraceptives, a relatively heavy and, at times, unpredictable and unwanted reproductive responsibility for the family will no doubt be lessened. The answer to whether the family as we know it today is really meeting human needs will lie in differentiating which needs it does meet and which needs it does not. The family probably meets fewer overall human needs than fifty years ago. With this decrease, there has been an increasing emphasis on individuality and the realization of one's identity. Concomitantly, there has been a lesser emphasis on necessary mutuality. Most people still conceive of their family in terms of experience and function, like the family at the turn of the century that focused to a substantial degree on survival economically, educationally, and socially but often to a lesser degree emotionally. The discrepancy arises from outmoded social expectancy on one hand and contemporary emphasis on self-realization and individuality on the other. Essential mutuality, however, has not changed. It has merely shifted from economic and physical forms to more psychologically and emotionally directed forms. Children need not work to support most families anymore; they must learn, nevertheless, to assume responsibility in the joint outcome of the family in other ways.

What to Be or What Not to Be, That Is the Question

Can human needs be better met in some other form of human living than the family? The answer lies not in discarding the idea of the family but in changing our expectations and images of what the family can be. What families have done and what they can continue to do is to attempt to meet human emotional needs. Some families do this much better than others. This is no reason to dispense with the family, but to see how human needs can best be met.

At the present time the idea of what a family should be is a social expectation that is out of touch with current awareness of humans as evolving, living need systems. People change over time. They are not the same at twenty-five as at thirty-five, forty-five, or seventy-five. At all ages, however, there are needs, some similar, some different. Meeting these needs is vital to the continued emotional existence of the person. Whatever lives must be nourished. That nourishment must come from another who is aware of what needs must be fulfilled. To give and to receive in a relationship is a reciprocal necessity, if emotional needs (e.g., support, affection, concern, encouragement) are to be met. Such reciprocity is derived from open awareness of need and mutual negotiation toward solution, rather than "love." Affectionate response is more the result than the cause of reciprocal need meeting. Such prelove is, in reality, a romantic evasion of uniqueness, replete with unilateral expectations and fantasies of self-enlargement.

While man remains essentially the same in emotional nature, his ways of social living seem to be forever changing. Hopefully, ways of living together change to better meet physical and emotional needs of our human nature. To the degree that social institutions and practices do not, they are dysfunctional. This must include expectancies aroused by social learning within the family and the larger society, for example, the myths of romantic love as the basis for marriage or peace at all costs as the way of maintaining supposedly conflict-free family relations.

Part of man's basic nature would appear to be his rather insatiable need to perceive himself as a uniquely significant being, to be loved, adored, rewarded, cheered, overpaid, always happy, cheerful, creative, thoughtful, intelligent, and an all-around hero. All of these conditions, however, smack of unilateral hedonism rather than reciprocal mutuality, reflecting an either/or question of the mutual meeting of needs or the actualization of self. Self-actualization, a term used by psychologist Abraham Maslow, refers to a person with an enriched and more functional life outcome. A self-actualizer is aware and experiences; he is not a user or exploiter. But self emerges from a social experience. How are human needs to be met so that self may be actualized at the same time?

We all became the kind of persons we are because of a combination of inherited material and social experience. It is hard to conceive of any self being realized, or even initiated, without the social experience of the family. Perhaps such social experience did not help in the actualization of self but rather acted to produce a frightened, defensive, and rigid automaton—a person who always sees in terms of an experienced past and thereby misses the opportunity for expansion of self-growth in his identity. Again, the focus must be on what kind of emotional experience within the family will lead to mutual self-actualization. Identity is, after all, a matter of differentiation from and similarity with others.

Self-actualization results from progressive emotional growth, which emerges from experiences of nurturance, support, and committed direction within the context of a relationship system that can meet evolving, living needs. One does not emotionally grow alone. One grows and expands his self and more fully realizes himself as a result of relationships with others. Mutuality does not interfere with self-actualization; *it is absolutely essential to it.* The withdrawn, self-centered, or narcissistic individual is not self-actualized; he is, rather, stultified and fixated in his own self-grip. If one is to grow in the context of human relationships, he must be willing to accept responsibility for the growth of others—both child and adult—in order to reciprocally involve himself in their growth-giving nurturance to him. There can be no self without other, nor other without self.

The so-called changing role of the American woman in the family provides us with a focal point for the interrelationship between family systems, human needs, and self-actualization. The mother's function and satisfaction in the family is reciprocally related to the other members of the family. It is not she alone who has changed in her behavior and responsibilities. The expectations and behavior of husband and children are also different. With his wife's greater social and economic freedom (she can vote, hold office, and work), man is less a protector, and more of a collaborator. Children are no longer labor assets and dependent automatons but participating emotional members and sharers of the family experience. This, in turn, sets up a circularly reciprocal and reinforcing series of behaviors within the family.

From the perspective of the woman, as our machine technology advances and proliferates, the physical and mechanical tasks of the mother in the home lessen. Fewer hours are required for food preparation, cleaning, and child care, especially compared to twenty-five and fifty years ago. The children too spend significantly more time away from home than they used to. Education is outside the family and in the school, often for an increasingly prolonged period of years. What has happened to the woman's opportunities for significant identity and a conviction of worthiness of her contributions to family life? Neither the home nor the children need her as much. The emphasis has shifted to the quality of relationships between mother and the others in the family. The female of the human species has no instinctive maternal behavior. It is learned, acquired, and experienced. "Mothering" in actuality can be done by either a male or a female, as can child rearing. Only the mother, however, can bear and give birth to a human infant. This is a biological-emotional experience that, at least in the beginning, ties mother and child together. Her work, her strivings, her ambitions are necessarily interrupted by childbirth. She was a unique person prior to childbirth, and has a need to be so after the child comes. How is this to evolve with new responsibilities and a triadic relationship with husband and child, instead of the former exclusive marital dyad? All three now become emotional recipients of a joint outcome.

If, after bearing the child, the mother leaves home to work and the child is largely reared by another, who nurtures and is responsible for him, it makes a significant difference in the child's emotional perception. If, on the other hand, the mother remains with the child throughout the preschool years, when the elementary years come, she may be left home for large parcels of time with relatively little to do. Where then does she realize her self as significant, productive, and worthy? Where does the child realize his identity if his support and protection are in actuality mother's bitter frustration? How does husband relate to a changing wife, no longer the bright, cheerful, and energetic lover she was before the child was born?

Technology, which frees woman from the drudgery of mechanical tasks, also allows time for creative homemaking. A woman who identifies herself as a homemaker is significantly different from one who identifies herself as a housewife. As a housewife she perceives herself as "married" to the house. The implication is that the marriage may not be going well. It smacks of an involuntary, rather than a voluntary, commitment. To make or to create a home, however, is a significant elaboration over "taking care of the house." Unfortunately, it is the values of the society itself that place an emphasis and reward on career achievement rather than creative homemaking. No woman, unless she is a masochist, spends her whole day bending over a hot stove. What does she do all day?

The modern home is a rather complicated technological system in one sense. Caring for it requires both engineering and maintenance foreman skills. In any case, it does not require the same skills, attitudes, and type of work that was required of a mother thirty years ago. There is both a dilemma and a challenge involved here. How does a woman, unaccustomed by her own previous learning, adapt to the continuously changing role of homemaker? At times she is emotionally required to be mistress, nurse, chef, waitress, maintenance supervisor, child-care expert, and executive officer.

If she leaves the home for part-time or full-time work, she competes with the traditional role of the male, who is not always happy with this situation. He too is caught up in the dilemma of new opportunities for identity realization that conflict with outmoded family and social preconceptions. For the husband this may require, for example, frequent absences from the home to realize his vocational responsibilities and objectives. What happens to his emotional support of the family members? It certainly changes or at least lessens. If, in fact or in fantasy, the mother's work is competitive with the father's, then a radical renegotiation of who is who and who does what is required. If this does not take place, not only does the affectional and emotional nature of the relationship between husband and wife change, the repercussions are felt throughout the entire family. Competition replaces collaborative support; mutual emotional outcome becomes unilateral achievement. Support and nurturance lessen, emotional distance increases, and eventual isolation and fear of abandonment arise.

The woman may often be caught in the dilemma between privilege and responsibility. She may wish to work outside the home like the husband and then expect the others, in addition to their own home tasks, to help her with her usual tasks. After all, these are essential and must be done by someone. Is this actualizing herself or burdening others? The answer resides in the joint negotiations entered into by the members of the family.

Partners in Awareness

To meet the triad of survival needs, idiosyncratic needs, and the influence of social and technological change, the family requires an attitude of partners in awareness—awareness of needs, of consequences of behavior, of the necessity for collaborative support to negotiate joint outcome. The focus, of course, would not be on technology or society as such but on the effect of technology and society on people in a specific family. We must learn to view a family as a small, living social system that is affected from within as well as from without, a system of relationships that is constantly changing, but requires a kind of dynamic stability achieved only through mutual negotiation to function adequately. Together family members will do something about the changes that confront them. There will be a constancy of responsibility among the family members to keep all aware of individual perceptions of change and need and to struggle toward more satisfying joint outcome.

Meeting human and survival needs requires an emotional awareness and acceptance of the mutuality of self and other as a basis for psychological survival. If there is to be sense and order in a family, there must be a clear commitment and a clear communication of commitment to one another: to negotiate, not merely tolerate; to support and encourage. If each member of the family is to feel productive and meaningful in the family's functioning and work output, he must manifest his uniqueness so that it may be utilized. Each family member must help others to become aware when he requires nurturance, support, limitation, and cooperation. As Eric Berne has said, "If you don't receive stroking, your spinal cord will shrivel up." Emotional nurturance is necessary within the family to keep the spinal cord loose and relaxed and to allow people to achieve and to produce unencumbered from anxiety and defensiveness. Finally, if the members of a family are to reach the intimacy possible in close relationships, they will need to value differentness. They will have to be able to view self and other as different and to accept that differentness in itself produces some conflict that can be worked out.

The basic emotional problem to be solved in the family is how to live with differentness without destroying individual identity. We need to learn from one another and, in turn, to teach our children to value the individual selves in a family. We must likewise be able to value our own self as unique and different from other. We need not be what our father or mother was, or our great-aunt, twice-removed cousin, or eminent grandfather. We need only to be what we are, as long as this includes an awareness of the needs of others and an attitude of mutual and reciprocal responsibility.

The fact that we are different from one another within our family does not mean we are better than one another. We must give up infantile and narcissistic conceptions of self as the center of human focus and accept each other out of necessity for the mutual benefit to our psychological survival. Identity is defined by acting with security and freedom in one's unique differentness, out of a conviction of worthiness born from mutual confrontation with others in respect and awareness.

Why live in families? For mutual emotional survival derived

from satisfying joint outcome. The family that attains this in a changing environment would have three basic qualities:

1. The parents and children are *emotionally aware and focused.* They can report their feelings and observations openly without fear of hurting self or other. How they feel about self and toward one another is not valued in itself but used to achieve greater meaning to one another.

2. The family members view their being together as a *mutual survival system.* They are aware that what affects one, affects all. They each have a stake in what goes on among and between them. Meaning and purpose to life comes from their mutual relationship. It therefore requires clarity, specificity, and congruence of communication if sense and order, productivity, and intimacy are to be achieved among them.

3. The interrelationships in the family represent an open, negotiated system. Joint outcome is arrived at not accidentally but by the awareness of differentness and the acceptance of such as the beginning of the negotiation of an emergent solution to joint outcome.

While we can discard and disregard marriage and family relationships for a time, we cannot likewise disregard the fundamental mutual human needs that made marriage and family relationship an emotional survival necessity.

Chapter 19

Intimacy and Relationship

In previous chapters much attention has been paid to the way in which the family meets human emotional needs necessary to ensure psychological survival. Sense and order, productivity, and intimacy give meaning to life for the human individual. These are not only the reasons for emotional living but the lubricant and substance that encourage and perpetuate the will to live, as well as the experience of finding such living emotionally satisfying. Although each of these three needs is, to a large degree, interrelated to the other two, our deep emotional need for intimacy with another person is perhaps the most emotionally significant to marital and family life.

Intimacy is, among other things, the ability to share private experiences, thoughts, attitudes, and feelings for another. It is also the ability to care about another and to have another care about us, to have another show concern in our welfare, to contribute to, but not be entirely responsible for, our satisfaction and happiness. Intimacy within marriage and family relationships is also the vehicle of emotional nurturance in the relationship, carrying much the same meaning as physical nourishment; it is that part of the relationship between persons that encourages growth by giving confidence and support to one's self-esteem. High self-esteem, in turn, allows the human individual to deal with a new experience more effectively. When experience can be perceived and reacted to with confidence and hope, a person can enlarge his self—to grow emotionally and to effect appropriate outcome from a unique present experience without a repetition of past expectations. To deal with new relationship experience is to expand personality, to emotionally mature and grow as an individual in relationship with other people, not only within the family but to outside individuals as well.

Emotional nurturance in an intimate relationship reveals itself in behavior that involves physical touching and holding. It is closely akin to comforting and assuring the other person of their worth by open and direct physical support. The nurturant aspect of an adult intimate relationship, therefore, gradually leads to a physical sexual intimacy. This, however, is the result of, not the cause of, the more fundamental emotional intimacy between two persons. It is a mistake to think that physical intimacy and emotional intimacy are the same thing or, in fact, that sexual intimacy may precede emotional intimacy. Such sexuality does not derive from an evolving intimacy in a face-to-face relationship. Intimacy, after all, begins face to face, not genital to genital. The genital expression of intimacy, when it is a vehicle of affection and concern and not a vehicle of exploitation, is a result of the relationship.

The romantic love of adolescence and courtship is also not to be confused with emotional intimacy. Intimacy requires years of shared experience and emotional vicissitudes for solid trust and confidence to build. Romantic love is a necessary bridge between the security and affection of our family of origin and the eventual security and affection that will come from our family of procreation. It gives us something to be secure about in that interim when we belong to no family but on our own seek out a mate to eventually begin one. People fall in and out of romantic love. While there are some nurturant elements, these stem from a desperate need to validate oneself and are basically unilateral expectations. Intimate mutuality can only evolve from long-term shared experience. The potential for true intimate relationship, therefore, fundamentally exists in a marriage and family where the true sharing of experience can occur over the years. Of course, the fact that one is married or part of the family does not in itself ensure shared experience. This is only true of functional marriages and families. In dysfunctional marriages and families one finds total strangers, by no means intimately related to one another but only living together under the same roof.

Romantic love is a necessary bridge between parental love and marital love. It is often the forerunner, the springboard from which the intimate and nurturant love of an enduring and shared marital experience derives. A romantic attachment is an illusion of intimacy, a false, unreal, and overidealized relationship that is basically a desperate mutual admiration society. This kind of attachment gives a temporary meaning and value to a beginning heterosexual relationship from which a negotiated, realistic, and committed intimacy can emerge. This can occur only if mutual commitment, responsibility, and honest negotiation are central to the latter development of the relationship.

Our Emotional Humanness

To all appearances the human individual has a rather critical need for closeness, emotional warmth, and protection in his relationships with another. When this becomes a part of the shared experience of a relationship, it leads to confidence and, as Eric Berne would put it, "a relaxed spine." It results in that confident glow of worthiness as a human being as a part of a relationship with another and, within the context of the family, as part of a larger system.

At the same time the emotional nature of man also presents the potential for vulnerability. When one is close to and confident with another, one is also very open and revealing of oneself. In terms of a relationship reciprocity, each partner is most vulnerable to the other because of this very closeness. To allow oneself to be undefended in revealing and sharing, is also to risk being vulnerable to the negative feelings of the other. If the feelings of the other, whether positive or negative, can be accepted, as Virginia Satir says, as a gift rather than as an assault, relationship is enhanced. Risk, revelation, and lack of defensiveness are not, in reality, a kind of vulnerability to anything but nurturance, growth, and satisfying joint outcome.

If such vulnerability to the feelings of the other leads to self-disappointment (because our cherished illusions are challenged), this disappointment may be construed as attack and interpreted as self-annihilation. This fear may stem from the disappointments we experience when the other does not live up to our expectations.

Even in a close and reliable relationship, constant individual growth of the two partners is always taking place. They are forever changing, growing, expanding—not only from the family relationship but from outside relationships as well. This means we can consistently predict our or other's behavior only to a limited degree. We are limited by the very nature of human growth. This growth risk, however, can, to a large degree, be ameliorated by checking out meaning with the other, by constantly using an emotional and communicational feedback, so that we know the other not only from our perceptions of them but from their own self-revelations. Relationship expectation is therefore based on reality rather than wish or image. Relationship can only progress and evolve with time if the persons involved risk and grow rather than play it safe and stagnate.

Perhaps the basic dilemma of emotional intimacy in marriage and family relationships is its achievement without loss of personal identity, that is, for one to be intimately related to another and still be an integrated self, separate from the other. This, in a sense, is the functional ideal of human relationship: to experience emotional intimacy that supports identity—and gives the kind of confidence and support that allows openness and shared experience with one another—and the capacity to leave the other and operate confidently in other relationships. To know oneself is to experience self from our inner feelings and as the significant persons in our life respond to us openly and honestly. We are not only what our inner feelings and thoughts are but what our behavior is and how other people react to it. In a sense, they serve as mirrors to oneself; they give an opportunity to view oneself from an outside point of observation. We can then correct our own personal distortions, see ourselves more accurately, and relate to another in terms of the reality of that relationship, rather than our fantasy of how we hope it will be.

When we risk being open and honest with another, we experience more directly the inherent human differentness between ourself as a husband and other as a wife, between ourself as a father and the other as a child, and so on. But this risk is also the beginning of creative identity. As we share ourselves openly and directly with another, they may accept us for what we indeed are. We can, in turn, take their reflections on us as an attempt to promote shared experience and develop a confident and realistic idea of ourself as a person. Emotional intimacy, then, comes from this openness and sharing. When we realize the true qualities of the other person we can more easily relate in a warm, close, and affectionate way to them. This becomes a part of the mutual experience of the relationship that builds confidence, loyalty, and satisfaction. At this point we become more a part of the life of the other, while at the same time continuing to possess our own unique qualities. We gain the confidence and support to be a unique identity as well as part of a meaningful intimate relationship.

There is a common saying that "familiarity breeds contempt." Is this what happens in a close relationship after years of shared experience? Does the familiarity, the knowing of the other person, the awareness of their true qualities breed contempt? Or does the saying refer to the familiarity of a shared experience that has been deceptive, closed, unrevealing, and basically defensive? Perhaps familiarity brings about the disillusionment of dysfunctional and often neurotic change fantasies we have about ourselves and family members. If romantic love does not evolve into something more intimate and realistic, it becomes the springboard of an "illusion of fusion." It results in an expectation of survival because we cling so tenaciously and desperately to one another as to become one. We hope the other will be responsible entirely for our support and growth, but often they have the same fantasied expectation. In such a relationship whatever qualities are seen as negative and undesirable in the other will be thought to change as the result of love. This, however, is unilateral selfish love that is labeled noble but in reality covers up a desperate need for unilateral self-vindication.

There are periods in all marital and family relationships (usually around the birth of children or when they leave the family to go to school or to assume a career) when we have expectations that are not fulfilled, when we feel disillusioned and let down. Intimacy, after all, is forever building and changing. We do not come full-blown functionally into a relationship; we must build it through intimacy, and we must be aware of the human tendency toward disillusionment when our self-vindicating fantasies are not met. It is, rather, a fantasy of familiarity that breeds contempt.

There is an apparent dilemma in intimate relationships that involves the qualities of closeness that present both the potential for vulnerability and the protection from loneliness. If one keeps safely apart from another in order not to be hurt or to have one's expectations disrupted, one loses any potential for support or reinforcement of intrinsic worth as a human being. Any contempt that stems from familiarity represents a failure to establish esteem and identity on the basis of sameness. Differentness cannot be seen as true uniqueness but as a threat to one's own cherished self-aggrandizement. If one must fuse with another to feel worthwhile, there is neither identity or intimacy, only evasion, denial, and suppression of one another's real qualities in order to maintain the fused state. This is, of course, impossible to maintain, except for severely emotionally disturbed people.

The Past and Present Dilemma

Intimacy is always possible with all human beings, yet it is remarkable the number of persons whose relationships produce more dysfunctional outcome than functional outcome, where closeness is viewed as threat, and where sameness and detachment are considered protection from hurt.

We often tend to emotionally predict the future and the present in terms of the past. As intelligent human beings, we apply our logical and inductive powers to our past experience in order to deal with the present and future. We have a foresightful ability to anticipate the future and to project plans into the future. With emotional relationships, however, this often leads us to overlook the obviousness of the present and miss the opportunity of seeing it as a unique transaction between ourselves and another that can be dealt with in terms of its own manifest behavior. We look to the past and we hope for the future, but we tend to evade the present. In so doing, the present may turn out dysfunctionally. We confuse similar experience (reacting to hurt) with identical experience ("It's just like childhood"); realistic solution is submerged for neurotic reenactment of earlier, unresolved conflict. The present problem may, in fact, go unresolved in favor of a unilateral self-protective and self-righteous defense of our personal esteem. The result is dysfunctional to satisfactory joint outcome. The unsatisfying present becomes, in turn, part of our past, which we project into the future in terms of a negative expectation. We are on the interpersonal merry-go-round illustrated in Figure 16.

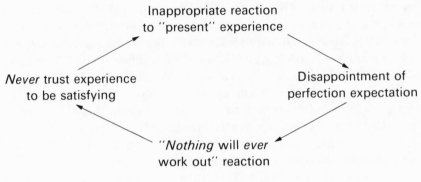

Figure 16

If our past experiences have been negative, we tend to anticipate and expect that present and future experiences, especially in human relationships, will also be negative. We have a remarkable but dysfunctional ability to engage in self-fulfilling prophecies. This means that if we expect relationships to turn out badly, we behave in such manner as to bring about the very result we fear. Instead of culminating our relationships as a satisfied but ordinary person, we end up as unhappy but accurate prophets. Psychologically, we control our destiny, even in determining how many relationship tragedies we are to experience in a given year. Precipitous hurt and rejection is replaced with unconsciously calculated and expected disaster.

In previous chapters various patterns of human relationship within marriage and the family have been explained and illustrated, with their crucial, perpetuating nature; that is, if a young man who anticipates a negative relationship in his marriage eventually marries, he strongly tends to marry a woman who, in fact, will help him to realize this dysfunctional ambition. For self-fulfilling prophecies to materialize, it is necessary within human relationship to have an active and willing collaborator. If we are to understand marital and family relationships, we must focus on not only what the persons bring to the marriage, but more importantly how marital partners collaborate together to perpetuate a dysfunctional pattern. They can compulsively repeat their childhood experiences within their current family, only if their spouse or children help them to perpetuate this expectation within the family. All the dysfunctional patterns presented in this book can be resolved by breaking the perpetuating cycle in the relationship, so that a new alternative is called for in the behavior pattern.

Often persons in marital and family relationships cannot refocus on other possible alternatives in their relationship. I would question for example, whether a person labeled as a masochist actually enjoys suffering in relationships or whether he is unaware of an alternative way of relating.* (Remember the "Joan of Arc Rides Again" pattern.) The suffering mother, the pained father, and the hurt child do not behave that way because they need to suffer emotionally but because they seem unaware of any other alterna-. tive in the relationship. If persons have been brought up in a family where they have been a scapegoat, the butt of hostility, and never praised or admired, they expect such treatment from all people. They feel it is their just due, their lot in life, and they may know no other alternative from their experience.

If one operates on the basis of past experience only, it becomes apparent that one exists in relative ignorance of other possible, and perhaps more functional, alternative ways of relating. Intimacy is not possible to any significant degree where there is eternal confusion of past and present. In a dysfunctional marital or family relationship, one can only build up shared experiences of threat, not of closeness, warmth, and protection. This, again, is the kind of familiarity that breeds contempt and not intimacy.

While we seek to be secure by being able to predict our future, we may evade and ignore immediate reality. This excuses us from responsibility to negotiate outcome and places it potentially in the hands of self-fulfilling prophecies. We may feel secure in our prophetic ability but very shortly end up feeling quite insecure in a basically nonintimate and dysfunctional relationship. To be a successful prophet of doom is hardly a satisfying experience. It is, perhaps, the self-vindicating achievement of having been right at the expense of foregoing any potential for a negotiated and deeply satisfying intimacy.

---

* Originally the term masochism specifically applied to a sexual deviation in which sexual pleasure and satisfaction were derived from physical abuse by another. We may have misapplied this label to a person who behaved as if he could only suffer in general in his relationship with another.

Intimacy in Marriage and Family Living

The feature that inhibits the growth of intimacy in many marriages and families is infantile disillusionment and disappointment of hopeful expectations of an ideal, exclusive relationship with another. These expectations are constantly bombarded with reality changes that make their realization impossible. We seem to regard such disappointments as threats to intimacy in marriage and the family, because of our common delusional conviction that only "perfectness" and complete fulfillment in a relationship represent intimacy. Any lack of perfection must be repudiated and displaced as a disappointment, rather than a false and unreal narcissistic expectation. In other words, if the person or persons in our meaningful emotional lives do not live up to our expectations, it is they who are disappointing us, not our inability to accept changing reality—physical and emotional—and deal with it. Our ability to deal with such changing reality evolves around our willingness to accept the present for what it is and to work with the other toward a negotiated outcome based on what fits rather than on manipulation. Intimacy emerges from a shared experience of relationship awareness, negotiation of joint outcome, and mutual responsibility.

Three fundamental areas of unexpected change occur in the history of marriage and family life that are emotionally significant to the intimacy of the marital partners.

1. The realization that one's spouse does not change because you are in love with one another. Change in a relationship can only occur through negotiation and patience. A marital relationship represents not an exclusive parent–child prototype but a meeting of two uniquely different adults who need one another's care, concern, and nurturance. The awareness of the love-change myth occurs shortly after the marriage has taken place and has been described earlier in this chapter.

2. The coming of children into the family presents a basic disruption in the original exclusive marital pair relationship (mutual adult—adult caretaking).

3. As the marriage progresses, there is a gradual separation of responsibility for family functions and work between the husband and wife. This leads to different spheres of influence and activity

but further tends to separate and differentiate the relationship between husband and wife. Some married people experience this
progressive differentiation as a lessening of intimacy between them.

The responsibility for children interrupts for a considerable
period of time the exclusive marital relationship. Unless each spouse
in the marital relationship can face the additional problem of how
to make room psychologically for three instead of two, they will
experience the coming of children as a critical disruption of their
own marital intimacy. The more desperate their emotional needs
to foster an exclusive relationship with one another through the
marriage, the more they will experience the coming of the child as
a break in that rather idyllic arrangement. In fact, the early years of
the marriage when there is only an exclusive marital pair resembles
to a degree the kind of early exclusive parenting that a child receives from his parents. As adults, however, married couples alternate in giving and receiving. Early in the marriage there are no other
responsibilities to interfere with this. Primarily each gives exclusively
to the other in the hope of "making him happy." If negotiation of
joint outcome does not begin very early in the relationship, needs
will be met entirely on the *assumption* of love and concern, rather
than awareness and negotiation of differentness. With the arrival
of children, the failure to give exclusively to the spouse may be
interpreted as a breakdown of love and concern.

With the coming of children, the parents need to work out the
problem of making room for another and then later two and perhaps three more. This, however, greatly complicates the original
exclusive dyad that was the marriage. In Figure 17 it is easy to see
how the simple dyad of the marriage is turned into a thrice-compli-
cated triad with the coming of only one child. The presence of two

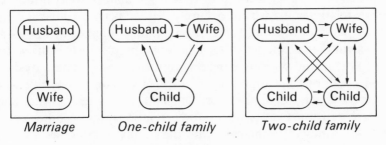

Marriage   One-child family   Two-child family

Figure 17

children is six times more complicated in terms of mutual relationships than was the original simple marital dyad. The progression of emotional and interactional complexity in family relationships increases as a geometric rather than an arithmetic function. Making room for the other means that one is required to develop multiple and shifting dyadic relationships to numerous others in one's family in addition to the originally chosen spouse. There is no reason, however, why intimacy cannot become an aspect of *all* these relationships rather than simply the marital relationship. The kind of intimacy characteristic of a marital pair is, of course, not the same kind characteristic of a parent–child relationship. Different kinds and levels of intimacy must develop.

The spouses will need to concentrate and to work together on differentiating between their marital and familial intimacy. They must evolve a way to regard both as important, for each is both spouse and parent. Neither emotional commitment need be diminished for the sake of the other, except in emergencies when extra support and attention is necessary (e.g., sickness, physical injury, and the death loss of friends and relatives.)

If the commitment to parental obligation is seen as secondary, rather than equal to, marital obligation, the result is defective parenting of dependent children. If the commitment to marital obligation is seen as secondary rather than equal to parental obligation, the result is a gradual breakdown of marital intimacy. If spouses do not meet one another's, as well as their children's, needs, the children often become displacement objects for the lack of marital need satisfaction. This, in turn, may lead to family "splits"— exclusive pairs or triads relatively unrelated to the remainder of the family. Such splits represent exclusive relationships within the family and are a psychological unreality in view of the interlocking reciprocity of the relationship system. Attempts to continue exclusive relationships within a family, either between husband and wife or parent and child, represent a dysfunctional coalition within the system that precludes other relationships and fosters the setting up of hostile and warring camps within the family. These dysfunctional coalitions are especially disruptive to family security when they cross generational lines (e.g., husband–daughter vs. wife–son).

Each self must invest in multiple relationships of differing degrees and kinds of intimacy within the family. It becomes a matter of assuming "we are surviving physically and emotionally together."

In primarily functional families psychological survival is enhanced by virtue of different kinds of intimate relationships within the family. There is more growth of individual identities when differentness is used to enlarge and expand a view of oneself and in the variety of our relatedness to others. One can derive worth and meaning from a relationship with the spouse as well as from the child without overprotecting and living off the accomplishments of the child or demanding to be overinfantalized by the spouse.

It is helpful for the parents to be consciously aware of the dilemmas and the challenges that come with children's entering the family system. They must recognize and specifically concentrate on the necessity for maintaining a marital responsibility toward one another along with parental responsibilities. They can direct and concentrate efforts to enjoy one another intimately, both emotionally and physically, in addition to meeting the rather sizable tasks and responsibilities involved in the parenting of children. With the gradual separation of responsibilities and spheres of influence in the family between husband and wife, they must be alert not to let these responsibilities come to represent a separation of intimacy between the two of them. Again, room must be made for both kinds of relationships within the family. This quite obviously is not an easy task; it is a most difficult one and part of the responsibility that comes with marriage and parenthood. If it is overlooked it will lead gradually to dysfunctional separation between husband and wife, which will then come to a crisis point when the children leave the home and the marital pair discover they no longer have a meaningful relationship to one another. It is also quite valuable for children to directly observe the intimate relationship of the parents to one another exclusive of physical sexuality. They learn from this that one may relate in an intimate fashion, that closeness, touching, support, and comfort are part of human relationship. The parents serve as a model with this for their children whether they wish to or not. Physical sexuality, however, remains the exclusive and special separate part of the intimacy of the parents that is not shared with the children. It remains the private and exclusive intimacy of the parents.

The nature of human relationship in marriage and the family does not preclude intimacy realization, but neither does it guarantee it. Intimacy is the shared experience of awareness, negotiation, and honest commitment. It is tempered by the everyday realities of living together that diminish unreal hopes and wishes but is enhanced by mutual and realistic efforts. Neurotic expectation and manipulation destroy the potential for intimacy, while open self-revelation promotes its attainment. Intimacy is forever building and changing, or it is substituted by disillusionment and despair. Foremost, intimacy is the result of joint struggle and awareness; it is not an expected outcome but evolves from determined effort.

Chapter 20

Technology and Human Relationship

Man's inventive technology forever changes the methods and ways in which he can meet his needs. Man's human emotional nature, however, remains relatively the same. His wants for sense and order, productivity, and intimacy remain, and his need for psychological survival continues to exist. Technology represents a challenge to rigid and stereotyped behavioral customs: It forever forces upon us the recognition that needs may be met in a variety of ways. There may exist, in fact, no single best way. What is crucial is not the technology as such but the way in which man uses it. The question is not whether technology goes hand in hand with progressive alienation between people but whether man, if he wishes to alienate himself from another, can use his technology as a barrier in a relationship as well as an instrument to gratify his needs.

Man both designs and programs his machines. If science fiction becomes science nonfiction, as it does to a surprising degree, man will eventually design machines to build, program, and repair all his other machines. Part of his responsibility for decision may be given over to a sophisticated machine. But how much, when, and in what way still remains his responsibility. Man has the fundamental choice when he assigns responsibility to machines. He may abdicate and evade his own responsibility or he may not. This is a human choice and a quality of man. The methods and means of applied technology as it touches on man's relationship to spouse and child, lover and dependent, remains man's choice.

May I Introduce You to Yourself?

One of the results of our greater use of technology is the increase in leisure time. There has also been a corollary increase in time members of a family or marriage spend with one another without critical responsibility for essential physical survival. The machine has freed us from arduous labor and leaves us face to face with one another without a responsible task to bind the relationship with purpose and meaning. The characteristic American setting at the turn of the century was primarily rural and task-oriented to "getting the job done." Relationships were predictable, highly structured, and held a common purpose in the joint labor of the family toward economic survival. When we became urban, technological, and more economically secure, the era of the fat American was ushered in. Exercise is not as often provided through our daily work but more through our recreation and leisure. The family no longer has the common economic purpose they all directly worked on together as they used to. Joint family activities now tend to show up in the area of leisure time, rather than in day-to-day work. The day-to-day activities of the family are likely to be quite uniquely different from one another. The home has come to represent more of a physical location for emotional security and nurturance than the arena of the actual physical work of the family as the farm did.

Many people comment that "the machine alienates man." The question is sometimes raised whether the time we have now to really know one another better often ends in alienation because man cannot use his human relationships constructively. Is there something we are unaware of in human relationships, especially within a marriage or a family, that prevents us from making the maximum survival use of these relationships? Why does it seem so difficult for some persons to feel satisfied and nurtured? Why, at times, do they become so easily alienated from spouses and children?

Only recently have we begun to look at what human relationship is and how we can become more aware of its constructive achievement, which is often influenced by irrational elements. Each of us lacks by our very human construction one vital ability in perpetuating a positive relationship, the ability to see ourselves, from a point of observation outside ourself, as we affect the other; that is, to see us in the relationship with other as other is able to see us. I do not mean by this the capacity for empathy or the capacity to put one's self in the other guy's shoes but more the real objective capacity to view ourselves and the relationship as an observer outside of self and the relationship. This can be more easily understood if we keep in mind several very basic facts: We cannot literally see ourself as others do because our eyes are inside our head and we are looking out. Even when we look into a mirror, we see a reversed image. Nor can we hear ourselves as others do, because when we talk the sound of our voice resonates within our skull. The voice does not sound the same to us as it does to another person. We lose the basic objective viewpoint that comes from the subtle nonverbal clues to the relationship that are embodied in voice tones and facial expressions. We cannot accurately perceive the "observable self" and are then aware of how we seem to the other and how we affect that relationship.

Without the ability to actually see ourselves functioning from an observer position, we limit the amount of informational feedback we can use to correct and alter our own ways of relating when there are dysfunctional elements in our relationship to another. The use of videotape for home and office has given us a valuable tool. Videotape apparatus is now coming into wide use in the mental health professions. One can, in a very significant sense, see an instant replay of relationship behavior within seconds or minutes after it actually occurs. Its value is immeasurable in aiding members of a dysfunctional family system to view themselves for the first time outside of their own self-system. Ian Alger, a psychiatrist in New York City, often uses videotape playback with families he sees. They not only view their own behavior shortly after it happens, but he also allows them to do some of the video filming. By doing this they gain a new awareness and sensitivity, especially to the nonverbal forms of communication between members of a family. Using a similar apparatus, Norman Paul of the Tufts Medical School in Boston attempts to reach people who are inhibited and resistant about revealing their deeper feelings. He exposes them to segments of videotape of other individuals who can openly express their psychological pain. These tapes permit a stimulus toward and identification with the process of open self-revelation. There is often a rapid empathy with the more expressive, but "pained" other that helps to break down the barriers of inhibition in the observing person.

Both of the above examples illustrate ways in which a technological apparatus can be used to help man become more aware of himself, to develop a sensitivity to the nature of his relationship with others in his intimate family and marriage, and to learn how to express oneself more openly and honestly. In this way technology is not an evasion of, but an aid toward, a more constructive use of humanness and intimacy. Self-viewing is a serious use of videotape. It is not important that one sees oneself on television as a narcissistic gratification; its importance lies in the opportunity to become more aware of oneself in our relationship to others. If videotape in this use becomes an entertainment, it loses its self-awareness quality and becomes an intimacy evasion and medium of aggrandizement. If the use of videotape becomes an "I can't bear to watch it" phenomenon, we only deceive ourselves. We cannot turn off or deny what other can so easily view and what might well be a significant part of the relationship. Only we can alienate our *observable self* from our *acceptable self*. Videotape viewing offers us that rare and heretofore unrealized opportunity to confront one with oneself and from this confrontation to enhance the potential to change and alter oneself to relate more functionally to others.

Sex, the Pill, and Intimacy

The widespread use of the oral contraceptive, often called "the pill," has ushered in an era of both anxiety over its possible uses and reduction of anxiety in regard to an unexpected pregnancy. Some have become concerned that the widespread use of the pill will also usher in an era of unprecedented immorality. There does appear to be some correlation between the improved reliability of contraception during the past three decades and a corresponding change toward more liberal and open sexual *attitudes*. However, there is little evidence to indicate that *behavior* has changed appreciably over this period of time. Kinsey's studies in the 1950s provided information that indicated that our spoken attitudes and beliefs did not always match our actual behavior. What was often frowned on in attitude was rather common behavior in actuality. We seem to have been more constricted in attitude than we were in behavior, and this was, at best, a self-deception.

As contraceptive devices became more reliable and effective, fears of unplanned for and unwanted pregnancies subsided. With this, some persons feared that easy sex would become all too prevalent. The pill was designated as the culprit. Numerous persons have been concerned on the surface about sexual morality; underneath they really seem to be anxious about a more fundamental social problem—the care and responsibility for the illegitimate child. It may be questioned whether these persons are really against private sexual experience as long as no illegitimate child results. However, until reliable contraceptives were available, illegitimate childbirth was always a significant possiblilty. An unwanted child was often the result of passion, poor control, or plain indiscriminate sexual behavior. Was premarital sex undesirable or immoral because of some basic quality of premarital sex or because of the real possibility of an insoluble social problem? Abortion leaves emotional as well as physical scars. Forced marriages are often dysfunctional marriages.

Only within the marriage or the family did the potential exist for mutual caretaking and protective child rearing. These two basic functions of marriage and the family are crucial to the ultimate security and stability of a human person. Children who do not have both parents or who do not have a stable and responsible family environment experience significantly more emotional problems than children who do have these benefits. A child born into an existing marriage or family also assumed reproductive legitimacy. More important, however, was the provision of responsible caretaking and child rearing. The real emphasis, therefore, appeared to be on providing the child with a solid emotional base for his future emotional security through the social regulation of reproduction. It was assumed that if a prohibition existed, at least on paper, against premarital (or extramarital) sexual experience, there would be some inhibition of desperate adolescent passion or lonely despair that would prevent the possibility of an illegitimate child.

The contraceptive pill made it quite apparent that it would be possible for couples to enjoy full genital sexuality prior to marriage with complete protection from a possible unexpected pregnancy. The pill, to a large degree, does away with the concerns about social responsibility for the potential child. Of course, while the pill is almost foolproof, fools are not. Pregnancies occur if the pill is not taken, forgotten, or unconsciously avoided in order to force a reluctant lover into a marriage or a despairing marriage into "joyous" parenthood. Many of the problems the unwanted child has posed in the past will now gradually begin to diminish. Sexuality without reproduction is now possible with reliable predictability.

It is assumed by some that immorality will now increase. In this way of thinking, immorality is viewed as consistent with direct sexual expression prior to marriage and, subsequently, an ever-increasing behavioral pattern of acting out impulses without regard to their consequences. This, it is feared, may lead to less stability and responsibility in human relationships.

One other important change has occurred that may be relevant to the progressive liberalization and openness in regard to sexuality prior to marriage. Reproductive maturity in the human body occurs in early adolescence, for girls, usually between ages eleven and fourteen, for boys, usually between the ages of thirteen and sixteen. Before reliable contraceptives were available, after these ages, the potential of the illegitimate child was present. At one time, however, the persons married a great deal younger than they do at present. The gradual increase of the age of marriage has been brought about in large part by the extension of the educational process for youth in our culture. When the eighth-grade education was typical, a youth could move out into the labor market and assume economic responsibilities for a family at a much younger age. As the length of education has increased in this country, so has the discrepancy between the age of reproductive adequacy and the age of assumption of economic responsibility.

At the present time the American ideal is completion of a basic four-year college education. In fact, in the past seventy-five years our educational expectations have increased approximately eight years, creating the additional dilemma of exposing youth to eight more years of natural biological urges and desires that must be rather stringently controlled until economic responsibility is achieved and a marriage and a family can be adequately supported without financial stress and worry. We have expected, to an extent, that a youth will be able to forestall his own increasingly strong biological urges while he seeks eventual economic responsibility under the dependency of his parents. It is not at all clear whether this has worked out as well in actuality as it has in theory. It has pitted biological maturity against foresightful economic hope, perhaps an unfair pairing in view of the natural attractiveness of sexual experience versus the unrealized potential of the completed college education. It is also quite apparent that the pill truly represents the possibility of completing one's expected education and allowing sexual satisfaction without any discrepancy between hoped-for economic outcome and sexual needs.

At one time we regarded kissing on the lips as immoral, improper, and the first stages of moral decay. Today this is rather openly and commonly accepted by the great majority of people as a suitable aspect of an expression of the physical relationship between adolescent youth. Indeed, it seems quite possible that the widespread use of the pill may eventually make sexual intercourse as common in the future as kissing is now. It is entirely possible that the technology (the pill) that has resulted from increased understanding of the metabolic functioning of a woman, will make possible a continued liberalizing and changing of *attitudes and behavior* about the expression of sexuality. The real question may not be morality versus reality so much as how comfortable we are with our own sexuality and the correlation between sexuality and intimate human relationship.

Moral, technological, and emotional considerations in human sexuality prior to and during marriage have often been confused as these have been affected and altered by the pill. Is it a matter of good or bad? How can we understand the pill's implications for responsibility in human relationship? Does the lessening of traditional sexual morality preclude responsibility in human relationship? What connections are there between a technical device (the pill), relationship outcome (marriage), and social outcome (interpersonal responsibility)? The confusion to some degree results from the association of sexuality with intimacy and, in fact, at times defining intimacy in terms of sexuality. However, it is quite clear that intimacy can exist without sexuality and that sexuality can exist without intimacy. In the relationship sense, intimacy is a shared experience of thinking and feeling, of knowing the other person in depth as a total person through shared vicissitudes and joys. If sexual contact between two persons in a relationship is taken as a necessary prerequisite to intimacy, the cart has been put before the horse. In most deeply intimate human relationships sexuality emerges from that intimacy and becomes a part of it, but it is not to be confused with intimacy exclusively. (See Figure 18.)

(A)   SEXUALITY ⟶ INTIMACY   =   "RELATIONSHIP"?

(B)   INTIMACY ⟶ SEXUALITY   =   RELATIONSHIP

Figure 18

In (A) of Figure 18 sexuality is used as an inducement for supposed subsequent intimacy. Often it is a bribe out of desperation. ("I will only love you if you have sex with me" or "He can only love me if I allow him to have sex with me.") These relationships usually, if not always, terminate in suspicion, distrust, and eventual disillusionment, as the question invariably arises afterward as to whom this has gone on with before. Intimacy cannot derive from initial sexuality unless the intimacy has already been well established before. Let's not confuse experimentation and hormonal secretion with intimacy. This is a form of exploitation either by mutual collusion or unilateral need desperation. In (B) the intimacy of the relationship precedes the sexuality, and the sexuality evolves from it. When people begin to know one another closely and become concerned in each other's mutual welfare, the nurturant and supportive elements of the relationship eventually reveal themselves in physical nurturing, including mutual sexuality.

One can compare the two sequences in Figure 18 by saying that (A) represents "being screwed" while (B) represents sexual intercourse. Intercourse implies mutuality and relationship; being screwed implies unilateral, but perhaps joint, lust. (Similarly, preschoolers who play in the same sandbox at the same time and enjoy the activity as such do not have any relationship with one another. Their being together avoids loneliness only.) With the increasing use of the pill one might suppose to some degree that there will be an increased confusion between sexuality and intimacy. The opportunity of sexuality preceding intimacy without fear of childbirth will, no doubt, be common. It may then become a matter of whether mutual exploitation and experimentation are to be taken as intimacy. Freedom of expression and appropriate and responsible use of self-expression may be confused. The real issue is how one builds a trusting, confident, and mutual relationship as opposed to unilateral self-aggrandizement through collaborative exploitation. The latter is really a form of mutual masturbation through the collaborative use of genitals instead of hands. The essence of intimacy is the depth of regard and mutuality one has with another in a relationship. This certainly allows room for sexuality but, again, as the result of, rather than the cause of, intimacy. One does not come to know a person nearly so well by sharing genitals as by sharing a very wide range of experiences, thoughts, and feelings over a long period of time. Intimacy cannot develop in weeks, months, or even in several years.

It is entirely possible that use of the pill might be a symptom of the evasion of intimacy in the same way that a kiss on the second date is. Obviously there can be no substantial intimacy at the end of a second date, yet the mutual kiss serves as a physical reassurance that each is able to show some affection, however shallow and superficial, and to receive such as a validation to some degree of one's self-worth. But this is not intimacy. In much the same way, sexuality in relationship still requires emotional maturity if it is to result in a trusting, confident relationship that in the long run supports and enhances self-esteem.

We are gradually coming to accept talking and thinking about sexuality and its pleasures more readily, openly, and realistically. This may not be so much a change in behavior as a change in the open manifestation of attitudes and beliefs. A more open and honest awareness of self as a sexual person in a relationship may be revealed. Pills do not, however, remove responsibility and honest awareness; only persons can do that. The pill provides only protection from precipitous reproduction, not reciprocal commitment and mutual caretaking. Brazen exhibitionism is not to be confused with intimacy, confidence, or self-esteem.

Within the marital relationship the use of the pill can unquestionably relieve a great many anxieties over precipitous and unplanned childbirth. It can enhance the sexual relationship between husband and wife toward a more open, enjoyable, and relaxed experience. Sexual love making (not the only kind of love making) can be a part of planned reproduction by choice rather than chance. At other times sexuality can become part of the relationship experience without any connection to reproduction, part of the total intercourse of the relationship.

It is obviously no longer true of our physical survival as a species that reproduction need be random and indiscriminate, occurring by chance in order to sustain the species. We are troubled now by overpopulation and impending fears of extinction by competitive overcrowding, not by a progressive lessening of people. The pill can increase the comfortableness of the marital sexual relationship and lead to purposeful, planned, and, therefore, more spontaneous acceptance of, children. Children can then be the result of mutual planning at a point in the dyadic relationship when there is room for one more.

Marital and family life was instituted in part, to enhance our chances for psychological survival. This in no way conflicts with our evolving technology. In our marital and family relationships, and in the human relationships that precede them, we are the ones who choose how this technology is to be used. It can lead to an enhancement or an inhibition of the relationship; this remains our choice and responsibility. We can either increase our awareness of our self and our relationship with others, as was illustrated by the use of videotape, or we can defensively regard such innovations as an invasion of our privacy and miss this opportunity. By the same token, our use of the pill can be one of the ways to enhance our achievement of intimacy in our premarital and marital relationships, or we can use it to disguise mutual exploitation and unilateral self-aggrandizement under the name of intimacy. In essence, any problem of technology and human relationships, premarital, marital, or familial is not a question of machines, pills, and sexual organs but of awareness, responsibility, and honest commitment.

Chapter 21

Family Dysfunction:
Dilemma or Challenge?

Toleration and Forbearance or Promotion
of Emotional Growth

When individual members of a family system feel it is necessary to put up with behavior that is upsetting, painful, or otherwise dysfunctional, they assume a lack of more functional alternatives in their living together. They may have the patience to tolerate the status quo of their relationships with one another, but they do not seem to have the patience and awareness to work with the essential "humanness" of persons in a relationship. Essential humanness includes resistance to change, fear of risk, needs to be cared for and feel worthwhile, protection of one's cherished hopes and values, and irrational defensiveness when under attack. These are characteristics we all possess, and they enter into all relationship behavior and outcome. However, these characteristics of our humanness are counterbalanced by a capacity for spontaneity, awareness, flexibility, and rational negotiation. It is often a matter of which characteristics are focused on in the relationship consciously and with purpose. The impulsive relationship, often called spontaneous, is based on an unconscious program based on past experience and is without a purposeful focus on here-and-now awareness and negotiation. Alternatives to conflict and disillusionment are blocked by the compulsive repetition of previously learned assumptions of relationship.

While ignorance and lack of experience may help create the illusion of a lack of more functional alternatives in a disturbed relationship, dysfunction is more likely to come from self-centered, vested interests and a need for unilateral realization. No matter how noble, righteous, or intellectually rational a facade we erect, we obscure from our awareness other alternatives to the relationship. If self is viewed only in a unilateral relationship to other, mutual reciprocity is ignored for the hope of unique self-satisfaction.

Our childhood family experiences often help to develop this unilateral principle. There is a great emphasis in our culture on individual attainment and achievement. "Getting along" is stressed, but as a ploy to make the other person think you are nice and acceptable, worthy, helpful, courteous, kind, etc. There is no mutuality here, only unilateral manipulation in the form of a personal public relations program—getting along with others in order to get what you want. If we understand humanness, we understand that such unilateral expectation is one of our more fundamental desires in interpersonal relations. Disguising this unilateral expectation in noble and elegant facades of self-deception is not understanding humanness, however. It is more important to accept this expectation as human and to use it in a mutually beneficial way. While we can accept our wanting exclusive satisfaction in a relationship as wanting self-centered validation of our identity, we are aware that only mutual negotiation and openness will result in actual attainment of this want. When we commit ourselves, for whatever reasons, to a relationship, we are stuck with the consequences of a reciprocal system, not a unilateral, self-system. The outcome of a relationship is far more than the summation of the individuals involved.

We do not need to tolerate dysfunctional behavior; we can promote emotional growth within marriages and families. But in order to guarantee emotional growth and satisfaction, it is imperative to recognize that any relationship system becomes functional because of several well-defined reasons.

1. The joint outcome of the relationship is worked at. Satisfactory joint outcome does not come easily; it must be accomplished through open negotiation and requires both considerable effort and patience. The results are not manipulated, but *risk is taken* with basic and very personal feelings to insure the negotiation

will result in an outcome that emotionally fits the people involved.

2. The system will remain functional only as long as there is a constant vigilance and observation of its own functioning. In essence, this means that communicational feedback is used constantly to evaluate joint outcomes, the feelings of individuals, and points of crucial conflict that may be negotiated rather than evaded.

3. Difficulties are to be expected. The marriage or the family is not romanticized on the basis of projected wishes but is seen as a system of unique, faulty human beings struggling together for a common psychological survival. There is nothing noble, romantic, or satisfying about this, *unless* the persons involved work *actively* toward a satisfying joint outcome.

4. There is a confidence among the persons in the system that the relationships and the persons will survive, both physically and psychologically, if they mutually accept responsibility for joint outcome.

Without the above conditions the family all too easily becomes a dysfunctional and irrational system—one based on unconscious assumptions that are never openly spoken about and feelings of unilateral desperation that structure the rules of relationship within the marriage or family. Under these circumstances, there will only be a perpetuation of dysfunctional behavior and outcome from day to day within the family and a propagation of dysfunctional expectation and behavior from generation to generation.]

While persons may tolerate dysfunctional behavior on the erroneous assumption that some relationship is better than none at all, the basic result of an irrational behavioral system is mutual psychological self-destruction. Man has both physical and psychological needs for survival; he may survive physically but exist without meaning and purpose. Psychological self-destruction in the irrational system has three primary features.

1. Irrational systems are governed by an assumption of threat and defended against by continuous counterattack. Relationships within this system, therefore, are basically attacking and defending rather than nurturing.

2. The fundamental rule of an irrational system is to protect yourself and to strike the other before you are emotionally annihilated. Such a fundamental rule is rejection provoking by its very nature and, thus, is destructive to any attempt at mutual relationship.

3. The irrational system in time results in a fundamentally paranoid life experience that is serially perpetuated. In other words, the more you attack to protect yourself the more others see you as attacking and, in fact, do reject you (in order to protect themselves). The fear that you must always defend against attack is, therefore, realized by your own provocation. The conviction develops that you cannot trust, rely on, or be open with the so-called intimate others of your marriage and family. Since your defense activates their attack and vice versa, it is a serial perpetuation of dysfunctional outcome.

If persons in an irrational relationship system put up with their dysfunctional outcome, they continue to perpetuate the very process that is destroying their mutual relationship and individual identity. They can only come to eventually lose meaning and purpose in their human relations. This need not be tolerated. Forbearance and patience are unnecessary, futile, and dysfunctional. If we wait for time to cure all in an irrational system, nothing happens except that the people involved despair more and more.

Emotional growth is not possible in the irrational system. Persons are too busy attacking or defending; they have no time to be aware of themselves as individuals with emotional lacks, with needs and feelings, who require nurturance in relationship to survive with meaning in human existence. A human relationship system can promote growth only if the focus and goals of the members of that system are turned away from *behavior content* (how you and I "ought" to behave) and are directed toward a *process* of working out satisfying joint outcome (how can *we* survive more satisfactorily). Four basic conditions are necessary:

1. *Sensitivity*—Persons can learn to tune in to both the verbal and nonverbal messages of their significant others and not to deny or evade these signs. What will develop is a sensitivity that indicates that they are alert to and will use all cues between self and other in working toward more satisfying joint outcome.

2. *Awareness*—When people have developed a sensitivity to the cues in the interpersonal–transactional environment that indicate human needs, points of conflict, and individual uniqueness, they can begin to see these observations combined in a meaningful pattern. They become aware of the complex of human factors that is the nature of their relationship. They may directly use this awareness in the negotiation of more satisfying joint outcome.

3. *Willingness*—The more each person in the marriage or family is willing to contribute to the joint outcome in that family, the more satisfying that joint outcome will be. There is no room here for persons who are looking for a 50–50 relationship. If each is willing to contribute 110 percent they may very well end up with a 220 percent relationship. There must be a willingness to give of oneself in terms of effort, feeling, and commitment.

4. *Patience*—It is understood that change takes time, but change can occur if it is consistently worked at. The negotiation of a combination of needs and behaviors in several persons concurrently is needed. However, if we sit around patiently and wait for change to occur, no change occurs. On the other hand, if attempts are made to force change without the consent and participation of others, this depersonalizing intrusion will be reacted to as threat. We must be patient with our natural humanness, which includes a reluctant and groping awareness and willingness to change behavior.

These fundamental conditions allow for openness, nurturance, and shared mutual experience. This secondary triad of factors is the more basic springboard toward emotional growth in a relationship, whose basic formula may be stated as follows:

OPENNESS   +   NURTURANCE   ⟶   GROWTH

(Undefensive   (Mutual exchange of   (Expand our means
communication)   support and affection)   of dealing with
                                                     relationships)

Growth is the enlargement of self by the risk of self-revelation, confrontation, and negotiation. Growth expands our means of dealing with differentness, change, and newness with confidence and satisfaction. Relationship growth has its clearest manifestation in the way in which self is used openly in the communication of wants and perceptions with another in a reciprocal negotiation. Growth comes from the security that we are engaged in a relationship that has a commitment and a method toward accomplishing satisfying joint outcome. We grow because we are undefensive in our approach to others. We can then take our experience with other and willingly alter ourselves to be more responsive, communicative, and giving.

This is what emotional growth is. We can change, we can be different, we can adapt to reality, we can live without romantic fantasies and noble hopes because we fully enjoy the fruits of our own mutual labors with significant others in our family experience. This comes from openness, risk taking, and negotiation. But how can people be educated or prepared to use a growth orientation to enhance the emotional functioning of their relationships?

The Pound of Prevention

Public health practice in this country has demonstrated overwhelmingly that an ounce of prevention is worth a pound of cure. In the area of family dysfunction and in the more general area of mental and emotional health, the fractions may well be reversed. The potentials and possibilities for prevention are so great and the resources for cure in the development of therapeutic measures are so limited that the formula should perhaps read, a pound of prevention and an ounce of cure. Certainly there is every reason to believe much more can be done to prevent family emotional dysfunction by types of emotional-educational procedures that are already known to us.

Before these procedures can be utilized to enhance relationship outcome, however, considerable public education is necessary. Vigorous, substantial, and long-term efforts must be made to refocus people's conception of marriage and the family. This requires some radical reorientation in our society to the way in which we view these relationship systems. We have come to take relationships so much for granted that we devote less time and attention to critical analysis in selecting a mate, or dealing with a marital problem, or in facing a family crisis than we do selecting a used car. At one time, public health measures in regard to sanitation needed substantial public understanding and acceptance before many prevalent contagious diseases were eradicated. Marital and family emotional health have a similar cultural resistance to deal with.

It is necessary to alter how we, as a culture, have viewed marriage and the family in four basic areas. Only with this refocusing will it be possible to planfully enter into a period of realistic appraisal of these relationships with a basically humanistic yet practical preventive program.

1. We must first of all view marriage and the family as a joint commitment to survival and as a reciprocal relationship system. Common welfare is involved, both in marriage and the family. People often enter marriage for social, emotional, and other reasons that basically start the relationship off with no commitment other than unilateral desperation. Only when relationships can be seen as reciprocal in their consequences can marriage and family living be realistically considered. Marriage and family life is the most single difficult life task any individual will enter into. While he may contribute to and be a part of the experiences of that relationship system, only through negotiation can he influence the joint outcome of these relationships.

2. We must see marriage and the family not as a romantic escape from reality, unpleasantness, and boredom but as a singularly serious and far-reaching responsibility for all members of the system.

3. Premarital preparation for marriage must be substantially altered to include a long-term, serious and participant-involved study of the relationship prior to the marriage. This would involve not fact giving, advice, or well wishes. Nor would it include exhortations, platitudes, or "just wait" catch phrases. It must include a long series of interviews with the couple, either alone or in a group of couples, in which they can directly examine their relationship experience in the light of reality and the appraisal of objective others, not for its rightness or wrongness, its properness or impropriety, but from the point of view of the kinds of manipulations, gains, and dysfunctionality that are apparent but unconsciously used in their relationship. This cannot be done adequately in less than a six-month period before the marriage. The principal purpose of this experience would be to give the couple a realistic awareness of their relationship and to help them begin to devise methods of functional negotiation to guarantee more satisfactory joint outcome in the years to come.

4. We must regard marital and family health in the same way as we do physical health, stressing the importance and value, if not the necessity, of a continuous check on marital and family functioning through periodic transactional system checkups.

There are several methods that may be utilized in the realization of the above goals. The most crucial of these might well be the establishment of well-family clinics whose primary function would be to encourage, demonstrate, and educate persons for functional family living. Significantly dysfunctional families would be referred to appropriate therapeutic facilities. The well-family clinic could operate on premarital, marital, and family levels. The philosophy of this clinic would involve a basic orientation toward the ideas of joint commitment in a reciprocal relationship system and the nature of responsibility and negotiation within relationship systems. Such a clinic could also provide the premarital preparation sessions and the continuous periodic transactional system check-ups for existing marriages and families. It is strange to note that at the present time there is much comment, criticism, at times hysterical reaction to certain facets of family disruption and disintegration, especially divorce statistics. Yet it is also apparent that amid the talk and discussion little is being done prophylactically on the community and on the public health level to provide a facility similar to the well-family clinic.

For some years considerable use has been made by some practitioners in mental health practice, both under public and private auspices, of a device called the structured family interview. This was first developed at the Mental Research Institute at Palo Alto, California. It is basically a device through which a family can view, analyze, and be more aware of their total functioning with one another by the experience of a series of structured questions and tasks. The interview evaluates individuals, dyads, triads, and the total family unit in terms of family productivity and conflict resolution. In fact, it provides a way of viewing all the critical variables that have been discussed in this book as significant for family functioning, whether toward growth or disintegration. The interview is a device that could be realistically applied and utilized in, for example, a transactional family system check-up. It is a usable, viable procedure that is already available, but more is needed.

In research little has been done recently with paper and pencil questionnaires that might be used as marital prediction scales. The scales available in the past have not proven to be very accurate or valuable predictors of marital function or dysfunction. Recently, however, some preliminary studies with a questionnaire scale that measures the positiveness of an individual's self-esteem show some promise. Both the man and the woman complete the questionnaire and a comparison measure of the relationship between the two scales can be obtained. When the results of couples who were not experiencing significant difficulty in their marital relationships and had not sought any kind of therapeutic help were compared with those of couples who had been involved in marital therapy of one kind or another, there was a clear separation between nonclinic couple scores and clinic couple scores. While much further refinement and additional testing will be necessary, this simple device that takes approximately twenty minutes to complete may prove to be an effective predictor, at least of the need for therapeutic intervention in a marriage, which may be taken as an indicator of dysfunctional process. In any case, there is no reason why we should not pay as much attention to the nature of relationships of persons who are dating or who intend to marry as we do to purchase of a used car.

Perhaps the most useful procedure in both evaluating the nature of a relationship and offering constructive leads toward initiating a functional and negotiated relationship may reside in the use of experiential groups. Historically, these groups evolved somewhat under the joint influence of group psychotherapy and the T-groups of the National Training Laboratories. They sometimes are still called T-groups or sensitivity, awareness, or encounter groups. They have been vividly described by William Schutz in his book *Joy*. Such encounter oriented groups might both be used in terms of premarital preparation as well as marital evaluation and continuous awareness training. The principles utilized in encounter groups may also be well put to use in family awareness sessions. A couples' group might be composed of four to six couples with a principal focus on encouraging members of the group to experience with one another and their spouses a significant range of feeling—doubts, concerns, anxieties, pleasures, and despair. There would be an emphasis both on the teaching and learning of functional communication and the establishment of a more meaningful awareness of the relationship of the spouses as individual identities. The same principles could be applied to family meetings. Incipient dysfunctional processes could be isolated, and couples could be helped to become aware of them and how to manage them toward more functional outcome through the process of interpersonal negotiation. This is one particular way in which premarital counseling could become a significantly more meaningful preparation for marriage than is now generally practiced.

Growth-experience groups could also be conducted on a marathon basis, where the sessions cover periods of time from eight, twelve, or twenty-four consecutive hours to allow for more complete working out of relationship barriers in a socially intensive and, therefore, more realistic experience. Many variations of this procedure are possible, depending on the needs of specific couples and families.

Such a preventative program could be part of the function of a well-family clinic, which itself would be part of the larger program of a family institute. The institute would represent a program to study patterns of family interaction, both healthy and pathological, and to develop from these studies methods by which marital and family interaction could be enhanced toward more creative and meaningful relationships.* In brief, a family study center would have research, service, and educational facets. The basic responsibility of such a center would be to develop an understanding of the nature of family relationships as representative of an emotional social system. We are only beginning to learn about how to promote more healthy family functioning; much more experiential research is needed in this area. The service aspect of the program would specifically put into practice the research findings and the clinical knowledge and experience in the therapy of human relationship systems; these could include the well-family clinic, a family counseling clinic for dysfunctional families, and a training and education program in marriage and family therapy for professionally trained persons. The educational facet of the program would involve the dissemination of information coming from the institute's experience in research and service areas to the professional mental health practitioneers and agencies in the human community: clergymen, lawyers, public welfare personnel, physicians, police, etc. The center and its total conception would represent a creative integration of research, practice, and training. The financing and administration of such a family study center would most productively be undertaken under private auspices to insure its separation from other institutional social systems with vested interest in the *status quo*. Private financing would permit a wider range of creative ex-

---

* The Appendix contains a proposal that describes the structure, function, and purpose of such a family institute. The interested reader is encouraged to view this in terms of the potential significance such a center could have toward the influence and realization of more functional family life. Persons interested in knowing more of the work of a partially developed center may contact the author at: The Family Institute, 2600 Euclid Avenue, Cincinnati, Ohio 45218.

ploration and application, while allowing for integration with existing community services, both public and private.

If the talk and discussion about the problems of the American marriage and family could be operationalized in the creation of a national family study center, this would be the beginning of a move toward a more meaningful integration of the American marriage and family with our contemporary technological society. It would be an expression of the pound of prevention.

The Ounce of Cure

For marriages and families in which dysfunction—ranging in degree from mild to severe—is already significantly present, public and private therapy facilities exist in most communities. All too often, however, couples and families come to practitioners with very chronic relationship problems. The relationship system presents itself to the practitioner with well-established patterns of dysfunction in which defensiveness, fear, and withdrawal are deeply ingrained. For some of these families and marriages the help they seek often offers too little, too late. While they can be helped, there is a limitation to the degree of functional realization that may emerge from prolonged therapeutic intervention.

Present-day therapeutic programs, not only in the marriage and family counseling field but in mental health practice in general, are only now becoming family-oriented (in a social systems sense). There is still a large focus on the treatment of the individual outside of the context of his family, and there is a lack of public awareness of family-based emotional disturbance and the consequent value of a family-system therapeutic approach. In essence, the primary purpose of this book is to inform the educated public of these trends and potential developments. A greater appeal to individual treatment remains because it is both unilateral and self-centered and, therefore, supports the narcissism of both the patient and the therapist. If we are essentially correct in our experience and research on marital and family dysfunction, we may question whether individual therapy does not often support the pathologic pattern rather than help alleviate it by the focus on exclusive inner perceptions and symptoms, without appropriate *actual involvement* of the individual's social-relationship context—his marriage or family.

In the light of recent clinical experience with human relationship systems, it has become apparent that it is necessary to have practitioners who are basically well-trained psychotherapists who can work with individuals, groups, *and* families—clinically trained persons who will not lose sight of the total complex configuration of human interaction in the family or marriage and who will be able, because of thorough clinical training, to intervene in any appropriate way, whether in an individual session, a group meeting, or a family session.

Even today ever-increasing numbers of counselors and therapists, from the fields of psychiatry, psychology, and social work, have obtained additional training and experience in conjoint family therapy (where one or more therapists see a total family or marital unit at the same time in the same room). Persons with marital and family disturbance who wish help with their relationship problems must inquire from the agency or practitioner in question as to his experience in working with transactional family units. This applies both to private practitioners and to staff members of public and private clinics. Such persons are most likely to be found among private practitioners in clinical psychology, psychiatry, and psychiatric social work and on the professional staffs of community mental health clinics and family service agencies that are accredited by the Family Service Association of America.

It is entirely possible to change relationships if we can disrupt the perpetuating cycles of behavior rather than go back historically with insight to change personal feelings and convictions about original experiences. The person with marital and family troubles must be aware of this, and he should also seek out marital and family practitioners who have conjoint and transactional experience. This approach, in the hands of a skilled, clinically trained professional, may make significant inroads into the dilemma of existing family dysfunction.

EPILOGUE

What This Book Has Been All About

This book has described despair and realistic hope. Its intent throughout has been serious: to point out the realities of evasive and crippling dysfunction in marital and family relationships, as well as the roads to satisfying joint outcome. Relationship dysfunction is not inevitable, except where neurotic repetition prevails over honest and direct mutual negotiation. When we can openly confront one another with the consequences of our humanness, realistic enjoyment can surmount hopeless manipulation. Awareness, commitment, and responsibility may replace evasion, withdrawal, and manipulation. If there is to be meaning in our existence, that meaning must come from the realized (not fantasied) intimacy of our living together in mutual relationship.

The humor has also been with serious purpose: A spoonful of sugar helps the medicine go down, and a humorous tone helps promote that characteristic of our humanness that allows us to laugh at our desperate fumblings for godhood, lest we fall victim to our own pompous illusions.

APPENDIX

Proposal for a Family Institute

The following is a proposal for the establishment of a family institute that might be a part of a university, an existing family service agency or the auspices of a private foundation. This description is given in a series of levels of conceptualization from general to exact program, administrative, and staff specifics. The first two of four anticipated levels are described.

1. General schema
2. Functional organization
3. Administrative and staff patterns
4. Specific program content

A reciprocal feedback research model is used. In other words research (study) and application (service) are designed to mutually feed one another. Both clinical and experimental data and normal and pathological processes are studied and used. Clinical hypotheses can be tested, and research data can be applied.

The institute would represent an interdisciplinary program to study patterns of family interaction, both healthy and pathological, and to develop from this study, methods and means by which marital and family interaction can be enhanced toward more creative and meaningful relationships.

First Level of Description—General Schema

As envisioned the institute's program would include:

1. *Research Unit* for the scientific study of family interaction as a social–interactional unit. This would encompass healthy as well as pathological features.

2. *Service Unit* for the testing out in practice of research findings and the development of methods of useful application of study findings. Three subunits would include: a well-family clinic, a family therapy clinic, and a training and education program in marriage and family therapy.

3. *Education Unit* to sponsor and promote interdisciplinary seminars and workshops on family study and therapy for: (a) the staff of the center and relevant university faculty, (b) the mental health community in the general area and in the state (clinics, agencies, etc.), (c) the professional groups who often work with families, (clergy, lawyers, public welfare personnel, school personnel, both academic and guidance, physicians, police, etc.).

Combined Interdisciplinary resources of many orientations would be required, for example, child development and family life, family sociology, clinical and social psychology, psychiatric and family social work, psychiatry, anthropology, home economics, social welfare.

Second Level of Description—Functional Organization

A *Research Unit* would be headed by a project coordinator who would:

1. Keep an integrated picture of the research at universities relevant to findings, data, etc., on family interaction as a unit in interpersonal functioning via liaison with departments of universities likely to be similarly engaged in family research and through liaison with other study centers and universities engaged in similar research (Integrative Function). The unit would produce yearly integrative and summary reports of current and completed research on the family unit as an informational service.

2. Offer research consultive services to faculty, graduate students, and clinical facilities so engaged in family interaction research and therapy (Consultative Function). This could be done either directly by the institute's research director or by having well-qualified social research personnel on a consultive contract to the institute.

3. Initiate, instigate, encourage, and promote relevant family interaction research by center staff and graduate students in relevant university departments and family agencies and clinics through research project grants (Direct Research Function).

A Service Unit would be headed by a coordinator of family services with the purpose of providing families and couples with direct evaluation and therapy interviews and providing the center staff with persons for training of clinical personnel. The following functions would be carried out in this unit:

1. *Well-Family Clinic* (Healthy Family Function) For the evaluation and study of families without apparent serious distress in their interrelations. Functions would include: (a) family evaluation regarding emotional health akin to the yearly physical check-up; (b) a method of defining early case finding relative to initiating preventive prophylaxis; (c) experimenting and developing methods to help families achieve new levels, avenues, and areas of intra-family awareness and creativity, in essence a family growth center; (d) premarital evaluations and counseling; (e) emotional family life education.

2. A *Family Therapy Clinic* (Distressed Family Function) including: (a) a crisis resolution unit for apparent acute and emergency situations, (b) a chronic family disturbance unit, (c) an ongoing study of therapy effectiveness, (d) consulation to community agencies and clinics on a contractual basis.

3. A *Training Program in Family Therapy* including premarital, marital, and family unit approaches: (a) to train college graduates (Degree Program Function) with a background in the social or behavioral sciences to the application of a knowledge of family interaction and the clinical professions in developing a confidence in a method of assistance to distressed families; (b) to train es-tablished professionals (Continuing Education Function) in the application of family interaction data and the methods of the clinical professions in the assistance of distressed families. This is

to be done by specific part-time course work over a period of time in the local community area;* (c) a learning systems research project (Training Methods Evaluation Function) that would represent a continuous evaluation of the nature and effectiveness of training methods in the program.

An Education Unit would be primarily intended as an information-giving service and *brief* continuing education service and an informational orientation service to both the academic and public community of the general area as well as the state and nation. This unit would be headed by a coordinator of education who would no doubt, frequently work with university continuing education centers in actively promoting and establishing seminars, workshops, and institutes of from several days' to several weeks' duration to convey in an integrated and planned fashion the research findings of the center and the implication of these findings for utilization in service facilities. It would serve in the following ways (Stimulator and Refresher Function):

1. As a suitable grounds for a cross fertilization of ideas, concepts and research data between and among the staff of the center and other relevant departments of universities and clinical facilities.
2. As a source of information and stimulation to the mental health community of the area including suitable clinics, agencies, etc.
3. As continuous or periodic stimulation and informational service and as a source of interdisciplinary cross fertilization with professional groups who work with families such as clergy, lawyers, public welfare personnel, school personnel (academic and guidance), physicians, and police, etc.

---

* (a) would be part of a definite degree program for full-time students while (b) would be a part-time or evening study program for the interests of professionals, not specifically oriented toward a degree but encompassing the same course length and material as under (a).

Suggested Reading List

This brief and selective reading list of books and articles offers opportunity for further exploration into the marital and family behavior patterns, processes, and concepts discussed in this book. An asterisk indicates technical material written for the professional mental health practitioner and trainee.

*Ackerman, N. (1958), *The Psychodynamics of Family Life*. New York: Basic Books.

*———— (1966), *Treating the Troubled Family*. New York: Basic Books.

*Alger, I., and Hogan, P. (1968), Enduring effects of videotape playback experience on marital and family relations. *American Journal of Orthopsychiatry*, 39:86–96.

*Andrews, E. (1972), Conjoint psychotherapy with married couples and families. *Cincinnati Journal of Medicine*, 53:318–19.

*———— (1973), The adolescent in family therapy. In *Group Therapy for the Adolescent*, ed. N. Brandes. New York: Jason Aronson.

Bach, G., and Deutsch, R. M. (1970), *Pairing*. New York: Avon Books.

————, and Wyden, P. (1969), *The Intimate Enemy*. New York: Morrow.

Berne, E. (1964), *Games People Play*. New York: Grove Press.

———— , (1970), *Sex in Human Loving*. New York: Simon and Schuster.

*Birdwhistell, R. (1966), The American family: Some perspectives. *Psychiatry*. 29:203–212.

*Gehrke, S., and Kirschenbaum, M. (1967), Survival patterns in family conjoint therapy: Myth and reality. *Family Process*, 6:67–80.

*Haas, W. (1968), The intergenerational encounter: A method in treatment. *Social Work*, 13:91–101.

Harris, T., (1967), *I'm O.K., You're O.K.* New York: Harper and Row.

Jourard, S. (1968), *Disclosing Man to Himself*. Princeton: Van Nostrand.

*Laing, R. D. (1964), *Sanity, Madness and the Family*. New York: Basic Books.

———— (1969), *The Politics of the Family*. New York: Vintage Books (1972).

Lederer, W., and Jackson, D. (1968), *The Mirages of Marriage*. New York: Norton.

Maslow, A. (1968), *Toward a Psychology of Being*. Princeton: Van Nostrand.

Morris, D. (1969), *The Naked Ape*. New York: Dell.
*Mullan, H., and Sanguiliano, I. (1964), *The Therapist's Contribution to the Treatment Process*. Springfield: Thomas.
O'Neill, N., and O'Neill, G. (1973), *Open Marriage*. New York: Avon Books.
Otto, H. (1970), *The Family in Search of a Future*. New York: Appleton-Century-Crofts.
*Paul, N. (1968), Self- and cross-confrontation techniques via audio- and video-tape recordings in conjoint family and marital therapy. Paper presented at the 45th Annual Conference, American Orthopsychiatric Association, Chicago, March 1968.
Reik, T., (1949), *Of Love and Lust*. New York: Farrar, Straus.
Rogers, C. (1961), *On Becoming a Person*. Boston: Houghton Mifflin.
———— (1972), *Becoming a Partner: Marriage and Its Alternatives*. New York: Delacorte Press.
Salk, Lee (1972), *What Every Child Would Like His Parents to Know*. New York: David McKay.
*Satir, V. (1964), *Conjoint Family Therapy*. Palo Alto: Science and Behavior Books.
———— (1965), Conjoint marital therapy. In *The Psychotherapies of Marital Dysharmony*, ed. B. L. Green, 121–133. New York: Free Press.
———— (1972), *Peoplemaking*. Palo Alto: Science and Behavior Books.
Schutz, W. (1967), *Joy*. New York: Grove Press.
*Sheflin, A. (1965), *Stream and Structure of Communicational Behavior*. Philadelphia: Eastern Pennsylvania Psychiatric Institute of Behavioral Studies, Monograph No. 1.
Shostrom, E., and Kavanaugh, J. (1971), *Between Man and Woman*. Los Angeles: Nash.
Viorst, J. (1968), *It's Hard to Be Hip over Thirty and Other Tragedies of Married Life*. New York: New American Library.
*Watzlawick, P. (1966), A structured family interview. *Family Process*, 5:256–271.
————, Beavin, J., and Jackson, D., (1967), *Pragmatics of Human Communication*. New York: Norton.
*Wildblood, R., and Weiner, B., (1968), Self-concept and ideal-self concept in therapy and non-therapy couples. Unpublished paper, available from The Family Institute, 2600 Euclid Ave., Cincinnati, Ohio 45219.
*Zuk, G., and Boszomenyi-Nagy, I. (1967), *Family Therapy and Disturbed Families*. Palo Alto: Science and Behavior Books.

Index